LAW AND ECONOMICS

IN A NUTSHELL

THIRD EDITION

By

JEFFREY L. HARRISON
Stephen C. O'Connell Chair
College of Law
The University of Florida

Prepared with the assistance of
McCabe G. Harrison

Mat #40160830

COPYRIGHT © 1995 WEST PUBLISHING CO.
COPYRIGHT © 2000 WEST GROUP
© 2003 By West, a Thomson business
        610 Opperman Drive
        P.O. Box 64526
        St. Paul, MN 55164–0526
        1–800–328–9352
Printed in the United States of America

ISBN 0–314–14759–4

For

*McCabe
Casey and
Connor-Blue*

*

PREFACE TO THE THIRD EDITION

This edition reflects an effort to expand on the scope of the previous editions and to refine the analysis found in those editions. The book, as before, includes the straightforward or conventional application of economics to law. In addition, it discusses the implications of ongoing research into the validity of the assumptions economists make. In effect, it continues to reflect my belief that a complete examination of law and economics requires both the conventional application of economic principles to law and a study of the philosophical implications of the methodology. The purpose is not to discount economics but to convey an understanding of its uses and limitations. In fact, it has always been curious to me that economists seem more willing to examine the underlying assumptions and value of their work than those who apply it in an interdisciplinary context. Yet it is precisely when economics is applied to law that one must be mindful of what economics can and can not do.

In this edition there are many specific additions. Chapter Seven, on criminal law, which first appeared in the second edition, has now been expanded to include criminal procedure. Chapter Eight, which covers the basics of antitrust, now closes with a discussion of *Alcoa* and *Microsoft*. In Chapter Nine, on government regulation, I now include a brief section on regulations that seem clearly to reflect an interest in social justice. Some of the economic issues raised by intellectual property law are discussed in Chapter 10, which is new. Other smaller additions are found throughout the book, including a discussion of "takings" in Chapter Three.

I would like to thank those who have contacted me with observations and recommendations for improvements and even those who have pointed out mistakes. This edition was prepared with the able assistance of McCabe Harrison who contributed substantively, caught mistakes that had survived two previous editions, and identified areas in which my explanations could be improved.

JEFFREY L. HARRISON

Gainesville, Florida
2003

OUTLINE

*

TABLE OF CASES

References are to Pages

TABLE OF CASES

TABLE OF CASES

*

LAW AND ECONOMICS

IN A NUTSHELL

THIRD EDITION

*

CHAPTER ONE

INTRODUCTION

Although without much fanfare, lawyers have long recognized economics as a complementary discipline. For example, Oliver Wendell Holmes wrote in 1887, "the man of the future is the man of statistics and economics."[1] In addition, the economic underpinnings of the famous Hand Formula, which defines negligence as the absence of cost-justified preventive action, is obvious. Similarly, well before legal scholars began to think and write about law and economics in the late 1960s and early 1970s, economists were hard at work providing litigation assistance to attorneys in the areas of remedies and antitrust.

Economists have always been conscious of the importance of the relationship of law and economics. Evidence of this is found in the earliest studies of economic matters as well as in the writings of Adam Smith and Karl Marx. In the early part of the last century, scholars like John R. Commons, Robert Lee Hale, and Irving Fisher discussed the importance of understanding the impact of legal institutions on economic development and the ways in which economic change may encourage legal

1. Oliver Wendell Holmes, "The Path of the Law," 10 *Harv.L. Rev.* 457 (1987).

change.[2] In fact, it is possible that these earlier scholars of law and economics and the "Institutional Economists" made a greater effort to fully address the complex interplay of law and economics than more contemporary writers.[3]

The most recent wave of law and economics, associated with the University of Chicago, roughly began with the appearance of Ronald Coase's famous 1960 article "The Problem of Social Cost—"[4] now the most cited article in legal scholarship. It gained its real impetus among legal academicians with the publication of Richard Posner's *Economic Analysis of Law*. This period of law and economics was and is marked primarily by efforts to describe what law would look like if courts adopted efficiency as their guiding standard. Often the conclusion is that it would look much like it does. The Chicago period has also seen efforts to study the evolution of law to determine whether laws move inevitably toward sets of rules that are efficient. In addition, there have been attempts to address the moral justifications for adoption of efficiency as a desirable standard. More recently, there have been increased efforts to assess individual behavior in legal contexts with empirical studies. Throughout this book,

2. Steven G. Medema, "From Interwar Pluralism to Posner," 30 *History of Political Economy* (Ann. Supp., 202) 1998.

3. See generally, A. Allan Schmidt, "Institutional Law and Economics," 1 *European Journal of Law and Economics* 33 (1994).

4. Ronald Coase, "The Problem of Social Cost," 3 *J. L. & Econ.* 1 (1960).

ideas drawn from this approach to law and economics will be referred to as "conventional."

The post-Chicago era of law and economics began almost as early as the appearance of Chicago School ideas and is really divided into two branches. The first branch seeks to discredit the Chicago School directly by maintaining that there is an ideological bias inherent in the application of economics to law.

The second post-Chicago development is less critical in a direct sense. Instead, it can be viewed as an effort to incorporate law and economics into a broader spectrum of interdisciplinary theories about law. The criticisms from this quarter are largely by implication. Its primary goal is to add a measure of behavioral realism to the purely conventional approach. In a sense, this approach—the Socioeconomic approach—is similar to that of the Institutional Economists. This time around, however, this broader examination has caught the attention of legal scholars.[5]

An interesting element of this second branch is to question whether the assumptions of the conventional or Chicago School approach are realistic, especially when economics is applied to an area in which morals and social norms are important in influencing behavior. In this regard it relies a great deal on the work of behavioral economists whose experiments over the last 30 years suggest deviance between the economist's "rational self-interest" as-

5. Robert Ashford, "Socio-economics: What is its Place in Law Practice?" 1997 Wisc. L. Rev. 611 (1997); Jeffrey L. Harrison, "Law and Socioeconomics," 49 *The Journal of Legal Education* 224 (1999).

sumption and actual behavior. The legitimacy of this work was affirmed in 2002 when the Nobel Prize in economics was awarded to Daniel Kaheman and Vernon Smith, two of the leaders in economic experimentation.

This book proceeds from the assumption that a properly taught course in law and economics, whether in an economics department or in a law school, will include more than a single-minded examination of the conventional application of economic analysis to law. A good deal of attention to the criticisms of law and economics can assist one in having a better understanding of the area. Similarly, it is valuable to consider the ways in which the theory of law and economics can be improved by considering information about human behavior provided by other disciplines.

The next Chapter is an introduction to basic price theory, including the fundamentals of supply and demand, and to concepts of efficiency. Although the concepts are not always obviously connected, it makes sense to become acquainted with them as they are likely to be relied upon at various points throughout the remainder of the book. Much of what is described in Chapter Two will be elaborated upon in Chapter Eight in the context of antitrust law. Chapter Three focuses on some of the controversies that arise in the application of economics to law.

Chapter Four discusses the foundation of law and economics—the Coase Theorem—and many of its applications to property-related issues. Chapter Five examines the various concepts typically found in a course on contracts and contract remedies. Chapter Six does the same with respect to tort law with emphasis on unintentional torts and the Hand formula. The premise of Chapter Six is that the economic function of tort law is to minimize the sum of accident costs and efforts to prevent them. Chapter Seven offers a sampling of the many efforts to apply economics to criminal law.

Chapter Eight covers much of the economic theory behind most antitrust law. Chapter Nine is devoted to the economic justifications for the regulation of business. These justifications range from regulating natural monopolies and allocating inherently scarce resources to efforts to control pollution and limit the destruction of endangered species. Chapter Ten extends this analysis to intellectual property.

Finally, in Chapter Eleven, the newest area of law and economics—public choice theory—is examined. Public choice has been the focus of social scientists for many years. While conventional economics deals with decision-making and the expression of preferences in traditional markets, public choice addresses the same issues in contexts in which the mode of expression is voting. Public choice may be especially relevant to an understanding of the criticisms of applying economic analysis to law. This is because people may tend to vote in a way that expresses their generalized preferences for certain values or notions of fairness or justice. In traditional markets, they are more likely to vote—with their dollars—in a manner that expresses individualized "tastes."[6]

6. See Kenneth Arrow, *Social Choice and Individual Values*, (1963).

The application of economics to the decisions that involve law probably occupies some middle ground in which both general values and individualized tastes play a role.

Before beginning a detailed examination of law and economics, one final notice is warranted. A study of law and economics requires the student to adopt a different orientation from that required for conventional college courses. Law and economics is not really a single topic but a series of topics ranging from microeconomics to game theory, sociology, and jurisprudence. Although one can find a wealth of implied and expressed economic analysis in judicial opinions, the basic materials are really scholarly writings found in law reviews and economics journals. These writings are landmarks in the same sense as judicial opinions are landmarks: they set new standards or signal turning points.

CHAPTER TWO

ECONOMIC TOOLS AND CONCEPTS

This Chapter is devoted to the fundamental tools and concepts that economists use to study law, beginning with a discussion of supply and demand. It then considers elasticity and compares perfect with imperfect competition. Together, these concepts make up what is known as "basic price theory." For those who wish to follow up on this Chapter's discussion of basic price theory, Chapter Eight extends the analysis to another (but still basic) level with respect to antitrust law. This Chapter also examines externalities and the forms of efficiency that are most commonly discussed in law and economics.

A. DEMAND, SUPPLY AND MARKET EQUILIBRIUM

1. DEMAND

"Demand" has a very specific meaning and is often used in a confusing manner in the popular press. When economists speak of demand, they mean a *range* of prices and the amount of a good or service that individuals are willing and able to purchase in a given market at a given time at those prices. It is critical to note that demand does not account for those who either cannot afford the good or service or are unwilling to pay. Also, one cannot speak about demand without expressly or implicitly limiting the market both time-wise and by location. Thus, one might ask what is the demand for gasoline from 7:00 A.M. to 9:00 A.M. on Monday in Oscarville. The appropriate answer to that question would be a list or schedule of possible prices and the amounts of gasoline people would be willing and able to purchase during the time specified. Table 1 might be the answer.

Table 1: Demand for Gasoline

Price per gallon	Quantity
$1.00	800
$1.05	750
$1.10	700
$1.15	650
$1.20	600

From the Table, one can determine the *quantity demanded* of gasoline at each price. As the Table indicates, the quantity demanded declines as the price increases. For example, at $1.00 per gallon, the quantity demanded is 800 gallons. At $1.05, the quantity demanded is 750 gallons. Typically, the relationship between price and quantity demanded is depicted on a graph. In Figure 1, the Y or vertical axis is price, and the X or horizontal axis is quantity. If the demand for gasoline were graphed, the price/quantity combinations could be connected by a straight line. In Figure 1, D_1 is called a demand curve and is a graphical representation of the demand in Table 1. In this particular graph, only a few of the possible prices and quantities are illustrated.

Figure 1

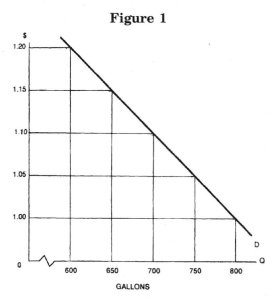

Demand curves almost always slope downward. This is consistent with people being willing and able to purchase less as prices increase. They purchase less both because they look to buy substitutes and because an increase in the price of any product lowers their purchasing power generally.

A change in demand is represented by a shift of the demand curve so that at all prices the quantity demanded either increases or decreases. In Figure 2, D_2 represents a decrease in demand while D_3 shows an increase in demand. It is important not to confuse a change in demand with a change in the quantity demanded.

Figure 2

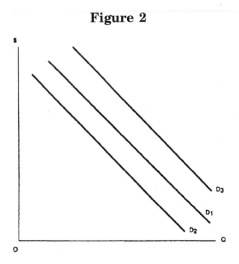

A change in quantity demanded occurs when a change in price results in movement to a new position on the same demand curve. A "shift in demand" or "change in demand" means that the entire curve shifts and that a different quantity is demanded at every price on the schedule.

Shifts in demand can be the result of changes in the tastes and preferences for the good or service. They can also be the result of a change in price of other goods and services. For example, complementary goods are those that are typically used together. Thus, tennis balls and tennis rackets are complementary goods. If the price of tennis rackets increased, the demand for tennis balls would be likely to decrease. If the original demand for tennis balls was D_1 in Figure 2, the new demand curve would be to the left, perhaps D_2, indicating a downward shift in demand.

Another possibility is that goods are substitutes. In other words, to one degree or another, they can be used for the same purposes. Thus, to some extent jogging can be viewed as a substitute for playing tennis. If the price of tennis rackets increases, the demand for jogging shoes may increase. This would be illustrated as a shift to the right of the demand curve for jogging shoes. D_3 in Figure 2 represents an increase in demand over D_1.

2. SUPPLY

The proper definition of supply is comparable to that of demand. Supply is a schedule of prices and the quantities that would be available for sale at each price in a given market at a given time. Thus, the supply of gasoline in Oscarville between 7:00 and 9:00 A.M. might look like Table 2.

Table 2: Supply of Gasoline

Price per gallon	Quantity
$1.00	600
$1.05	650
$1.10	700
$1.15	750

Price per gallon	Quantity
$1.20	800

As with demand, supply is often plotted on a graph. In Figure 3, the quantity is along the X axis and the price is along the Y axis. S_1 is the supply curve for gasoline in Oscarville between 7:00 and 9:00 A.M. As the Table and Figure indicate, quantity supplied generally increases as price increases. To understand why, one must understand the concept of marginal cost. Marginal cost is the increase in cost associated with the production of one additional unit of output. Thus, if the total cost of producing 4 units of output is $4.00 and the total cost of producing 5 units of output is $5.00, the marginal cost of the fifth unit is $1.00.

Figure 3

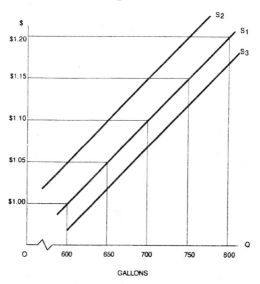

GALLONS

One can plot marginal cost on a graph and illustrate how the costs of producing one more unit of output change as output increases. This is the marginal cost curve, and the part of that curve that is relevant for this analysis is upward sloping. In fact, the relevant part of the marginal cost curve is the supply curve just as depicted in Figure 3. The reason why the marginal cost curve and the supply curve are identical is because a producer will be willing to sell an additional unit of output as long as the price offered for that unit is at least equal to the marginal cost of producing that unit. Thus, in order to answer the question of how many units will be made available for sale at each price, the producer would consider the marginal cost of producing each unit.

Like demand curves, the entire supply curve can shift. Again, it is important to distinguish this from a change in the quantity supplied. A change in quantity supplied occurs when a price change results in movement to a new position on the same supply curve.

Typically, a shift in supply is a response to an increase or decrease in the cost of inputs. Thus, if the item involves the use of labor and the cost of labor on an hourly basis increases, one would expect the supply curve to shift upward and to the left. In Figure 3, this is illustrated by the curve S_2. At each price along S_2, sellers are willing to sell a lower quantity than they were before the increase in the cost of labor. Or, to put it differently, at each quantity, it will now take a higher price to get the producer to make that quantity available for sale. Conversely, a decrease in the price of labor will result in a shift from S_1 to S_3. This is an increase in supply.

3. MARKET EQUILIBRIUM

By combining supply and demand, as depicted in Figure 4, one can determine the equilibrium price and quantity for a given market at a given time. This does not mean that a price and quantity will be established and not change. Instead, there will be a tendency for the market to gravitate toward the equilibrium price and quantity. In the case of

Oscarville, the equilibrium price will be $1.10 and the equilibrium quantity will be 700 gallons.

Figure 4

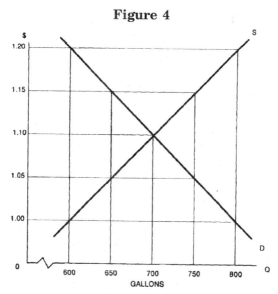

To understand why, consider the reaction if the price were $1.20. The quantity demanded would be 600 gallons and the quantity offered for sale would be 800 gallons. With more offered for sale than individuals are willing and able to purchase, there is a surplus in the market and price will tend to fall. In effect, suppliers would compete against each other by lowering price to eliminate the excess. At a price of $1.00, the quantity demanded would be 800 gallons and the quantity supplied 600 gallons. In this case, there is a shortage, and suppliers will find that they can increase price. Only at a price of $1.10

would the quantity supplied equal the quantity demanded. Price will gravitate toward this level and the quantity sold will gravitate toward 700 gallons.

B. ELASTICITY

1. GENERALLY

Just as important as the fact that demand curves generally slope downward and supply curves upward is the question of just how steep the curves are. Put differently, just how responsive are sellers and buyers to changes in price? The economist's label for this measure of sensitivity is "elasticity." Elasticity is expressed as a number which is:

% change in quantity/% change in price.

In the case of demand, if the percentage change in quantity exceeds the percentage change in price, i.e. the above ratio is greater than one, demand is said to be "elastic." In short, buyers are relatively responsive to price changes. If the ratio of percentage change in quantity to percentage change in price is less than one, demand is said to be "inelastic." The primary factor accounting for the elasticity of demand is the availability of substitutes. If prices increase and many substitutes are available, individuals will move away from the good or the seller who has increased price. A classic example of an inelastic good would be emergency medical care. If you need emergency treatment it is a necessity for which few substitutes exist. An example of an elastic good would be a luxury item such as diamond necklaces, because one can easily substitute away from diamond necklaces by buying different kinds of jewelry.

The implication of different elasticities is illustrated in Figure 5. The graph includes two demand curves. D_1 is relatively steep, while the slope of D_2 is relatively slight. At P_1 on both curves, the quantity demanded is Q_1. If price increases to P_2, the quantity demanded on D_1 is Q_2 and the quantity demanded on D_2 is Q_3. In other words, the same price increase results in different responses. The steep curve is relatively inelastic; buyers are relatively unresponsive to the price change. Among other possibilities, this suggests that there are not many good substitutes for the good represented by D_1. Along D_2, the response is greater. D_2 is relatively elastic and buyers alter their spending in response to the price change.

Figure 5

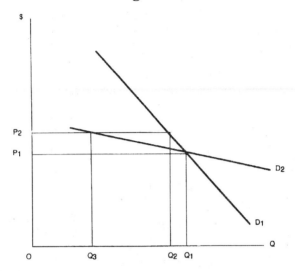

Elasticity of supply can be calculated the same way as the elasticity of demand. Here again, the more responsive sellers are to price increases or decreases, the more elastic the supply curve is said to be. The critical determinant of supply elasticity is the rate at which costs of production increase as output increases. For example, if a seller has excess capacity and if inputs are relatively inexpensive, a small increase in price may result in a large increase in output.

2. INCIDENCE ANALYSIS

Incidence analysis is devoted to determining who actually pays more when costs of production or taxes increase. Elasticity is an important determinant of which groups of possible payers are affected. This can be illustrated using the supply and demand for gasoline in Oscarville. In Figure 6, the initial equilibrium price is P_1 and the equilibrium quantity is Q_1. Suppose a new government regulation is enacted that requires all service station owners to pay ten cents per gallon sold to a fund established for cleaning old service station sites. This would have an impact, initially, on the supply side of the market, making it more expensive to sell gasoline. The supply curve would shift upward and to the left. In Figure 6, S_1 is the supply before the regulation and S_2 is the supply after regulation. The curve shifts up by exactly the amount of the charge because at every level of output, the marginal cost of gasoline increases by the same amount—in this case, ten cents.

Figure 6

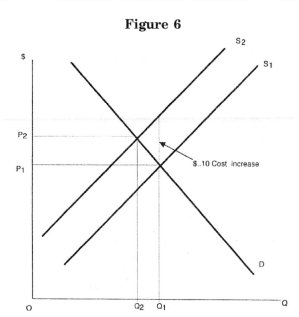

Here the question incidence analysis addresses is how the extra ten cent cost will be allocated between the buyers and sellers. For example, in Figure 6, the cost of gasoline increases to P_2 per gallon and the quantity sold drops to Q_2. Thus, some consumers pay more and some do not buy as much gasoline. The increase in price is not, however, equal to the ten cent increase in the cost of production.

Contrast Figure 6 with Figure 7. Here the two supply curves are the same as in Figure 6, but the demand curve is very steep or relatively inelastic. As the demand curve indicates, price increases do not result in much of a response in terms of quantity demanded. Thus, after the regulation, the price of gasoline goes up to P_2 and quantity decreases to Q_2; most of the extra cost of production is paid by consumers. One could repeat this exercise with a very flat or elastic demand curve and the result would be that the price of gasoline would barely rise at all; more of the cost would be absorbed by producers. As it turns out, the elasticity of both supply and demand determine upon whom the extra cost will fall.

Figure 7

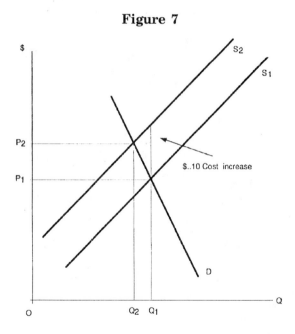

C. PERFECT AND IMPERFECT MARKETS

While supply and demand curves are useful tools for economic analysis of law, they may not be representative of how markets are actually structured. For example, total market demand in Oscarville might be determined by asking each resident how much gasoline he or she would be willing to buy at each price along the schedule and then adding those quantities of gasoline to get the total market demand. The same process might be done on the supply side. All the sellers of gasoline might be asked how much they would be willing to sell at each price on the schedule. These quantities would be added together to get the supply for the market. This would also be the sum of all their marginal cost curves. This is called "horizontal summation" since the prices are not added, but the amounts offered for sale at each price are.

The analysis so far assumes that there are in fact a number of suppliers. In this context, the sellers can do no more than passively react to the market-determined price. In fact, the basic demand and supply model involves the assumption that the sellers are selling homogeneous products, that buyers and sellers have complete information about prices and any other relevant factors, that it is easy to enter the industry, and that no seller is large enough to effect price by increasing or decreasing its output. Economists call this perfect competition.

Under these conditions, each seller is a "price-taker" and simply sells all it wants to sell at the market-determined price.

If any of the above conditions are absent, the market becomes imperfect. Imperfect markets are ones in which sellers cease to become passive price takers and, for one reason or another, are able to raise prices above what they would be in a competitive market. For example, consumers may not be able to get information easily or one seller may be able to convince prospective buyers that its product is different from the others—that is, it is differentiated. These imperfections can be sources of market power. The more market power a seller has, the more it will be able to raise prices above competitive levels. Moreover, the firm with market power is no longer a price-taker. As market conditions increasingly differ from those under perfect competition, simple demand and supply analysis begins to lose its validity. Instead, individual firms will set prices above competitive prices and decrease output to levels below that under competitive conditions. A more detailed explanation of the economic implications of imperfect competition is reserved for Chapter Eight, but the actual process of determining price is discussed here.

In order to determine how price determination differs, assume all the service stations in Oscarville merge into one big supplier. Assume the new supplier's marginal cost curve would be derived by horizontally summing together the marginal cost curves of all the small firms. In other words, it would be the same as the supply curve for the whole town before the merger. The one firm will also be faced with the entire Oscarville demand.

That does not mean it will price where demand and supply intersect. Instead, it will want to pick the one price that will maximize profit. It will make a profit on each unit sold as long as the addition to total revenue from selling that unit exceeds the increase in total cost associated with producing that unit—marginal cost. The extra revenue from selling an additional unit is the marginal revenue.

It is now useful to turn to Figure 8. The demand from Figure 2 is included in the graph as is the supply from Figure 2. Here it is labeled MC for marginal cost and not S for supply because the firm really is not willing to offer different amounts for sale at different prices but is searching for a single price. The curve that is new is labeled MR for marginal revenue. Marginal revenue—again, the extra revenue from selling one more unit—is consistently lower than the price for which that unit is sold. The reason for this is simple. If the seller wants to sell more, it must lower the price for all units. Thus, the increase in revenue from selling additional units when price is lowered is partially or completely offset by the decreased revenue from all those units that now have lower prices.

Figure 8

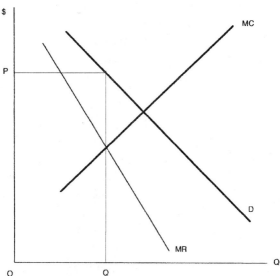

The firm would like to sell all those units that generate more in terms of marginal revenue than their marginal cost. In the graph, this is true for all units for which the marginal revenue curve is higher than the marginal cost curve. Thus, the firm will produce and sell up to level Q. Of course, it will want to set the highest price possible for Q. The price on the demand curve that corresponds to quantity Q is price P. This will be *the* price set by the seller.

Obviously, the degree of competitiveness has many important implications. Although explored more fully in Chapter Eight, it is worthwhile to point out some of them here. First, under perfectly competitive conditions, firms will tend to make the minimum profit necessary to stay in business. This is called a "normal profit" and economists treat it as a cost along with other costs of production. A profit in excess of a normal profit is called an "economic profit." The reason why firms in perfectly competitive industries tend to make only a normal profit is because entry into the industry is so easy that anything above a normal profit will attract competitors and the increase in supply will drive prices and profits down. Under imperfect competition, this is less likely to occur and firms can make long term economic profits. In addition, prices will tend to be higher under imperfect conditions and the level of output lower. This, as one might expect, has important implications for antitrust policy.

The competitiveness of the industry also plays a role in incidence analysis. Under perfectly competitive conditions, any costs that are passed on at all must be passed on to consumers. This is because the firms in the industry are only earning a normal profit—the minimum necessary to survive. This does not mean that prices will necessarily rise by the full amount of the cost increase. As firms raise prices to cover the cost increase, some consumers will drop out of the market and fewer firms will be needed to serve the remaining buyers. With fewer firms, the demand for the inputs used in that industry will fall and the price of inputs may decline. If so, the cost increase may be partially offset by a decrease in the price of other inputs and, overall, price will not increase by the full amount of the cost increase. If anyone "absorbs" the cost increase, it is the consumers who continue to buy, those who have left the market to buy less desirable products, and the firms that have left the market.

On the other hand, if the industry is imperfectly competitive, it may be that firms are enjoying economic profits or "rents." In these instances, the part of the cost increase that is not passed on to consumers may be absorbed by the firms that remain in the market in the form of lower profits.

D.   MARGINAL ANALYSIS GENERALLY

An important tool of economic analysis generally and in the application of economic analysis to law is marginal analysis. Marginal analysis is essentially a decision-making technique in which one compares the benefits and costs of decisions. As already described, in its most traditional economic application, firms apply marginal analysis to determine their level of output.

In the context of criminal law, one might reason that a motorist will speed as long as the advantage from speeding exceeds the expected fine for speeding. Here the expected fine would be the fine if caught multiplied by the probability of being caught. The marginal benefit would be whatever advantage is gained by arriving earlier than if the speed limit were observed.

The usefulness of marginal analysis is obvious and many would say that it is the "rational approach" to decision-making. For example, suppose an inventor spent several years and several thousand dollars attempting to invent a special hair growing tonic and was getting no closer to the magic formula. He might reason, "I can't stop now, I have already devoted so much time and expense to the effort." This would not be marginal analysis. The time and money spent are "sunk costs." The supposedly rational approach would be to ask what the costs of further efforts are likely to be and what are the likely benefits. This may be, however, a bit of an oversimplification in that there may be adverse psychological effects associated with giving up on a project. This does not mean that marginal analysis as a decision-making strategy is flawed. It suggests that there is a tendency in economics to define the marginal costs and benefits of decisions too narrowly.

E. EFFICIENCY

In one form or another, the concept of "efficiency" is an important tool in the study of law and economics. Typically, the term "efficiency" is associated with the notion of accomplishing an outcome at the lowest possible cost. The term for that type of efficiency is "productive efficiency." Productive efficiency is, however, just one of a number of "types" of efficiency one encounters in law and economics.

1. ALLOCATIVE EFFICIENCY

Allocative efficiency is typically reserved for considerations of whether an industry is producing the "right" amount of a specific good or service. This is different from the question of productive efficiency, which deals with whether any particular level of output is produced at the lowest possible cost. Allocative efficiency can be understood by referring to the basic supply and demand model. The demand curve tells what a particular product is worth to individuals. As one moves down the demand curve, the value of additional units of output decline; that is, the price people are willing to pay decreases.

The supply curve, on the other hand, really tells the cost of producing additional units of output. This is because when the seller is considering how much he or she will offer for sale at each price, a direct comparison is made of the price offered to the cost of producing additional units. Of course, the cost of producing additional units is determined by the cost of inputs and the cost of those inputs is determined by the price others are offering to use the inputs in the production of other goods. Thus, in a real sense, when an input is used to produce one good, the "social cost" is the value placed on the use of the input in the production of other goods.

It makes sense, in terms of efficient resource allocation, to produce an item as long as the value attributed to it by buyers exceeds the social cost of its production. Since demand tells us the value attributed to the item being produced and supply tells us the social cost of producing extra units, it makes sense to produce until demand and supply intersect.

This can be seen in Figure 9, the demand and supply for Vespa motor scooters. Demand and supply intersect at 15 Vespas. At the quantity of 14 Vespas, the price people are willing and able to pay exceeds the cost, as indicated by the supply curve, of additional production. Thus, society values the production of additional units more than the social cost of additional units. At 16 Vespas, production would be too high. Since demand lies below the supply curve at this level of output, the social cost of the 16th unit exceeds the value of that unit. The "right" amount of inputs is "drawn" into the production of Vepas at 15 units. This is said to be allocatively efficient.

There is an important caveat to this explanation of allocative efficiency. The entire analysis, since it is dependent on supply and demand, is based on preferences and the strength of those preferences as they are expressed in markets. And, as indicated earlier, supply and demand depend on "willingness and ability to pay." It is possible that it is desirable to produce goods and services that people cannot afford. This does not mean that the economist's definition of allocative efficiency is necessarily wrong. Instead, it just means that one may legitimately believe that allocative efficiency is but one concept to be weighed in making normative decisions.

Figure 9

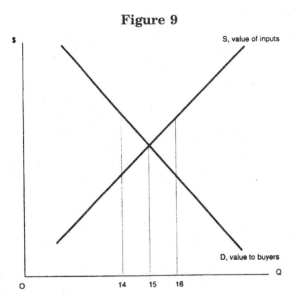

2.   THE THEORY OF SECOND BEST

Now that you have learned about supply and demand and how competitive markets result in allocative efficiency, an important additional concept comes into play. The "theory of second best" has received scant attention in the field of law and economics.[1] This is unfortunate, as its implications

1. The work of Richard Markovits is an important exception. See Richard Markovits, "A Basic Structure for Microeconomic Policy Analysis in our Worse–Than–Second–Best World: A Proposal and Related Critique of the Chicago Approach to the Study of Law and Economics," 1975 *Wisc. L. Rev.* 950.

are important and have the potential to undermine a great deal of economic-based policy. One can understand the theory by thinking back to the concept of allocative efficiency. Demand indicates the value attributed to the good by buyers and supply indicates the cost of production in terms of resources used that could be used to produce other goods. Presumably, the efficient amount of inputs are drawn into the production of the good at the level of output determined by demand and supply.

Suppose, however, that there are two goods—buttons and zippers—and that they use the same inputs except that buttons require plastic and zippers do not. In addition, assume all inputs are sold under competitive conditions except plastic. Since the price of plastic will be determined under imperfect market conditions, its price will be higher than it would otherwise be. In addition, due to this inflated price, the supply of buttons will be lower and the price higher than it would be if plastic were sold under competitive conditions. Unlike the model used to describe allocative efficiency, now the supply curve does not tell us the cost of button-making in terms of the cost of resources.

In addition, since the price of buttons is higher, consumers will shift their purchases to zippers, a good substitute for most purposes. Resources will flow into zipper production even though, but for the imperfect conditions in the plastic market, those resources would be more efficiently used in the production of buttons.

The solution to the problem may seem simple: somehow arrange for the plastic market to behave competitively. As one might expect, though, this may very well be impossible. If one decides that all the markets cannot be competitive, the question then becomes whether it makes sense from the standpoint of efficiency to make as many markets competitive as possible. The answer is that efficiency may not be furthered by a policy of making as many markets as possible competitive when you know that ultimately all markets will not be competitive. In fact, there may be a "second best" solution that actually allocates resources more efficiently by allowing for comparable levels of imperfection.

The theory of second best illustrates the interdependence of markets. It also calls into question analyses that speak in terms of efficient levels of damages or sanctions without examining the structure of the "market" involved and related markets.

3. PARETO OPTIMALITY AND SUPERIORITY

The concepts of Pareto optimality and Pareto superiority are discussed in any study of law and economics. To understand their use, consider Jack, who would like to sell his 1965 Ford Mustang, and Sally, who would like to buy the Mustang. Suppose Jack asks for a price of $10,000, but would be willing to accept an offer of $8,000. This means that Jack would prefer or feel better off with any sum in excess of $8,000 than he would feel if he continued to possess the car. Put differently, Jack would derive more utility from $8,000 than he would from possessing the Ford. Similarly, suppose Sally offered Jack $7,000, but was willing to pay as much as $9,000. Here again it can be said that Sally would feel better owning the car than she would feel if she possessed anything else $9,000 could buy.

Obviously, we have a range of possible prices that would leave both Jack and Sally feeling better off. That is, there would be a range of prices that would be consistent with increasing the utility of both parties. This increase in utility could be regarded as a movement to a more efficient allocation of resources. The range of prices that would achieve this in the example would be from $8,000 to $9,000.

Sometimes this range of prices is referred to as the "contract curve." It describes a number of prices that would make both Jack and Sally feel better off. If they are better off and no third parties are worse off, the reallocation is Pareto superior. In more general terms, a reallocation is Pareto superior when at least one party is better off and no one is worse off.

Suppose an exchange does take place—the car for $8,500—and we then consider adjusting the price. In other words, having chosen a position on the contract curve, we then consider the possibility of adjusting the exchange so that it is at another place on the contract curve. For example, one might decide to let Sally have the car and require Jack to refund $100. Or one might allow Sally to keep the car but pay Jack $200 more. In both of these cases, the movement from one price to another would not make both parties feel better off. In fact, any movement from the $8,500 would leave either Jack or Sally worse off. When resources are distributed in such a way that they cannot be reallocated without at least one party feeling worse off, the original distribution is said to be "Pareto optimal."

In short, an allocation is Pareto superior if achieving it means at least one person is better off and no one is made worse off. It is Pareto optimal if any movement from that allocation would make at least one person worse off.

Although voluntary exchanges are the best way of assuring that a Pareto superior allocation is achieved, it is also possible to achieve Pareto superiority through involuntary means. For example, Sally may simply take the Mustang from Jack and leave him 85 crisp one-hundred dollar bills. If the money makes Jack feel better off than possessing what Sally took and no one else is adversely affected, the outcome is Pareto superior.

The problem is that there are only three sources of information that tell us what amount Jack needs to make him feel at least as well off as he did before Sally took his car. Sally is one source, but there is no guarantee that she can accurately determine how much Jack valued the Mustang. Jack might be another source, but it is not clear that Jack will be dependable when, after the fact, he is asked what amount the court should require Sally to pay in order to restore him to at least his previous level of well-being. Finally, there could be outside sources that would testify as to the fair market value of the car. The problem here is that Jack may attribute a greater value to the car than the fair market value. Thus, if the involuntary exchange achieves Pareto superiority, it may be more a matter of coincidence than anything else.

The public policy implications of Pareto standards of efficiency are extremely confining. Strict adherence to these standards would either rule out all involuntary exchanges or require one to employ inherently unreliable *ex post* measures of compensation. For example, it may seem quite clear that resources would be allocated more efficiently if money were taken from the very wealthy and then used to pay for food and shelter for the neediest. And, for all anyone knows, the amount of benefit for the poor would greatly exceed the loss experienced by those from whom the money is taken. While this may seem obvious to some, the problem is that economics as a science is not equipped to make any assurances about the relative gains and losses from such a redistribution. Such an analysis involves what economists call an "interpersonal comparison of utility." Pareto standards avoid these comparisons, but their application would result in a public policy straitjacket.

4. KALDOR–HICKS EFFICIENCY

Paretian concepts of efficiency, if applied to all public policy decisions, could lead to very limited government action. After all, everyone would have to agree with the policy. Another version of efficiency, Kaldor–Hicks or wealth maximization, responds to this problem. (Although Kaldor–Hicks and wealth maximization can be distinguished, they are often considered and discussed together.) For something to be Kaldor–Hicks efficient, those individuals made better off by the policy or change would have to be made sufficiently better off that they could compensate those who are made worse off. The key here is that the compensation is "potential," not actual.

Two aspects of Kaldor–Hicks efficiency are critical. The first is that the unit of measurement for well-being is not utility but "wealth," "value," or "price." This introduces the notion of "ability to pay." What is maximized is an imperfect substitute for utility and for actual well-being. For example, suppose two individuals—one rich and one poor—both desire a gallon of milk. The poor person wants it desperately and is willing to give his or her last dollar for the milk. On the other hand, the rich person does not care for the milk but thinks it would be fun to open the container and pour the milk into a storm drain and, therefore, is willing to pay $1.50 for the milk. Under wealth maximization principles, the efficient allocation is to the rich person.

The second critical feature of Kaldor–Hicks efficiency or wealth maximization is that the consent of all those affected can be dispensed with. Thus, in the previous example, if the milk were already the property of the poor person, devotion to wealth maximization might require taking the milk from the poor person and simply transferring it to the rich person.

Obviously, although wealth maximization overcomes the inflexibility of Paretian concepts of efficiency, it does so at two prices. First, there is no guarantee that maximizing wealth maximizes any other measure of well-being. In addition, the protection of individual autonomy inherent in Paretian concepts of efficiency is lost.

Richard Posner, in particular, offers an argument that this loss in autonomy may be overstated. He does so by employing the concept of *ex ante* compensation.[2] In a simple form, the argument is that many, if not most, instances in which individuals find they are "worse off" are really the result of choices the individuals made to forego courses of action that would have prevented the loss. The riskier course of action is typically the less expensive and the "compensation" may be in the form of the money saved by taking that option. Thus, the individual "consented to" and was compensated ahead of time for the loss that is now experienced. Judge Posner's effort to reconcile the Kaldor–Hicks or wealth maximization approach with Paretian

2. Richard Posner, *The Economics of Justice* 94–95 (1980).

concepts of efficiency by use of the notion of *ex ante* compensation has met with substantial criticism.[3]

F. EXTERNALITIES

1. NEGATIVE EXTERNALITIES AND PROPERTY RIGHTS

a. Negative Externalities

Much of law and economics is concerned with what are called externalities. Externalities are either positive or negative. A negative externality results when the activity of one person or a business imposes a cost on someone else. The most commonly used example is that of the polluting factory. The owners of the factory may use a variety of inputs for which they pay suppliers. In addition, they may pollute the water and air, making them less useful to others, but not pay for the loss to others. The critical question is whether the activity imposes on others in a negative way.

Of course, the definition of what is a negative externality requires that one address the fundamental question of what rights a person has. If the people affected by the factory have no "right" to clear air or water, there is still technically an externality but the air and water are destined to deteriorate. Other examples of activities that create externalities include cigarette smoking, driving recklessly, and producing defective products. The

3. See e.g. Jules Coleman, "Efficiency, Utility and Wealth Maximization," 8 *Hofstra Law Review* 509, 534–540 (1980).

existence of negative externalities explains a great deal of environmental, tort, and property law.

b. The Tragedy of the Commons

A problem that illustrates negative externalities and explains the need for property rights is the "tragedy of the commons."[4] The problem, as described by Garrett Hardin, involves a group of herdsmen who make use of a common area for grazing. Each makes what seems be a rational assessment of the costs and benefits of adding one animal to his herd. For each one the benefit is the profit to be earned from one additional animal. The cost, however, is a general cost of over-grazing that is spread throughout the community. In effect, the full profit is internalized by the herdsman but the cost is not fully internalized. Since each person engages in the same reasoning, over the long run, the "tragedy" is that the commons are destroyed. The "tragedy of the commons" provides a powerful argument for the assignment of property rights. Such an assignment would mean that the costs of adding an animal to the herd would be fully internalized by the landowners.

c. The Prisoner's Dilemma

The tragedy of the commons is also useful to illustrate the advantages of cooperative behavior. In the case of the herdsmen, everyone is ultimately made worse off by pursuing what seemed to be his or her self-interest. If they could reach some sort of

4. Garrett Hardin, "The Tragedy of the Commons" 162 *Science* 1243 (1968).

agreement about the use of the commons under which they gave up some of their individual freedom, they would all be likely to benefit in the long run. Cooperative behavior could substitute for a public assignment of property rights.

The most commonly used construct in law and economics to illustrate the importance of cooperation is called the "prisoner's dilemma." The problem involves two prisoners who are being held apart from each other after being arrested in connection with a crime. Separately they are questioned. If both prisoners confess they will receive sentences of five years. If neither confesses they will receive sentences of two years. Finally, if one confesses and the other does not, the confessor will be given a one year sentence and the prisoner choosing not to confess will be sentenced to 10 years.

Without cooperating, each party will assume that the other will act selfishly and try to save his own skin. The result will be that each will confess and receive a sentence of five years. The alternative of not confessing is far too risky because it could mean a 10 year sentence. Of course, the best outcome would be for both parties to do exactly that—not confess. But this is an outcome that is unlikely to come about without some ability to form an enforceable agreement.

The Prisoner's Dilemma can be easily adapted to the "tragedy of the commons." Suppose that two farmers on adjoining land draw water from the same reservoir. If both attempt to draw enough water to maximize their output, the water supply will run out before the growing season ends, and the value of their output will be $50 each. If one farmer takes voluntary conservation measures in the form of rationing her use over the growing season, the conserver will produce output worth $30 and the nonconserver will produce $70 of output. If they both take conservation measures, the water will last the entire growing season, they will each have an output of $60, and joint production will be maximized.

In the absence of something more, the parties are destined to produce $50 worth of output each for a total of $100. Just like the prisoners, the rationally self-interested act is to assume the other party will try to maximize his gain. If that is so, it is rational for the counterpart to do the same. It is also rational to adopt the selfish strategy if one assumes the other party will adopt a cooperative strategy.

There are two ways out of the dilemma. The first is to assign property rights so that each party will have the right to exclude the other from unlimited use of the water. Too much use by a party would then give rise to an "externality" and give the other party a legal basis for stopping the overuse. Actually, as discussed in the next chapter, it may not matter to whom the "right" is assigned. The other way out is for the parties to cooperate and privately to create a system of "rights."

2. POSITIVE EXTERNALITIES, FREE–RIDING AND PUBLIC GOODS

a. Positive Externalities

Positive externalities occur when the activities of an individual or a firm result in benefits, the value of which the producer is unable to internalize or enjoy. For example, suppose a homeowner has his or her property beautifully landscaped and the effect is to increase both the value of the recently landscaped property and of the entire neighborhood. Here, the benefit to the neighboring property owners would be a positive externality.

b. Free–Riding

The possibility of positive externalities gives rise to the concept of "free-riding." Free-riding takes place when individuals are able to take advantage of the benefits of the activities of others without paying for those benefits. For example, without copyright protection, a composer might find that others are able to perform his or her music without paying. Similarly, without patent protection, an inventor of a new process may find that manufacturers are making use of that process without compensating the inventor. Positive externalities and free-riding explain the existence of copyright, trademark and patent law.

Just how pervasive free-riding problems are is an empirical question. It seems clear that not as much free-riding takes place as there are opportunities to do so. People do contribute to public broadcasting and to charities without any assurance that their contributions are really necessary for the success of the operation.[5] Thus, it is often hard to square these acts with the standard economic assumption that people are rational maximizers of self-interest.

c. Public Goods

Goods for which there are positive externalities and free-rider problems may not be produced in the quantities in which they would be produced if those problems did not exist. Specifically, they may not be produced at allocatively efficient levels. The problem is that even though potential buyers may desire the good, they may be tempted not to buy or produce it themselves in hopes that they can free-ride off the production or purchases of others. In effect, the private market receives an incorrect and weak signal with respect to the value of these goods.

For example, suppose my house is close to my neighbor's and, if either one of us purchased a watch dog, the dog would alert both of us to any intruder. I might not buy a watch dog because I hope my neighbor will buy one, and he might take the same approach. If so, neither of us will buy a watch dog, even though the value we place on the protection of a watch dog would more than offset the cost of buying the dog.

5. See Jeffrey Harrison, "Egoism, Altruism and Market Illusions: The Limits of Law and Economics," 33 *U.C.L.A. L. Rev.* 1309, 1338–1340 (1986).

Economists and game theorists use a construct called the "chicken game" to illustrate the free-riding problem.[6] Like the actors in the prisoner's dilemma, the participants in the chicken game have a choice of two actions. In the watch dog example, it would be to buy or not buy a watch dog. Here each party would prefer that the other party incur the expense of the dog. If a party were positive the other party would not acquire the dog, then he would be willing to buy it because the value of the dog would outweigh its cost.

The problem in the chicken game and in the case of free-riding generally is that the market receives a false signal as to the value potential buyers attribute to a good or service. This can be illustrated in Figure 2. D_1 is the actual demand of the good for which there are positive externalities and S is the supply. D_2 shows what the demand would be if people were not making an effort to free-ride. Put differently, D_2 shows the true value of the good. The actual quantity produced will be Q_1, but the allocatively efficient level of production would be Q_2.

6. Charles Goetz, *Law and Economics: Cases and Materials* 17–19, 29–32 (1983).

Figure 10

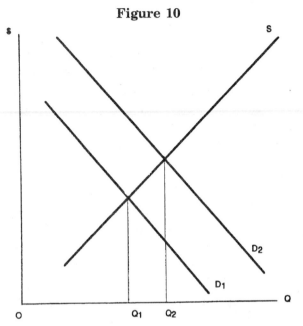

Often when the good in question is subject to these types of influences, it is provided by the government and financed by tax revenues. These types of goods are called "public goods," and the justification for government involvement is that the goods would not be produced in sufficient quantities without government action.

G. TAKINGS, EFFICIENCY AND EXTERNALITIES

An area of law in which many of the issues discussed here can be seen as coming into play is that dealing with takings. As you may know, the

U.S. Constitution prohibits government takings of property unless it is for public use and just compensation is paid. Some takings are obviously that—the government takes land, for example, from someone and uses it itself to allows someone else to use it. This might be the case if a highway were constructed. In other cases, the government regulates the use of property and, in some instances, this too is regarded as a taking. In the case of the highway, the objective is to build a public good—something would likely not be produced due to free-riding. In the case of regulation, typically there is a negative externality that the state seeks to control.

When a taking occurs, compensation is required. The fact that it is required does not mean that the taking is efficient. On the other hand, even it compensation were not required, the taking might still be efficient. First take the case in which compensation is required. Suppose the states pay $20,000 for a parcel of land that has a market value of $20,000 but the owners would not have sold it for less that $25,000 because it has been in the family for years that they attach sentimental value to it. The taken here, even with compensation is not efficiency from either a Pareto or Kaldor–Hicks standpoint.

Now suppose no compensation is required but somehow we know the public values a parcel of land as part of a highway at $10,000 and the owners value it at $8,000. Here a decision to take the land and not pay would be Kaldor–Hicks efficient. This assumes that taking the land produces not other costs. Frank Michleman has made the point that living in a society in which land may be taken without compensation may have a demoralizing effect.[1] If so, this too would be a cost the state would have to consider in making a Kaldor–Hicks evaluation. Interestingly, this means a policy of compensation could have the effect of lowering the cost of public projects.

It is even possible to work the idea of *ex ante* compensation into an analysis of takings law. One of the factors courts consider when determining whether a regulation amounts to a taking is "reasonable investment backed expectations."[2] The suggestion is that the probability of being subject to regulation may be reflected in the price one pays for property. For example, if a person purchases a business that produces externalities, the likelihood of eventual regulation could be reflected in the price paid. If so, a denial of compensation would be consistent with the view that the buyers actually did not possess a property right that had been taken.

1. Frank I. Michleman, "Property, Utility, and Fairness: Comments on the Ethical Foundations of 'Just Compensation' Law," 80 Harv. L. Rev. 1165 (1967)

2. See e.g. District Intown Properties Limited Partnership v. District of Columbia, 198 F.3d 874 (D.C. Cir. 1999), cert. denied, 531 U.S. 812 (2000) (J. Williams, concurring).

CHAPTER THREE

SOME COMPLICATIONS IN THE APPLICATION OF ECONOMICS TO LAW

This Chapter is devoted to some of the controversies and complexities encountered in the study of law and economics. The first section deals with questions that arise from the economist's assumption that individuals are "rational maximizers of self-interest." It is important to establish what this term means. Whether people actually are rational and self-interested is an inquiry that is important to economics generally and perhaps especially important when economics is applied to law. From there, the Chapter goes on to address the question of whether choices and preferences are consistent. This may seem like a strange issue, but economics is generally focused on maximizing some measure of social welfare based, in part, on the choices people make. If these choices are not consistent with actual preferences, it is comparable to sending an incorrect signal to the market. The Chapter's final section considers three problems encountered when one attempts to use economics as the basis for policy.

49

A. RATIONAL MAXIMIZER
OF SELF–INTEREST

Central to conventional law and economics is the assumption that individuals are rational maximizers of self-interest. These seemingly non-controversial terms can be broken into two components. Rationality would require most basically that the individuals not engage in acts that seem to be inconsistent. Often the critical matter that comes up here is the "law of transitivity." Under the law of transitivity, if an individual expresses a preference for apples over pears and pears over oranges, they could not then express a preference for oranges over apples. The importance of the rationality assumption is fairly obvious. Economics, above all else, is about getting the most out of scarce resources, and inconsistent, irrational behavior will impair the functioning of markets and render this goal impossible. The maximizing behavior assumption requires that decisions be made that advance some end. For example, if you wanted to be the richest person in the world, it would not be consistent to give money away unless you viewed it as an investment.

The self-interest assumption is more difficult to define. To some, it may mean to behave selfishly in the most common sense. Others, however, take the view that all rational conduct is self-interested. From this point of view, any choice that one makes is motivated by the fact that the selection is the one that "feels" better. If an option feels better then you prefer it, and to select options you prefer is to act self-interestedly. An example is a seemingly altruistic act. In the jargon of the most die-hard economists, the altruistic person gains more utility—satisfaction—from acting altruistically than from acting in a manner that would appear to be selfish. The altruistic act is explained by self-interest. The person who acts altruistically is really not uncompensated—she receives "psychic income." Psychic income attempts to explain everything but ultimately proves useless because one is still forced to distinguish amongst the different forms of self-interest. These different forms can be very important considerations when one applies economics to law.

Of the two ideas–rationality and self-interest–rationality is the more intriguing because of the numerous studies conducted by economists and psychologists over the last 30 years that suggest that people are not rational. It is important to remember that the criticism of economics is not whether the assumptions are perfectly accurate, but whether they are realistic enough that theories based on them are dependable in real world applications.

1.   WEALTH AND ENDOWMENT EFFECTS

One general observation that indicates that the rationality assumption is incorrect, or at least far more complicated than traditionally assumed, is that people tend to react differently to the same gain or loss depending on their starting point. This is, in fact, one of the elements of "prospect theory," an area of research pioneered by Nobel Prize winner Daniel Kahneman and coauthor Amos Tversky.[1]

One of the central problems associated with relying on choices made or statements about the intensity of individual preferences is the wealth effect. Although the wealth effect can present itself in a number of forms, one of the more perplexing is that a person may seem to value an item or a right more when they possess it than when it is possessed by someone else. For example, suppose an individual owns a piece of property with an ocean view and, because of a deed restriction on the height of structures on a neighboring property, the view cannot be obstructed. If asked by someone what she would take to give up her right to the unobstructed view, her answer might be $50,000. On the other hand, if she did not possess that right but it was offered to her by the owner of the right to build an obstructing dwelling on the neighboring land, she might be willing to pay only $20,000. The fact that expressions of value vary depending upon whether an individual is a potential buyer or seller has been empirically verified.

In some measure, the fact that individuals value things more if they own them can be traced to the fact that ownership means they actually are wealthier and, therefore, are capable of paying more for

1. Daniel Kaheman and Amos Tversky, "Prospect Theory: An Analysis of Decision Under Risk," 47 *Econometrica* 263 (1979).

the items than if they did not own them. The wealth effect, however, goes much deeper than this simple possibility. For example, it seems to hold even when the item at stake is of insignificant value. The problem this poses for law and economics is that the determination of preferences and the strength of those preferences may be contingent on whether or not the person currently owns the property. This is particularly troublesome for those who adhere to a concept of efficiency that seeks to maximize wealth where wealth is determined by how much one is said to value a particular item or right.

2. ULTIMATUM GAMES

The most interesting challenge to the rationality assumption has resulted from experiments conducted by economists and psychologists in which people do not behave as expected. The most important of these experiments is the ultimatum game, which works like this: Groups of subjects are broken into pairs. One person is given a sum of money and can give any amount of it to the other person. If the other person accepts the offer, they both keep what they have. If the other person rejects the offer, neither party receives anything. There is only one chance and the two parties do not communicate.

The rationality assumption would seem to require the first person to offer the second person very little or nothing. If he or she offers nothing, at least the second party is no worse off and would appear to have little reason to reject the offer. If the second person is offered a small amount there seems to be even less reason to reject the offer, since doing so means receiving nothing.

Repeatedly, the game results are that the first party offers more than a minimal share of the total, and the second party rejects offers of very small shares. The implications for rationality are obvious. If one prefers more wealth to less, why reject a sum that at least builds in that direction? Put differently, if a person would bend over to pick up a dollar on the ground, why would he or she reject an offer of a dollar out of a total of $10? The answer seems to be that people value both fair treatment and others' perceptions that they are fair.

The "sense of fairness" explanation is demonstrated particularly well in a game designed by Richard Thaler. Thaler asked a group of people to assume it was a hot day at the beach and that a friend has offered to go find a beer. Part of the group was told that the beer will be bought from a fancy resort bar. Part of group was told that the beer would be bought at a run-down grocery store.[2] Each group was then asked what was the highest price they would pay for the beer. Those who saw themselves as buying from the resort were willing to pay an average price of $2.65. The group buying from the grocery store were willing, on average, to pay $1.50.

One interpretation of the results of the experiment is that people questioned the fairness or the

2. Richard Thaler, The Winner's Curse: Paradoxes and Anomalies of Economic Life, 21–49 (1992).

right of a run-down grocery store to charge as much as the resort. Put differently, those buying from the grocery store would have felt a sense of unfairness if the grocery store had required resort level prices. What appears to be happening is that individuals seem to place an independent value on coming away from an exchange with a sense of having been treated fairly.

The possible existence of an independent value for fairness is complex enough, but it becomes even more intriguing when one realizes that individuals may differ on what they perceive to be fair. This creates the possibility that two people may attribute the same utility and value to a good or service if they possess it, but might express their preferences in the market quite differently. For example, one person could find the price of an automobile acceptable while another would regard the same price as a "rip off." And, it would make sense, in this context, for sellers to discriminate between groups of buyers with differing senses of fairness.[3]

It is not clear that ultimatum games prove that people are irrational. A dollar found on the ground is not exactly the same thing as a dollar share of a much larger pot, and it is easy to imagine a set of preferences that would be both consistent and allow one to pick up the lost dollar and reject the offered dollar. What the games suggest is that rational

3. See generally, Ian Ayres, "Fair Driving: Gender and Race Discrimination in Retail Car Negotiations," 104 *Harv. L. Rev.* 817 (1991); Ian Ayres, "Further Evidence of Discrimination in New Car Negotiations and Estimates of Its Causes," 94 *Mich. L. Rev.* 109 (1991).

people have complex preferences. If so, the implications for the application of economics to law are enormous. People who study law and economics tend to write about efficient levels of contract breach and crime based strictly on the dollar values involved. What the ultimatum games indicate is that this could be an overly simplistic analysis.

The issues of what people find acceptable and why are studied by sociologists in the fields of equity theory and relative deprivation rather than by economists. These are, however, critical matters for those who apply economics to law in the hopes of using that analysis to help formulate policy. These concepts go beyond economics alone and permit one to pierce some of the mysteries of market behavior in order to make more informed decisions about the use of law.

B. CHOICES AND PREFERENCES

As mentioned above, one of the important assumptions that must be made to apply economics to law is that people reveal their preferences in the choices they make. Of course, the biggest problem with this assumption is that people with extremely strong preferences may not have the funds to express those preferences in the market. Since law responds to more than just the needs expressed in markets, this is a crucial matter to consider. Beyond that issue, it's important to be aware of a number of other factors that can make people's choices inconsistent with their preferences.

1.   PUBLIC GOODS AND FREE RIDING

You were already introduced to one of the ways in which the choices made in markets can be misleading when you read about the chicken game and public goods in Chapter Two. To review, imagine a case in which you and a pal are enrolled in the same class and you both trust each other to take good notes. You hope that your friend will attend class and share the notes with you so that you won't have to do any work. However, if you have to, you will go to class to get the notes yourself. Thus, your preferences could be ordered as follows: friend goes to class and shares notes with you (#1 choice), you go to class and take notes yourself (#2), or you have no notes (#3). The problem is that to get your first choice you may have to act as though the notes are less important to you than they actually are. You engage in bluffing designed to convince your friend that the only way for her to get the notes is to go to class herself.

You can see the problem here for an economist who is trying to gauge your preferences but is not a mind-reader. For strategic reasons, your signal must be different from how you actually feel, and the "choice" or lack thereof does not reveal your preference at all.

2.   THE PRISONER'S DILEMMA

A similar problem arises in the prisoner's dilemma, which you also saw in Chapter Two. Again, the problem involves two prisoners who are being held apart from each other after being arrested in connection with a crime. They are separately questioned. If both prisoners confess they will both receive a sentence of five years. If neither confesses they will receive sentences of two years. Finally, if one confesses and the other does not, the confessor will be given a one-year sentence and the prisoner choosing not to confess will be sentenced to 10 years. The ideal strategy is for both prisoners to not confess because this means only two years of prison each. The big drawback to this strategy is that the other prisoner may then elect to confess and the non-confessor gets 10 years. As a result, each prisoner will attempt to save themselves and confess.

The way to get to the ideal outcome is for the prisoners to make an enforceable agreement–something the rules of the game exclude–or to cooperate. There is, in fact, a great deal of evidence that people do learn to cooperate, especially after repeated tries, in order to get to the best outcome. The problem for those who rely on choices to reveal preferences is that, unless the observer understands the game, the action adopted to achieve the best outcome will appear to be inconsistent with what is really desired.

3.   THE POSSIBILITY OF COUNTER-PREFERENTIAL CHOICE

The possibility of choices revealing preferences becomes even more remote if people are capable of counter-preferential choices. Nobel Award winning

economist Amartya Sen suggests this possibility
when he distinguishes sympathy from commitment.
To understand this difference, suppose you become
a vegetarian even though you love the taste of meat.
Maybe you empathize with the animals' suffering,
or perhaps you believe that all animals are sentient
beings and deserve to have rights, one of which is to
not be eaten. The standard analysis that your
choice in the market reveals something about your
taste for eating meat would miss the fact that you
actually do like the taste of meat and might buy
similarly-tasting products. More importantly, it
misses a complexity in the choice-making' process
that could be especially useful to understand when
economics is applied to law.

4. FALSE CONSCIOUSNESS

A failure to match choices with preferences, according to some, can result from the inability of an
individual to know or express what is in his best
interest. This is best understood if one uses the
notion of coercion as a baseline. A person who
chooses to give up his wallet instead of both giving
it up and being beaten has in a sense expressed a
preference. Still, we tend not to give much credence
to that choice as something the law should legiti-
mize. Moving from that point, the question becomes: when should the choices made be regarded
as free? When are the factors influencing a choice
legitimate and when do they prevent someone from
expressing his "true" preference? These are obvi-

ously open-ended questions without answers that will satisfy everyone. They are critical though, because choices that do not reveal "true" preferences can hardly be said to be consistent with efficient outcomes.[4]

Other than distinguishing choices that would be made if one were "free" to choose from those resulting from illegitimate influences, questions can arise when people seem unable to control their choices. For example, an alcoholic may prefer not to be an alcoholic and at the same time consume a great deal of alcohol. A similar case is the heavy smoker who also buys nicotine patches in a effort to give up smoking. Again, since economics is so crucially linked with preferences and the expression of preferences, it is a problem when there is a gap between expressions and actual preferences.

5. FRAMING PROBLEMS

The problem of determining preferences is also complicated by the fact that people seem to give inconsistent answers to questions that are substantively the same depending on how those questions are framed. In one famous example, individuals were asked to assume that a disease outbreak in the United States was expected to kill 600 people.[5] They were then asked to choose between two programs

4. See Cass Sunstein, "Legal Interference With Private Preferences," 53 *U. Chi. L. Rev.* 1129 (1986).

5. See Daniel Kahneman and Amos Tversky, "Framing Decisions and the Psychology of Choice," 211 *Science* 453 (1981).

stated as follows: "If program A is adopted, 200 people will be saved. If program B is adopted, there is a one-third probability that 600 people will be saved, and a two-thirds probability that no people will be saved." Stated this way, there was a strong preference for program A.

The choice was then presented as follows: "If program C is adopted, 400 people will die. If program D is adopted, there is a one-third probability that nobody will die, and a two-thirds probability that 600 people will die." This time choice D was heavily favored. The problem is that programs A and C are identical as are choices B and D. The difference is in the way the choice is perceived.

C. PREFERENCES, VALUES, AND LEXICAL ORDERING

One of the assumptions that makes conventional economics "work" is that all sources of utility or pleasure are similar in that the type of utility they generate can be reduced to a common denominator.[6] For example, if someone took your autographed copy of Kingsley Amis' *Lucky Jim* it might be a terrible loss. Under the conventional thinking, no matter how great your loss in utility, you could somehow be compensated and restored—perhaps by receiving a carton of Rod McKuen poetry books—to your original level of utility or happiness.

6. Nicolas Georgescu–Roegen, "Choice Expectation and Measurability," 68 *Q. J. Econ.* 503 (1954).

Of course, under this way of thinking, money is used for compensation because it can be exchanged for all sorts of worldly goods and services. Moreover, everything is ultimately for sale. After all, if you could be compensated for any involuntary loss, presumably you could be compensated at just a slightly higher rate and freely give up whatever is at stake. For a price, your arm is for sale as well as your children. In a more familiar legal context, it could mean that, if the price is high enough, you will break a promise, or breach a contract, drive recklessly through a playground, or enslave someone.

But what if you are guided by principle: You will not allow someone to break your leg at any price, no amount of money will entice you into driving recklessly through a playground, and you refuse to break the knees of, say, a competing figure skater no matter how much you are offered. When these things come up, the assumption that everything can be reduced to simple utility does not hold. Moreover, it is least likely to hold when the "goods" involved are associated with some moral obligation and oft times with law.

It is easy to say that in these examples, you are simply not offered enough, or you are acting irrationally. Another explanation is that some sources of utility are lexically or lexicographically ordered.[7] An example of lexical ordering is a dictionary. In a

7.   John Rawls, *A Theory of Justice* 42–43 (1971).

dictionary any word beginning with the letter "a" comes before words beginning with the letter "b." Even a word beginning with "b" and followed by an infinite number of "a's" cannot be placed ahead of a word beginning with an "a," even if that "a" is followed by a whole host of "z's."

Like words in the dictionary, some values are, no doubt, ranked in such a way that they are not interchangeable with values or sources of utility that exist at a different level. This means concepts like "compensation" and "incentive" may be more complex than conventional economics seems to allow. This is particularly important in the application of economics to law because law is about so many of these values.

The possibility of the existence of different types of values can be especially important at a very practical level. In order to understand why, it is important to understand that economists usually start from the point of view that a person's tastes and preferences are fixed. The term here is that they are "exogenously" determined. This would be important if one wanted to examine the impact of a price change on the sales of orange juice. It is only possible to isolate the effect of the price change if the taste for orange juice remains constant whatever the price. In other words, even though the price change will affect the amount of orange juice purchased, it must not affect how much people enjoy orange juice.

This requirement presents a problem when economics is applied to law. For example, instead of orange juice, suppose one wanted to determine the impact of higher fines on speeding. The idea, of course, is that higher fines will decrease speeding. The problem is that the increase in fines may actually effect how people feel about speeding. That is, a higher fine may signify societal disapproval and actually have an impact on the individual's "taste" for speeding. More technically, law may act as an endogenous variable, not simply an exogenous one.[8] This means that the "markets" that are the subject of law and economics are probably far more complex than the ones to which conventional analysis is applied.

To give you an idea of how this makes the economic analysis of law more complex than the economic analysis of more conventional markets, consider the behavioral assumptions specified by one leading law and economics scholar. The author states the usual assumption underlying his analysis, that individuals are rational maximizes of self-interest. He then explains that this means they do not obey the law out of a sense of duty.[9] This is not atypical, and there is nothing inherently wrong with making assumptions. It does, however, give

8. See Kenneth G. Dau–Schmidt, "An Economic Analysis of the Criminal Law as a Preference Shaping Policy," 1990 *Duke L. J.* 1; Jeffrey L. Harrison, "Class, Personality, Contract and Unconscionability," 35 *William and Mary L. Rev.* 445 (1994).

9. Robert Cooter, "Prices and Sanctions," 84 Colum. L. Rev. 1523, 1527 (1984).

one a sense of how the economic analysis of law may be limited. For example, people who obey the law because it is the law or who change their behavior when something becomes illegal—and not as a result of a cost-benefit analysis—may be left out of the economist's theory.

CHAPTER FOUR

THE COASE THEOREM AND RELATED PROPERTY ISSUES

A. THE COASE THEOREM

1. ALLOCATIVE IMPLICATIONS

Nothing is more central to the study of law and economics nor more responsible for its growth than the Coase Theorem.[1] The Coase Theorem says that, in many instances, the assignment of rights by courts or legal authorities may have little to do with who eventually possesses those rights. In the words of Mark Kelman, "the market, like an untameable river, will knock out attempts to alter its mighty course."[2]

Although the Theorem has implications for a wide variety of areas of substantive law, it is most easily explained and understood in the context of competing uses for resources. One of the cases that lends itself to a Coasian analysis is *Fountainbleau*

1. Ronald Coase, "The Problem of Social Cost," 3 *J. L. & Econ.* 1 (1960).

2. Mark Kelman, "Consumption Theory, Production Theory, and Ideology in the Coase Theorem," 52 *So. Cal. L. Rev.* 669, 675 (1979).

Hotel Corp. v. Forty–Five Twenty–Five, Inc. (Fla. App.1959). The dispute revolved around the right of the Fountainbleau hotel in Miami Beach to build a fourteen-story addition. The problem with the addition was that its shadow would fall over the cabana, swimming pool, and sunbathing areas of a neighboring hotel, the Eden Roc. The Eden Roc sought to enjoin the construction of the addition and eventually lost. In more technical terms, the shadow could be viewed as a negative externality—a cost imposed on the Eden Roc by the Fountainbleau's construction project. As it turned out, the Eden Roc was denied injunctive relief; the right to build the addition, even though it blocked the sun, was assigned by the court to the Fountainbleau.

The question from a Coasian perspective is whether it really matters how the court decided the issue. Obviously the "right" to build had some value in terms of the present value of the expected profit the Fountainbleau would earn from the addition. Suppose this value was $1,000,000. Suppose also that the Eden Roc executives had studied the matter and determined that the present value of the profits lost due to the fact that a sunless resort hotel is less desirable to tourists is $1,100,000. At that point, it would have made sense for the managers of the Fountainbleau and Eden Roc to determine whether they could have made an exchange that left them both better off—in a Pareto Superior position. Obviously, any price in excess of $1,000,000 would have made the Fountainbleu better off and any price less than $1,100,000 would have improved the position of the Eden Roc. Thus, at least at this initial level of analysis, the right to build should have been sold to the Eden Roc and the initial assignment would not have withstood the influence of market.

The critical element of the Coase Theorem is that the outcome in terms of which hotel eventually owns the right to build or to prevent building is not affected by the initial assignment of that right. Thus, had the Florida court decided that the Eden Roc did have the right to enjoin the construction of the shadow-casting addition, presumably, the parties involved would once again engage in their valuation process. The Fountainbleau would be unwilling to pay any more than $1,000,000 for the Eden Roc's "right" to enjoin construction, and the Eden Roc would not take anything less that $1,100,000 for that right. Here again, the addition would not be built.

It is important to see how the Coase Theorem applies to the typical case involving a factory which, in its production process, either pollutes the air or the water in a nearby river. In both instances, the pollution, like the shadow cast by the Fountainbleau's addition, could be viewed as an externality. The question the Coase Theorem answers is whether the amount of this pollution really will be affected by whether or not the polluting factory has a right to pollute. What the Theorem tells us is that, however the right is initially assigned, the eventual use of the water will be left to market forces and the level of pollution will be the same.

It is important not to lose sight of the breadth of the implications of the Coase Theorem. The battle between the Eden Roc and Fountainbleau illustrates the Theorem in very simple terms. Coase's proposition was initially illustrated by competing users of land, a cattle raiser with straying cattle and a farmer whose crops were endangered by the straying cattle. This type of example allows one to focus on the workings of the Theorem in a context in which marginal analysis—the mainstay of microeconomics—is easily visualized. In this famous example, the relevant comparison was between the value of each additional steer and the annual crop loss per additional steer. Again, regardless of the initial assignment, one would expect the land to be put to the use for which it generates the greatest profit. In this example, where the output of each user can be divided into individual units, it is likely to mean the land will be divided in some fashion between cattle raising and farming.

Further afield, the Theorem seems to apply quite readily to a standard contracts problem. Suppose Bud agrees to sell his 1957 Chevy to Bette for $10,000 and that Bud must pay Bette $5,000 if he breaches, due to an iron-clad liquidated damages clause. Suppose Bette attributes a value of $12,000 to the car. Her "benefit of the bargain" is $2,000. Now Jack arrives and offers Bud $13,000 for the car. Obviously, Jack values the car the most of the trio. The problem is whether the market will find a way around the fact that Bette is entitled to the car or $5,000 and steer it into Jack's hands. Here Bud would be willing to buy the right to breach for up to $3,000 and Bette would be willing to sell it for something in excess of $2,000. Presumably they will make the exchange and the car will be resold to Jack. As for the liquidated damages, Bud can just threaten to perform (which only gets Bette a $2,000 surplus) anytime she presses the issue of the liquidated damages clause.

2.   ASSIGNMENT OF RIGHTS AND DISTRIBUTIVE EFFECTS

It is important to note that the Coase Theorem focuses on allocative effects. In its simplest form, it can be viewed as saying that an initial assignment that is allocatively inefficient—assigned to the party who does not attribute the greatest value to the right—will be "corrected" by the market. This hardly means the assignment by the court, legislature or administrative body is irrelevant. That assignment can have huge distributive effects. For example, by assigning the right to build to the Fountainbleau, the court ensured that the Fountainbleau would keep the right or be enriched by someone who valued it more. Put differently, the assignment may not determine the ultimate allocation of various rights, but it will have an impact on the distribution of wealth.

Oft-times courts seem to react to the distributive implications even when the parties seem capable of bargaining around the initial allocation. For example, in a contracts case, *McKinnon v. Benedict* (Wis.

1968), the court was faced with the issue of whether to enjoin the land development efforts of one landowner at the request of a neighboring landowner. The parties had evidently had significant personal contact, and it seems clear that the parties could reallocate the development rights should the relative values attributed to those rights by the parties warrant. The court denied the injunction, favoring the party it characterized as having limited financial means and limited business experience. The decision had the effect of enhancing the wealth of the disadvantaged party and creating a situation in which the wealthier party would be required to purchase the defendant's right to develop the property rather than have it given to him by the court.

This particular example may give the reader pause, because it seems clear that had the injunction been issued, the party with the limited resources would not have been able to buy the right to develop from the other landowner. From the standpoint of conventional economic analysis, the inability to pay is really indistinguishable from the unwillingness to pay. The conclusion would still be that the relatively poor landowner did not sufficiently value the right. If this is disconcerting, conventional economists would remind the reader that if the land would be sufficiently profitable when developed, the poor landowner would be able to find investors quite willing to loan him the money to buy the development rights from the landowner to whom the injunction was granted.

An even more direct interest in allowing for both allocative and distributive effects is found in *Spur Industries, Inc. v. Del E. Webb Development Co.* (Ariz.1972). Spur operated a feed lot in an isolated area. Over the years, land near the feedlot was developed for residential purposes, resulting eventually in complaints that the feedlot was a nuisance due to the insects and odors it caused. Del Webb, a developer, successfully sought an order permanently enjoining Spur from operating the feed lot. The court granted the injunction. From a strictly allocative perspective, there would appear to be little reason for the court to go any further. The court, however, seemingly desirous of altering what it seemed to view as an unfair distributive outcome, ordered the developer to pay Spur for the expenses of relocating.

3. TRANSACTION COSTS

The Fountainbleau and Eden Roc dispute is an easy example of how the Coase Theorem might work. A problem, which Professor Coase readily recognized, is that virtually all exchanges have a cost. These costs are called transaction costs. It is important to note that a transaction cost is not the price of an item or a right. Instead, it is the cost of the transaction itself. These costs include search costs, information costs, the costs of meetings, negotiations, and any other costs incurred to make the primary exchange occur. If these costs exceed the gain from the exchange itself, the exchange will not take place.

In the Fountainbleau example, the gain from the exchange would be $100,000. That is, the right to the sunlight is worth $100,000 more to the Eden Roc than the right to build is to the Fountainbleau. Thus, it would make economic sense, assuming no one is made worse off by the exchange, for the right to eventually find its way into the possession of the Eden Roc. Suppose, however, that the transaction involved substantial attorneys' fees, long distance telephone calls, and air fares in order to gather the interested parties together. If the transaction costs exceed $100,000, which in this case they very well might, the surplus or profit created by the exchange will be offset by the costs of the exchange. Thus, transaction costs, like the friction encountered in a physics experiment, may keep us from observing what would actually happen if the market were completely fluid. In short, in many instances, the market will not overcome an initial, possibly inefficient, assignment.

Two additional facets of the transaction costs problem are important to note. The first concerns situations in which the possible exchange does not involve single entities on both sides of the bargaining table but, on at least one side, there are multiple parties. Here the difficulty of achieving an exchange is made more severe by the costs of contacting a number of individuals and reaching agreement among them as to an acceptable selling or buying price. This coordination problem exists even if the parties are perfectly willing to cooperate. Another possibility—that they are not so willing to cooperate—is discussed below.

The second factor is the implication of time limitations. For example, the well-known case of *Ploof v. Putnam* involved the efforts by an individual sailing with his family who was caught in a violent storm. When he tied up at the defendant's dock, the defendant untied his mooring lines and his boat was cast adrift. Ultimately the court assigned the right to the party in distress to use the dock of the landowner. In this type of situation, any misallocation would be difficult to overcome. Here the costs of the transaction may not be prohibitive in the abstract but, when they must be expended in a very short period, they may become prohibitive.

B. BARGAINING PROBLEMS

The Coase Theorem has its best chance of actually "working" when the parties do not have significant "market power." In this context, "market power" means the ability to hold out for more favorable terms without fearing that the other party will easily turn to another seller or buyer. The bargaining problem can arise in two distinct contexts.

The first and most extreme example of when "market power" can be a problem is when there is only one buyer and one seller. This is called a bilateral monopoly. First, consider the basic Fountainbleau example in its simplest form—the single owner of the Fountainbleau bargaining with the owner of the Eden Roc. In the example presented earlier, the building right was worth $100,000 more to the owner of the Eden Roc than to the owner of the Fountainbleau. The least the Fountainbleau would take for this right was $1,000,000 and the most the Eden Roc would offer was $1,100,000. The parties must, however, determine an actual sales price. Presumably, they will both use a variety of bargaining strategies in order to get the most favorable price possible. In other words, they will each try to get the largest share possible of the gain created by the exchange. As they parry back and forth in an effort to gain the upper hand, it may be that the time for a mutually beneficial exchange will simply run out.

Whether the delays associated with bilateral monopoly that mean the exchange may not take place are fairly termed transaction costs in Coasian terms is not clear. They may be viewed as a form of transaction cost or it may be that the Coase Theorem involves an assumption that the bargaining parties will cooperate in order to consummate the exchange. In either case, there seems to be general agreement that the bargaining problem creates the same kind of "friction" as traditional transaction costs.[3]

Much the same problem arises if the hypothetical is revised so that the Eden Roc is owned by a single individual, but the Fountainbleau is owned by several individuals, all of whom must agree in order for

3. See Robert Cooter, "The Cost of Coase," 11 *J. Leg. Stud.* 1 (1982).

the exchange to be consummated. The most obvious difficulty this presents is an array of variations on traditional transaction costs. A larger number of individuals means increased difficulties of coordination, contract drafting, etc. In addition, each seller or buyer will have the potential power to veto the exchange. In effect, each owner has monopoly power with respect to her ownership rights. Here again, the absence of a competitive market may mean that some individuals hold out for a disproportionate share of the proceeds from the sale. Of course, this may entail a fair amount of strategic behavior in the form of bluffing. The general problem is the same as that which exists between the buyer and seller in that the holdout has the power to undermine what would otherwise be an exchange that would leave all parties better off.

In addition to the problems associated with strategic behavior in bargaining, there may be another obstacle to the free exchange. Referring again to the Eden Roc example, it is clear that under a traditional analysis any price between $1,000,000 and $1,100,000 will leave both parties in a better position than the one in which they started. One would think that they would realize that it is more important to come to an agreement that improves the lot of both parties than it is to hold out for the very best bargain. Under this line of reasoning, once all the haggling and bluffing is over, the parties would agree to something. The additional problem that may arise here is that both parties may approach the bargaining with expectations about what a "fair" division of the surplus made possible by the exchange would be. These expectations may result from an inflated sense of entitlement resulting from social class or a simple desire to save face. If one or both of the parties takes the view that they will take none of the surplus before they will settle for what is seen as an inadequate share, the deal may still fall through despite their best efforts. This "equity" barrier is probably of greater importance when the bargaining takes on an interpersonal character.[4]

C. THE WEALTH EFFECT

One of the most frequently discussed criticisms of the Coase Theorem and of the economic analysis of law generally is the "wealth effect." To understand the importance of the wealth effect, one must recall that what the Coase Theorem guarantees is that, in a transaction-cost-free context, resources and rights will end up in the hands of those who value them most. The wealth effect introduces an element of circularity into the theory by suggesting that the one who values something most is, all other things being equal, the person who already possesses whatever is at stake. It also suggests a bias in favor of the *status quo* as far as resource allocation goes.

What this means in the Eden Roc example is that, if the right had been assigned to the Eden Roc and

4. Jeffrey Harrison, "Trends and Traces: A Preliminary Evaluation of Economic Analysis in Contract Law," 1988 *Ann. Survey of Am. L.* 73, 96.

the Fountainbleau was enjoined from constructing its addition, the bias introduced in the system is that the right will not be transferred. Conversely, if the right is granted to the Fountainbleau, as was the case, the bias introduced favors the right remaining with the Fountainbleau.

In its most fundamental form, the actual ownership of an asset affects the ability of a party to pay. In actuality, factors that have only a minimal effect on wealth or no effect also seem to create the same kind of inertia that the traditional wealth effect produces. One of best examples of how "wealth-like effects" can work at insignificant levels of wealth was illustrated in an experiment in which individuals, upon entering a room, were given either a lottery ticket or \$3.00.[5] After the nature of the lottery was explained, they were given an opportunity to exchange their lottery tickets for \$3.00 or to exchange their \$3.00 for a lottery ticket. The majority of participants, whether they were initially given lottery tickets or given \$3.00, elected to keep what they had. In essence, the mere possession of one item instead of another seemed to give rise to some form of inertia that precluded an exchange. The value one attributed to \$3.00 or to the lottery ticket was determined solely by whether he or she had been handed \$3.00 or a lottery ticket in the first place.

5. Jack Knetch & J. A. Sinden, "Willingness to Pay and Compensation Demanded: Experimental Evidence of an Unexpected Distortion in Measures of Value," 99 *Q. J. Econ.* 507 (1984).

An illustration of inertia resulting in a wealth-effect type of influence is the change in the mobility of professional baseball players before and after free-agency.[6] Until relatively recently, due to agreements among the owners of professional sports teams, a player would be drafted by one team and generally would stay with that team unless traded to another team. In effect, the right to the player's services belonged to the team owner. The services of that player would have a certain value to that team and the player could be sold or traded to another owner who valued those services more than the original owner.

Under a free-agency system, which allows the players to sell their services, one would expect the level of player mobility to remain the same. In other words, players would still end up playing for teams that attributed to them the highest value based on revenue-generating potential. In actuality, in the era of free-agency, players have turned out to be significantly more mobile as owners bid for their services. Since it is unlikely that actual revenue-generating potential increased, it appears that owners valued the players' services more when they owned the rights to those services. Another explanation for the inertia under the former system is that owners found it far easier to refuse offers made for the rights to their players than to actually incur an out-of-pocket expense of the same amount in order to obtain a player.

6. See M. Kelman, supra note 2, at 682–685.

It is not clear whether the wealth effect and effects having the same manifestations really undermine the Coase Theorem. At one level, the Theorem seems to hold. As a technical matter, the eventual allocation does end up being to the party who attributes the greatest value to the right or item in question. On the other hand, the person who that happens to be and the allocatively efficient outcome are in some sense predetermined by the fortuity of the initial allocation. A different initial allocation may mean a different distribution would be allocatively efficient. In a sense, *who* really values something the most is indeterminate.

One additional and very intriguing problem further complicates the issue of valid expression of value. As you have seen, valuation may be affected by ownership. Now add to this the possibility that one can be wrong about that ownership. In other words, whatever wealth effect there is may be based on an incorrect premise. For example, one recent study found that terminable-at-will employees believe they cannot be terminated arbitrarily when, in fact, they can be.[7] The question to untangle is what to make of any expressions the workers may make with respect to the value of those rights.

7. Pauline T. Kim, "Bargaining with Imperfect Information: A Study of Worker Perceptions of Legal Protection in an At–Will World," 85 Cornell L. Rev. 105 (1997).

D. REACTIONS TO TRANSACTION COSTS

1. DUPLICATING FRICTION–FREE TRANSACTIONS

An important issue that arises in the context of the Coase Theorem is whether a court should take note of the presence or absence of transaction costs in its delineation of legal rights. There are a number of possibilities. The most commonly discussed possibility, typically attributed to Judge Richard Posner, is that the court should assign the right as the parties would have if they were not hampered by transaction costs.

For example, take a case like *Boomer v. Atlantic Cement Company* (N.Y.1970), a casebook favorite dealing with the subject of nuisance. The dirt, smoke and vibration associated with the operation of defendant's cement factory resulted in $185,000 in damages to the eight plaintiffs who requested an injunction. The cement plant represented a $45 million investment and presumably had a current value well in excess of $185,000.

In Coase Theorem terms, there would seem to be little long-run allocative impact from any decision the court made. Supposedly, if it had granted the injunction, the factory owners would have purchased the right to continue polluting from the land-owners. Transaction costs might have been quite low, and certainly low enough not to cancel out the gain from an exchange in which the land-owners value the right at $185,000 and the factory values it at several million dollars. With eight sellers, however, the possibility of hold-out problems exist and if the injunction were granted, the factory could not operate. In addition, if the number of plaintiffs were increased, there would be an even greater possibility that the exchange would not take place. One solution is to simply assign the right to the party that values it the most—in this case the owners of the cement factory. After all, the reasoning goes, this is what the parties would have done if they could. In the case, the court did, but it also granted damages to the landowners.

The solution to the transaction costs problem of granting the right to the party who would have purchased it in a friction-free market is subject to both practical and moral questions. From the point of view of simple practicality, it is not clear exactly how a court or any rights-allocating body is supposed to gauge, consistently and accurately, the value of the right to the respective parties. While the Posner solution seems to envision some kind of giant auction, that is not what happens, and courts are left to their usual means of attempting to assess value. This means reliance on objective as opposed to subjective values and the possibility that the court will simply get it wrong.

More of a problem is presented by the question of whether courts *should* try to replicate the allocations that would occur in the market. It should be recalled that one possibly comforting implication of the Coase Theorem is that both parties would agree to any reallocation of rights. In other words, since both parties consent to the exchange, it seems they have made a Pareto superior move. Of course, this is all subject to the limitations discussed in Chapter Three with respect to the disconnection between choice and preferences.

One cannot make the same claim under the judicial assignment approach. Returning once again to the Fountainbleau case suppose the numbers are the same as above: the right to build and block the sunlight is worth $1,000,000 to the Fountainbleau and access to sunlight is worth $1,100,000 to the Eden Roc. Due to transaction costs, suppose further that it is clear that once the assignment is made, the parties will not be able to exchange the right. If the court chooses to assign the right to the party who would have ended up with it in a transaction-costs free environment, it would be assigned to the Eden Roc. In the context of the case, the court would have granted the Eden Roc's request for an injunction. Such an assignment would seem to be consistent with wealth-maximizing or Kaldor–Hicks standards of efficiency. After all, even if one wanted to view the decision as involving a reallocation from the Fountainbleau to the Eden Roc, the gain for the Eden Roc would exceed the loss to the Fountainbleau.

On the other hand, a one-time allocation may not be consistent with Pareto superiority. It will be recalled that a Pareto superior move requires that the position of at least one party be improved and that no parties be made worse off. In the example, the Eden Roc will be no worse off as it always claimed the right to unblocked sunlight. The Fountainbleau, however, must be viewed as being worse off. It may be true that the right to sunlight/right to build dispute had not been previously settled and that neither party had a clear foundation for viewing its version of the right as a settled part of its property. Still, until the decision, it did view itself as either owning the right or, at least, having some probability of owning the right. Indeed, this undetermined interest probably could have been sold— with a suitable discount. Certainly, neither party would abandon its claim without compensation. Thus, the court's allocation worsens the position of the Fountainbleau. Without consent and with one party being made worse off, the moral appeal of judicial assignment is weakened.

There is a subtle and suspect reason for arguing that the court's policy of mimicking the market does not leave the losing bidder worse off. Presumably, the amount paid by each party for his property included embedded within it an allowance for the fact that property rights, particularly with respect to future events and assignments, are inherently uncertain. One of these areas of uncertainty would be one's right to unrestricted access to the sun or the right to build. In the case of the Eden Roc, the argument would be that the owners would have been willing to pay more when the site of the Eden Roc was initially purchased if the title to the land included a covenant from the Fountainbleau that it would not build beyond a certain height. The argument is that the Eden Roc "consented" ahead of time to the risk of losing access to the sun. In addition, the owners were compensated for the loss by means of the lower price paid for the property. This is known as *ex ante* compensation. Again, whether this is consent in any meaningful way is questionable.

This situation can be distinguished from another in which it may be possible to achieve both wealth maximization and Pareto superiority. Suppose the right in question was oil drilling rights off the coast of Miami Beach and that neither party had expected that such activity would become legal. Now when the parties bid and the right is assigned to the highest bidder, that party is better off. Moreover, unless there is some ultimate adverse impact on the losing party's business, it is difficult to see how it is made worse off. In effect, the creation and assignment of a new right does not leave the losing bidder in any worse position than it would have been in had the new right not evolved.

The issue of how to react to transaction costs has one more wrinkle. Suppose you take the view that for one reason or another a court should not attempt to mimic the market in high transaction cost contexts, even if it can do so accurately. You are, however, perfectly willing to allow people to voluntarily exchange rights once a court has assigned them. The problem here is that the only thing determining whether an efficient allocation takes place is the existence of transaction costs. Unless there is some moral significance to the existence of these costs, the position that you and many others have adopted seems to have no morally principled underpinnings because it reduces to a view that efficiency is desired when transaction costs are low and not required when they are high.

2.   ASYMMETRICAL TRANSACTION COSTS

As already noted, determining which party attributes greater value to a right is not likely to be an easy task. Thus, even if one is devoted to wealth-maximization as a legitimate goal of courts and legislators, there is no clear formula that determines how to achieve that goal. Guido Calabresi, and perhaps others, has offered a kind of back-up strategy that indirectly would achieve the wealth maximization goal. This strategy calls for assigning the right to the party from whom it could be transferred less expensively.[8]

For example, suppose both the Eden Roc and Fountainbleau attributed significant value to access to sunlight, but there was a problem in ascertaining their relative valuations. If we knew that a transfer from the Eden Roc would involve lower transaction costs than a transfer from the Fountainbleau, the proper strategy would be to assign the right to the Eden Roc. If this turns out to an incorrect assignment, the chances that there will be a market correction are higher than if the incorrect assignment were made to the Fountainbleau.

8.   Guido Calabresi, *The Costs of Accidents* 150–152 (1970).

E. PROTECTING ENTITLEMENTS

Although it may be possible for parties to bargain and engage in exchange when the rights at issue are not perfectly defined, most would argue that the Coase Theorem is far more likely to work when the ownership of various rights or entitlements is clear. The question that remains open is exactly how these entitlements are to be protected. In an important 1972 article, "Property Rules, Liability Rules, and Inalienability: One View of the Cathedral," Professor Guido Calabresi and A. Douglas Melamed outlined the options and the justifications for each of three possibilities.[9]

The proposition set forth by Calabresi and Melamed is that entitlements can be protected by liability rules, property rules or a rule of inalienability. Liability rules are used when a person is permitted to invade the rights of another and then compensate him or her. Typical of this would be an accident in which the person at fault is required to compensate the victim for personal or property damage.

A property rule, on the other hand, is one under which a party must have permission from the affected party before taking or using the other party's entitlement. Finally, in some cases, the rule is that the entitlement cannot be sold or otherwise exchanged, making it a rule of inalienability.

9. Guido Calabresi & A. Douglas Melamed, "Property Rules, Liability Rules and Inalienability: One View of the Cathedral," 85 *Harv. L. Rev.* 1086 (1972).

For law and economics purposes, the important question is when it makes sense to apply these various means of protecting entitlements. As a general matter, when transaction costs are likely to be high, a liability rule has much to recommend it. For example, returning to *Boomer v. Atlantic Cement Company,* suppose the entitlement was that the homeowners had the right to be free from the dirt, smoke and vibration caused by the cement factory. Suppose further that, as the case states, the damage to the cement factory of being required to shut down would far exceed the damage to property owners if it were permitted to continue operating. In a transaction-costs-free environment, it would not matter if the court had "mistakenly" applied a property rule and enjoined the factory from operating. In that context, the factory could easily buy out the rights of the landowners.

It is possible, however, that rather than a smooth exchange, there might be significant transaction costs. Or, as suggested above, the landowners, any one of whom could submarine the whole deal, just cannot agree to sell their right to have the factory's activity enjoined. Here, the idea of permitting the factory to pollute and to pay the victims for their losses has appeal, especially to those who are interested in traditional notions of efficiency. As it turned out, the court basically applied a liability rule by granting an injunction but ordering it vacated once the factory compensated the landowners.

The same sort of logic applies to accidents. Obviously, in the case of negligence, it would be impossible for the person causing the damage to negotiate with the victim beforehand. Presumably, the injurer does not know the victim or even anticipate the accident. Transaction costs are virtually limitless and liability rules are thus employed in these kinds of cases. Calabresi and Melamed make the point that requiring the parties to negotiate in advance for permission would really require a great deal of potential accident-causing activity to stop altogether.

As attractive as liability rules are—due to the relative ease with which entitlements can be transferred, there are three drawbacks, all of which are absent if one relies on a property rule instead. First, use of a liability rule permits one to take the property of another without her consent. Even though there is compensation after the fact, and even if the compensation seems fair, those who value consent as an independent interest—perhaps superseding economic interests—will find the liability rule objectionable.

Second, liability rules are risky when it comes to recognizing the subjective valuations of individuals. Suppose someone dearly loves his home, in part for sentimental reasons. Perhaps it has been the family home for generations. If the home is then accidently destroyed through the acts of another, the victim may find he is only paid the fair market value for the home. This amount does not account for his attachment and would not have been acceptable compensation in a market transaction. The problem here is not just that the victim has not been adequately compensated, but that the "exchange" itself has not led to any version of efficiency. If the victim would not have consented to an exchange for a price equal to the damages he or she is awarded, the "exchange" is neither Pareto superior nor wealth-maximizing.

The problem of properly protecting subjective values helps explain why interference with the rights of others is addressed not by simple compensation but by criminal penalties. If everyone simply had to pay the fair market value for damages caused or for items taken (assuming they are caught), property rules would be changed to liability rules. Yet, as Calabresi and Melamed point out, liability rules may understate the value to the victim of what was taken and invite inefficient "transfers." Hence, when the transfer could have been negotiated— transaction costs are low—it makes sense to employ a property rule and add on a penalty for those who try to substitute a liability rule.

A third objection to the use of liability rules is based on distributive consequences. Suppose in the typical polluting factory case, like *Boomer v. Atlantic Cement,* the fair market value of the damage to the landowner is $50,000 and the value to the factory of continued operations is $100,000. Suppose further that the landowner is entitled to be free of pollution. If a liability rule is employed, the factory will continue to pollute and simply compensate the landowner. The landowner would receive $50,000. In effect, the factory is permitted to pay only $50,000 for a right or resource (the air) to which it attributes a value of $100,000. Put in contracts terms, the benefit of the bargain is $50,000 and all of that benefit is captured by the factory. The landowner, in effect, is required to sell and the factory is permitted to buy the entitlement for the landowner's reservation price—the lowest price that would have been acceptable in a market exchange. The problem is that the "forced sale" does not permit the landowner to acquire at least some portion of the gain or surplus created by the exchange. Although this is irrelevant as a matter of allocative efficiency, it does have obvious distributive implications.

In some instances, entitlements are "protected" to such an extent that the owners are not permitted to sell them. Some examples are votes, organs and sex. Although this is of little consequence to those who would not sell under any circumstances, in some instances it is clear that the rule interferes with the preferences of potential sellers. This leads to the question of how it can be efficient or even just to interfere with the expression of individuals in the market. As a general matter, rules that prohibit the exchange of one's entitlements are typically justified by the fact that some exchanges are morally repugnant. Put in economic terms, one could say that those exchanges have negative— perhaps only psychological—effects on those who are not parties to the exchange. In addition, there are paternalistic justifications based on the belief that the parties to the exchange really do not know what is best for them. This too can be put in economic terms by claiming that the preference that might otherwise be expressed by the party is one that, sooner or later, she would regret. Consequently, it is not ultimately utility-maximizing.

CHAPTER FIVE

CONTRACT LAW APPLICATIONS

Of the areas of law to which economic analysis has been applied, the best "fit" is probably found in contracts, torts, antitrust, and government regulation. The application of economics to contract law tends to be relatively easy to understand since both the Coase Theorem and the concept of Pareto superiority envision some form of exchange. This Chapter begins with the basic economic theory linking contract formation with increases in efficiency. It then addresses a number of contract law issues that can be approached from an economic perspective. Contract remedies are examined in the final section. In all cases, the discussion centers on whether or not contract doctrine can be squared with economic interests. Concluding that they can, however, does not necessarily mean that contract doctrine is the product of economic reasoning.

A. CONTRACT LAW: THEORY AND ECONOMIC GOALS

1. EXCHANGE, THE CONTRACT CURVE, AND PARETO EFFICIENCY

In order to understand the economics of contract formation, it is necessary to grasp the concept of an indifference curve. An indifference curve illustrates all the combinations of two products that would leave an individual feeling equally well off. For example, in Figure 1, numbers of sweaters is plotted along the vertical axis and numbers of oranges is plotted along the horizontal axis. The curve labeled with an "I" might illustrate all the combinations of oranges and sweaters that leave Juan feeling the same in terms of his utility. In other words, Juan has no preference for any point on curve I over any other point.

Figure 1

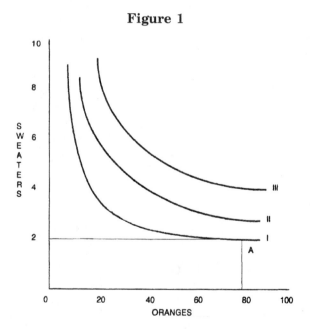

The graph also includes a number of other indifference curves; together they constitute an indifference map. As the curves move out from the origin, each curve signifies a higher level of utility. Thus, although Juan is indifferent to the points on any one curve, he would like to be on the curve farthest from the origin. In fact, what is really going on here is that this graph has a third dimension projecting out from the page, and the third dimension plots utility. Farther out from the origin is actually farther up from the page.

On curve I, point A is a combination of eighty oranges and two sweaters. Let's suppose that this is Juan's stock of goods at the moment. The notions of contract and exchange require that another participant be introduced into the model. Let's say Figure 2 illustrates the utility map of Lolita. Again, each curve indicates the combinations of sweaters and oranges that result in the same level of utility for Lolita. Further suppose that Lolita is currently in possession of 20 oranges and 8 sweaters. This would be point A on utility curve I. Given the uneven distribution of sweaters and oranges, Juan and Lolita may be potential traders.

Figure 2

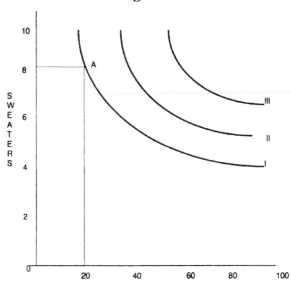

To illustrate the theory of why and how the trading might occur, it is necessary to convert the two sets of indifference curves into what is called an Edgeworth Box. The Edgeworth Box for Juan and Lolita is Figure 3. Although it looks a bit confusing, all that has happened is that the origin for Lolita's indifference map is no longer the lower left corner of the graph, but is now at the upper right corner. Thus, for Juan, utility increases as he moves upward and to the right, and for Lolita, utility increases as she moves downward and to the left. Point A is now common to both parties. For Juan, it is still 80 oranges and 2 sweaters, and for Lolita it is still 20 oranges and 8 sweaters.

Figure 3

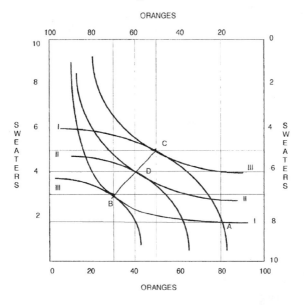

It is important to remember that each party would like to move as far from his or her origin as possible. In the context of this mini economy, they can achieve this by exchanging sweaters for oranges. But there are obviously limits on what "price" each will be willing to pay for what the other is offering. For example, consider point B. This is on utility curve I for Juan and curve III for Lolita. To achieve this outcome, Juan would have to give up 50 oranges in order to get one sweater from Lolita, leaving him with 30 oranges and 3 sweaters. Lolita would be giving up one sweater for 50 oranges, leaving her with 7 sweaters and 70 oranges.

Because this would put Lolita on indifference curve III, she would probably be delighted with the exchange. On the other hand, Juan would not be delighted or anything other than indifferent because he remains at the same level of utility. At point B, all the gains from the exchange would have accrued to Lolita.

Comparable to point B is point C, which is on indifference curve III for Juan and indifference curve I for Lolita. Here Juan exchanges 30 oranges for 3 sweaters and each party ends up with 50 oranges and 5 sweaters. Juan is on a higher indifference curve and Lolita is on her original curve.

Movements to point B or point C would both be to Pareto superior states because one party will be better off and no one will be worse off. These are extreme points, however, in that they involve cases in which the parties are willing to make an exchange that does not improve his or her position. Certainly, neither party would settle for terms that would result in movement to an indifference curve that would be lower than curve I, and movement to any curve above curve I is an improvement. Thus, all the points between Juan's indifference curve I and Lolita's indifference curve I are Pareto superior to point A. This oblong area between the curves is referred to as the "lens."

It is important to remember that both parties want to move to levels of indifference that are as far from the origins of their indifference maps as possible. This produces some particularly attractive points. These are the points at which their curves are tangent. In Figure 3, a line is drawn through the points of tangency between Juan's and Lolita's indifference curves. This is called the "contract curve." Points B and C form the extremes of the contract curve. Point D, at which Juan gives up 40 oranges for 2 sweaters, is also on the contract curve.

As already noted, any movement from point A to a point within the lens is a movement to a Pareto superior state. What is different about the contract curve as opposed to other points within the lens is that once the parties agree to an exchange along the contract curve, they have arrived at a Pareto optimal point. In other words, once on the contract curve, they cannot change the distribution of sweaters and oranges without making one of them worse off. This can be tested at point D, where Juan has 40 oranges and 4 sweaters and Lolita has 60 oranges and 6 sweaters. There is no way to move from this point to another distribution without one of the parties moving to a lower indifference curve.

The price that contracting parties agree upon is really a decision about which point on the contract curve will be selected. In the typical bargaining context, each party will prefer a point as close to the origin of the other party as possible. The issue of "price," or the point on the curve they select, directly implicates the distributive consequences of the contract. Simply arriving at a point on the curve increases general welfare and the utility of both parties. The actual point on the curve determines how the gain from the exchange will be divided between the parties. Thus, the Edgeworth Box allows one to consider both the allocative and distributive implications of the exchange. As will be discussed below, most of contract law, when it is viewed in economic terms, can be seen as responding to allocative or distributive issues. In fact, as the pages that follow illustrate, most of standard contract doctrine, ranging from offer and acceptance to consideration and competency, can be explained by an economic rationale. Before turning to those questions, however, a few more basics need to be addressed.

2.   WHY DOES CONTRACT LAW EXIST?

While the Edgeworth Box and the derivation of the contract curve explain why exchange is important, those constructs do not directly address the function of contract law. More specifically, why should executory contracts be enforced and what mechanisms should be used to further that end?

To be more specific, all the gains from the exchange just described between Lolita and Juan could be achieved if Juan showed up at a designated spot with his oranges and Lolita showed up with her sweaters and they swapped. In essence, the contract would be formed and executed simultaneously. In fact, if the parties made a point to thoroughly inspect the goods they were exchanging and adjusted the price to account for any uncertainty about the quality of the goods, contract law would seem to have little importance.

The problem is that the oranges for sweaters exchange is very primitive—it assumes a face-to-face transaction in which the entire contract is executed on the spot and the parties are able to make an assessment of what they are getting and what they are giving up. In reality, things are much more complex. For example, a general contractor may not be willing to bid on a large construction project unless he can be assured that numerous subcontractors will perform at specified times in the future. Similarly, if one's performance is to be financed with the payment received from the other party, simultaneous face-to-face exchange is not possible. Thus, a building contractor may need progress payments that are received before the contractor can perform.

In theory, virtually all of these problems could be and sometimes are overcome through the use of bonding arrangements and escrow agents. Of course, the bonding agreement and the contract with the escrow agent may themselves give rise to complexities that cannot be overcome by a face-to-face simultaneous exchange. In short, in the absence of contract law, the transaction costs of many day-to-day exchanges would be extraordinarily high. Consequently, exchanges that would be allocatively efficient may not take place. The existence of contract law lowers these costs and permits them to take place. As long as the cost of administering contract law is less than the gain from the exchange and less than efforts to create "private" contract law, it makes economic sense to have a body of law devoted to contracts.

3. CONTRACT FORMATION AND PRIVATE RISK ALLOCATION

The importance of contract law as a means of facilitating exchange leads to a closer examination of the substance of those exchanges. In large measure, contracts are means of privately allocating risks. For example, if Lonnie hires Bert to paint her house for $10,000, she is assuming the risk that no one will do an equivalent job for less and that she will not find another opportunity for spending $10,000 that she would find more attractive. Similarly, Bert is assuming the risk that someone will not offer him an opportunity that he would find more attractive and that the cost of the project will not exceed $10,000.

Of course, the risk allocation features of contracts are far more extensive than this example. In large commercial contracts that stretch over several years, the parties can be seen as purchasing insurance from each other. For example, a public utility may buy guaranteed deliveries of coal at a guaranteed price from a producer. That producer, perhaps on the verge of a substantial capital outlay, is looking for a hedge against a precipitous drop in the demand for and price of coal. In this type of instance, the private risk allocation may take the form of a requirements contract.

4. THE ECONOMIC GOALS
OF CONTRACT LAW

Given that the economic function of contract law is to facilitate exchange by overcoming transaction costs, it may seem odd that so much of substantive contract law is devoted to rules about what must happen in order for a contract to be enforceable. These rules concern issues ranging from the competency of the parties to formalistic notions of offer, acceptance, and consideration. Taken together, the rules of contract law seem to perform a number of economic functions. The first is to enforce only those agreements that are likely to result in increases in efficiency. The second function is to keep the cost of administering contract law as low as possible.

A third function is to allocate risks that are not expressly allocated by the parties. In this respect, contract law serves a gap-filling function. Gap filling pervades contract law but is dealt with most expressly when considering issues of ambiguity, breach, the proper remedy, and whether one party's non-performance will be excused. Even the mainstay lost profits case, *Hadley v. Baxendale* (Eng.1854) is a study in determining how the parties allocated the risk of consequential damages. From an economic point of view, it makes sense to allocate that risk to the party who can control the event or insure against it more economically.

Finally, it seems clear that much of contract law is devoted to concerns about the distributive consequences of the bargains people have made. Courts applying contract law often find ways to excuse parties from contracts that are deemed to be unfair. In this sense, contract law plays the role of setting limits on what is permissible bargaining behavior and encourages conformity with socially acceptable bargaining norms. This is probably the most controversial function of contract law, in part because there is great disparity in views about whether contract law should be used for this purpose and whether it is an effective means of addressing social injustice.

Often a court is faced with a question in which achieving one goal is inconsistent with achieving another. This tension between goals occurs most frequently when the court must choose between efficiency goals and distributive goals.

B. CONTRACT FORMATION

When one thinks of contract formation, a number of questions are raised:

1. Do the parties have capacity to contract?
2. Was assent the result of duress or undue influence?
3. Is there an offer?
4. Is there an acceptance?
5. Is there consideration?
6. Must the contract be in writing?

These questions can be seen as a means of determining whether both parties have truly consented to the exchange. Although there are no guarantees that utility will be increased if and only if the parties have consented, the probabilities are that consent and Pareto superiority go hand-in-hand. All of the questions associated with contract formation can be traced to a desire for clear signals that the parties have, in fact, made an agreement.

1.   CAPACITY

At one level of analysis, the basic rules about competency—whether applied to minors, those who are inebriated, or those who are cognitively or volitionally impaired—seem straightforward. Decisions made by those who are unable to understand what they are doing or unable to control those actions may not lead to Pareto superior outcomes. The decision that the party lacks capacity is really one that says that the perception of increased well-being is likely to be the result of a cognitive distortion.

While these limitations on contracts can be viewed as having an "objective" economic basis, the truth is that standards for capacity can vary from era to era. Decisions about who is capable of forming a binding contract are, therefore, political decisions about the limits of enforceable consent. Moreover, any examination of a sample of capacity cases leads one to believe that the economic concerns are not about efficiency as much as they are about distributive outcomes.

Still, some of the more specific rules pertaining to capacity and voidability can be reconciled with conventional economic interests. For example, the *Restatement (Second) of Contracts*, section 15, takes the position that a party may void a contract on the basis of volitional impairment or intoxication only if the other contracting party had reason to know of the impairment or intoxication. On the other hand, the power of minors to void contracts is not similarly limited. In terms of risk allocation, the contracting minor is less likely to be "stuck" with a contract he wants out of than someone who forms a contract while intoxicated.

The greater risk incurred by the intoxicated party is probably best explained by the judgements society makes about people who drink too much. In economic terms, there is a disincentive to become intoxicated. From a non-moralistic economic point of view, forming a contract that turns out, in hindsight, not to be to one's liking is a little like making a "mistake" or being involved in an accident. In the case of intoxication, the person who is arguably in the better position to avoid the mistake is given an incentive to do so. Of course, if the other party has reason to know of the intoxication, he or she is in as good or better position to avoid the accident and then the contract is voidable by the intoxicated party.

The same type of reasoning cannot be applied to the contracting minor. Supposedly, contracts are voidable by minors because they may exercise poor judgment. Thus, it is because they make "mistakes" and are vulnerable in their dealings with others that the protection exists at all. To then turn around and limit voidability to create an "incentive" to avoid mistakes would be inconsistent with the rationale for their treatment in the first place.

The capacity question in contracts raises concerns about paternalism and interference with autonomy and liberty. To some extent, these concerns may be offset by the fact that most of the rules about capacity make contracts voidable, not void. On the other hand, there are economic reasons why the importance of this distinction can be over-estimated. The fact that individuals lacking capacity can step out of contracts at their prerogative greatly increases the risk and, therefore, the cost of dealing with those lacking capacity. Since this discourages people from contracting with those who may be impaired, the actual outcome, in terms of choice, autonomy, and numbers of utility-increasing contracts may be about the same as it would be if the contracts were simply void.

As suggested above, distributive concerns are probably behind a great deal of the law that has evolved with respect to capacity. In other words, even if it could be shown that the contracts formed by those who lack capacity have resulted in Pareto superior outcomes, the contract law of capacity would still be applied to protect those who have not shared fairly in the surplus created by the exchange. For example, concerns about overreaching and advantage-taking are obviously at the heart of rules allowing minors or those who are mentally impaired to void contracts.

This is no more pointedly illustrated than in *Ortelere v. Teachers' Retirement Board* (N.Y.1969), in which a retired teacher made a retirement benefit election. Her choices were a lower payment that would extend through her life or her husband's, whichever was longer, or a higher payment through her lifetime alone. She died two months after electing the higher payment, and her election, upon being challenged by her husband, was found to be voidable. The decision is hard to view as being driven by concerns about efficiency. Instead, the decision was whether the pension fund should benefit, as a result of Ortelere's decision, when her husband would then be deprived of an extended period of benefits.

2. DURESS

Duress and undue influence are also doctrines that permit individuals to avoid contracts. Here again, the issue goes to the nature or the *quality* of consent at the point of contract formation. From the standpoint of economic analysis, duress and related doctrines address matters of both allocative efficiency and distributive outcomes. The concepts are difficult to grapple with because there is no bright-line test to be applied as in the case of the contracting party's age.

One of the factors complicating duress is that, once the party has made a decision while under duress, that decision may very well achieve Pareto superiority. Taking the simplest example, even the party who enters into a contract at gunpoint can be viewed as moving to a Pareto superior position, given the circumstances. Thus, the process of defining duress is really one of determining which decisions achieving Pareto superior outcomes are legitimate and which ones are the result of illegitimate pressure.

Section 175 of the *Restatement (Second) of Contracts* makes an effort to narrow the focus by defining duress as the use of an improper threat that leaves the victim "no reasonable alternative." The *Restatement* further defines what would be improper but, except for the examples of when the threat would amount to a crime or a tort, the language is very imprecise. Robert Nozick suggests that duress may be viewed as a situation in which the party is offered an option that he would prefer not to have heard about at all.[1] This makes a great deal of sense; the party who would have preferred not to have heard about the new choices finds his new set of options Pareto inferior to his prior state. In essence, he has been made worse off without compensation. It is hard to then "bootstrap" this into the type of exchange that leads to a legitimate form of Pareto superiority.

The *Restatement (Second)*, section 175, distinguishes between instances in which the threatening party is the other contracting party and when she is not. As one would expect, the contract is more easily avoided when the coercing party is a party to

1. For a discussion and criticism see Mark Kelman, "Choices and Utility," 1979 *Wisc. L. Rev.* 769, 789–790.

the contract. This reduces the incentive to make an improper threat and allocates the risk that one's threat may be deemed improper to the party in the best position to control the threatening behavior. The allocation of the risk is reversed when the party contracting with the victim has no reason to know of the duress and has given value or has relied on the transaction. It makes economic sense to allocate the risk in this manner because the coerced party is in possession of information that he is under duress and, by notifying the other party, could preserve his right to void the contract.

Use of the doctrine of duress is explained as much by distributive goals as it is by goals linked to allocative efficiency and risk allocation. In fact, under section 176(2) of the *Restatement (Second)*, bargains that are uneven are viewed as candidates for the duress label, which then creates in the "victim" the right to void the contract. A closer look at the contract doctrines that seem to foster distributive ends is reserved for Section C.

3. OFFER AND ACCEPTANCE AND OTHER FORMALITIES

Offer and acceptance are symbols of consent. Thus, requiring them to be present is consistent with the desire to enforce efficiency-producing agreements. In addition, to the extent that the law requires a fairly high level of specificity and a lack of ambivalence for a communication to qualify as an offer, the effect is to lower the costs of administering a system of contract law. The same is true with respect to the traditional "mirror image" rule in the case of acceptances.

In highly complex commercial transactions, rigid adherence to the "mirror image" rule could impede the formation of contracts. In effect, the transaction costs of finding a point in the negotiation at which all parties are in complete agreement with respect to every term in the contract could be quite high. Section 2–207 of the Uniform Commercial Code, which permits contracts to be formed in the absence of complete consistency between offer and acceptance, avoids some of these transaction costs. The consequence is that efficiency-producing exchanges are not thwarted by formal requirements. On the other hand and only partly in jest, whatever benefits may flow from section 2–207, might be offset by the disutility students and others suffer while trying to master it.

One of the standard rules of contract law is that the acceptance must be in exactly the form designated in the offer. This leads to the question of the appropriate type of response to an offer that is ambiguous with respect to the means of acceptance. For efficiency purposes, the risk of any confusion should be borne by the party who has created the ambiguity. This is basically consistent with the common law view as reflected by section 32 of the *Restatement (Second)*, which permits the offeree to accept by promising or by performing.

Another area in which softening the formal requirements may very well be consistent with economic efficiency is the creation of a limited number of instances in which silence may be construed as acceptance. It is important in this context to remember that, from an economic perspective, one purpose of offer and acceptance is to avoid the enforcement of "contracts" to which the parties did not consent. When it is clear that the offeror has good reason to believe that silence by the offeree signifies assent, there is no reason to insist on an expressed acceptance. This is generally in accord with section 69 of the *Restatement (Second)*, which lists the circumstances under which silence may be viewed as acceptance or that the risk that silence may be mistakenly taken as acceptance should be allocated to the offeree.

One more contract law standard that is susceptible to economic justification is the statute of frauds, which requires some contracts to be evidenced by a written memorandum. A writing has probative value with respect to consent. Moreover, to the extent any contract specifications are included in the writing, the cost of administering a system of contract law is decreased.

4.   THE CONSIDERATION REQUIREMENT

A black letter rule of contract law is that a promise must be supported by consideration in order to be binding. The consideration requirement is essentially that the promise or performance of one party be in exchange for the promise or performance of a counterpart. One implication for the economics of contract law is fairly obvious. The notion of "exchange" has an important symbolic value in terms of signifying consent. But it is equally clear that the rules pertaining to consideration reflect some ambivalence about its importance. Inconsistent responses to the consideration requirement may be the result of the tension between competing economic goals of contract law. This is illustrated by looking more closely at four specific areas.

a.   Adequacy of Consideration

The baseline rule is that, as long as there is consideration, the matter of "adequacy" of consideration is not at issue. This is the so-called "peppercorn" theory of consideration. The explanation for this, in economic terms, is that an assessment of relative amounts of consideration involves making an "interpersonal comparison of utility." In effect, to intervene when consideration appears to be lopsided amounts to an effort to compare the increase in utility experienced by one party with the increase in utility experienced by the other party. Such comparisons cannot be made. Consequently, once there is consent as signified by offer, acceptance and some kind of exchange, it makes no economic sense to attempt further inquiry. This particular view is consistent with viewing contract law as having the primary function of supporting Pareto superior exchanges.

The problem is that this rigid view of consideration gives way very often when courts address distributive goals. Thus, an uneven exchange can be viewed as evidence of duress or can be an element of unconscionability. In some instances, the distributive matter is handled by simply declaring that there was no consideration when in fact there was. A good example is *Newman and Snell's State Bank v. Hunter* (Mich.1928), in which the bank sold to a widow the promissory note of her deceased husband. The collateral for the note was in the form of the stock of an insolvent corporation. The widow received the actual note—certainly the equivalent of a peppercorn and quite likely the source of comfort. Yet the court held that there was an absence of consideration due to the fact that the note did not have monetary value.

b. Nominal Consideration

Another area in which this ambivalence is revealed is in the treatment of nominal consideration. The issue here is: what happens if the parties, conscious of the consideration requirement, observe the formality of reciting consideration? The earlier view as reflected by the first *Restatement of Contracts* was that nominal consideration was sufficient. This view was probably driven more by rigid adherence to the peppercorn theory than by any intuitive notion of the efficiency derived from enforcement of gratuitous promises. It made sense from the point of view of economic efficiency since both parties consented to a process they thought would create a binding obligation. Moreover, as discussed below, there are other economic reasons for enforcing gratuitous promises. The comments to section 71 of the *Restatement (Second) of Contracts* permit courts to pierce the formality of the arrangement and to make a finding that nominal consideration is not consideration at all. When all the other indicia of consent are present, it is hard to square this rule with economic efficiency.

c.   **Gratuitous Promises**

Nowhere is the ambivalence toward the consideration requirement more evident than in the trend toward enforcement of gratuitous promises. There are powerful economic arguments that this trend is well-founded. Once again, though, the support found in economic theory for enforcement of gratuitous promises does not mean that courts pursuing this course are driven by economic concerns.

Relatively recent arguments by law and economics scholars calling for the enforcement of gratuitous promises are based on possible increases in efficiency. There is some tension here, however, in that a system of contract law that includes a subset of rules that support enforcing gratuitous promises can be costly to administer. To some extent, reliance by the promisee as required by section 90 of both the first *Restatement* and the *Restatement (Second)* lowers these costs. This is especially true when the reliance has taken the form of an action, such as incurring out-of-pocket expenses, that seems unreasonable unless the action was induced by the promise.

Before describing some of the recent economic arguments in favor of enforcement of gratuitous promises, it is useful to note what actually occurs when gratuitous promises are enforced. Before development of promissory estoppel and section 90, the promisor remained, in effect, the "owner" of the promise. It created no particular entitlement in the promisee and, except for instances in which courts were willing to tinker with consideration and equitable estoppel, the promise could be withdrawn with impunity. The judicial evolution in this area has the effect of reallocating this right in favor of the promisee and creating a duty in the promisor.

It is tempting to think that this change can be justified by reasoning that the maker of a promise that is later broken is at "fault." In tort-sounding terms, one could say the maker of the promise puts the promisee at risk by making a promise upon which the promisee relies and then breaking the promise. Carrying the tort analogy one step further, however, if it were commonly known that gratuitous promises were not enforced, one would have to regard the relying party as contributorily negligent. Consequently, from an efficient risk-allocation point of view, it is not clear that gratuitous promises should be enforced. Thus, the reallocation of the promissory "right" cannot be based simply on the notion that broken promises may harm promisees. Something more is needed.

The question of whether the trend toward enforcement of these promises is consistent with economic efficiency is made more intriguing by the fact that it is not as simple as asking whether this reallocation of the promissory "right" means that it ends up in the hands of the parties who attribute the greatest value to it. This is because it is possible that both promisees and promisors may prefer that the right be allocated differently. If so, this may be one of those instances in which taking a right from one party and giving it to someone else may result in a Pareto superior outcome.

Before considering why, the issue can be narrowed. Assuming the parties are rational and self-interested in the conventional sense, the utility of the promisor will increase when the promise is made. Assuming the probability that the promise will be kept is greater than zero, the promisee is also made better off. At least one party is better off, no one is worse off, and the Pareto standard is satisfied. This still leaves open the question of whether it makes any economic sense for the law to increase the probability of performance so that the promisee does not have to rely solely on the trustworthiness of the promisor. Put differently, is there a good reason for making the promise the "property" of the promisee?

Richard Posner offers an economic justification for enforcing the promise.[2] An example goes as follows. Suppose I honestly desire to give my friend

2. Richard Posner, "Gratuitous Promises in Economics and Law," 6 *J. Leg. Stud.* 411 (1977).

a gift of $100 per week for the next 52 weeks. If I simply make the promise and my friend then discounts the promise due to the fact that gratuitous promises are not enforceable and I may change my mind, the actual perceived benefit to my friend may be less than $100 per week. Thus, by enforcing the promise, the value to my friend increases without any increase in cost to me.

Another way of looking at it is to assume I understand the discounting my friend will do, and I still want to give a gift that will be the equivalent of $100 per week. In order to actually give a perceived benefit of $100 per week, I may have to promise $125 per week. In other words, the promise will be more expensive to me. On the other hand, if my friend and I both know that the promise will be enforced, the promise of $100 per week will be worth its stated value or something fairly close. In short, the gift becomes less expensive to me and stays at the $100 per week value for my friend. The outcome is that promisors may prefer a rule that holds them to their promises.

In both versions of this example, it is important to note that the promisor does give up something that presumably has some value: the right to change her mind. Thus, for the change in the rule to lead to a Pareto superior outcome, the value attributed to the "right" to break promises must be exceeded by the gains to promisors associated with making promises more valuable. Of course, even if the rule change is not consistent with Pareto superiority, it may still be wealth-maximizing.

The efficiency-increasing effects of enforcing gratuitous promises also extend to the ways in which promisees may react to promises. Professors Scott and Goetz offer a useful way of viewing the ways in which increasing the dependability of these promises may increase efficiency.[3] Again, a simple example is instructive. Suppose I wish to make a gift of $5,000 to my friend in six months' time. I have two choices. I can make a promise now to give the gift in six months, or I can simply wait six months and give him the $5,000 as a surprise. Certainly, in either case, the gift will move my friend to a higher indifference curve than if there had not been a gift. But two things seem clear. The person who knows ahead of time about the future gift will alter not just spending patterns in the future but current spending patterns in anticipation of the gift. Thus, the friend is likely to move to a higher indifference curve if the gift is known about in advance. Goetz and Scott call this ability to anticipate and move to a higher indifference curve "beneficial reliance" and view it as "the principal social rationale of promising."

The second matter that seems clear is that, the higher the probability the gift will be given, the greater the degree of reliance on the gift and the greater the level of beneficial reliance. In other words, the higher the likelihood that the money will be paid, the more comfortable the promisee will be

3. Charles Goetz and Robert Scott, "Enforcing Promises: An Examination of the Basis of Contract," 89 *Yale L. J.* 1261 (1980).

about altering current spending patterns on the basis of the promise.

d. Contract Modification

As noted above, consideration performs the important function of signifying assent. This explains the long-standing rule that a contract modification is not binding in the absence of consideration. The rationale is that it makes little sense for a rational party, who is entitled to a certain level of performance by another, to pay more for the same performance. A modification without consideration, one might reason, is a sure sign that the modification was made under duress and does not increase the well-being of both parties. Both the Uniform Commercial Code and the *Restatement (Second) of Contracts* protect against coerced modification. However, under certain circumstances, both the *Restatement (Second)* and the Uniform Commercial Code permit modifications without consideration. They implicitly recognize that in the context of a contractual relationship, especially in light of the likelihood of repeated transactions, it may be in the rational self-interest of both parties to allow variations from the strict terms of the contract.[4] Efforts to anticipate and contractually treat every possible contingency would drive transaction costs up.

4. This is consistent with the findings of an empirical study undertaken by Russell J. Weintraub, *see* "A Study of Contract Practice and Policy," 1992 Wisc. L. Rev. 1.

C. CONTRACT LAW AND DISTRIBUTIVE GOALS

As noted at the outset of this Chapter, there is a fair amount of tension in contract law between efficiency goals and distributive goals. To put the issue in its usual terms, efficiency goals are those that are aimed at increasing utility or wealth without regard for who is actually made better off. Distributive goals focus on which individuals or classes of individuals are better off. There is a continuous debate about whether contract law should be concerned with distributive issues at all. Those who oppose this use of contract law, if they favor redistribution at all, would prefer the use of taxes and transfer payments to achieve those ends. Despite these philosophical differences, it is clear that much of contract law responds to distributive goals.

In terms of the contract curve in Figure 3, there are two situations that raise distributive concerns. The first deals with advantage-taking that is so extreme that one of the parties does not end up with an exchange that places him or her within the lens. This seems most likely to occur when one of the parties lacks the capacity to contract. In these cases, one party is made worse off by the contract and the outcome is Pareto inferior.

A different type of problem can arise when the parties bargain to a point on the contract curve. If the bargain struck lies at the extreme end of the curve, it indicates that one party has gained most of the surplus created by the exchange. In these instances, a refusal to enforce the contract has the effect of "undoing" what was a movement to a Pareto superior position. While such decisions may only mean that future bargains occur on different terms, there is also the danger that future efficiency-producing bargains will not occur at all. This presents the classic clash between allocative efficiency and distributive justice.

Another type of case involves instances in which the parties both seem to move to a position within the lens and perhaps on the contract curve, but after the fact it is determined that one of the parties is not better off at all. That party either regrets making the contract or something happens to make either the gain from the contract less valuable or performance more onerous. In the latter group of cases, the various doctrines that excuse non-performance come into play.

Many different theories are used by the courts to deal with these distributive concerns. Sometimes the distributive outcomes of contracts affect the way a court reacts to a formation question. The most obvious examples are the use of capacity, duress, and misrepresentation as means of upsetting bargains. But, as illustrated above, distributive concerns can also affect the way a court views the issue of whether a promise is supported by consideration. Beyond these justifications lie even less clear notions like unequal bargaining power, unconscionability, and contracts of adhesion. The precise theory is probably not as important as the effects of contract law decisions that seem to have a distributive purpose. The primary concerns are that contracts that benefit both parties will not be enforced and that there will be long-term implications affecting individuals who are not parties to the contract. These issues can be seen more clearly in the context of two common problems.

1.   EXCULPATORY PROVISIONS

A typical case involving an exculpatory provision is *O'Callaghan v. Waller & Beckwith Realty Co.* (Ill.1958) which concerned the enforceability of an exculpatory clause in the lease of an apartment. The implications of either a judicial or legislative determination that such a provision is unenforceable can be illustrated graphically. In Figure 4, D represents the demand for housing. S_1 represents the supply of housing. In the market depicted here, the equilibrium price will be P_1 and the quantity of rental housing available will be Q_1. Presumably the exchange of P_1 dollars for housing increases the welfare of both lessors and tenants. Lessors prefer P_1 dollars to possession of the housing unit, and the tenants prefer housing to keeping the money or spending it on something else.

Figure 4

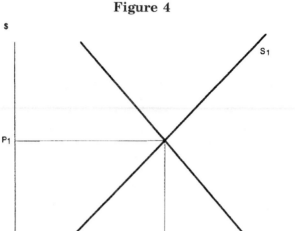

HOUSING UNITS

It will be recalled from Chapter Two that supply is also the marginal cost of production. A decision that the exculpatory provision will not be enforced is really a decision that tenants should get more for their rent payments. It can be viewed as an effort to transfer wealth from the lessors to tenants. If it is determined that exculpatory provisions are not enforceable, the cost of providing housing will presumably increase as lessors improve the housing or increase their insurance coverage. In theory, this will mean that the supply of housing will decrease. In other words, the supply curve for housing will shift upward and to the left. This is depicted in

Figure 5 in which S_2 is the supply of housing after the lessors purchase insurance. At least in theory, the result of this change in the law is an increase in the price of housing and a decrease in the amount rented.

Figure 5

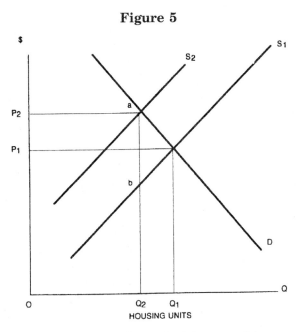

One way of viewing what has happened is to say that the efforts to make tenants better off has backfired in that some tenants—possibly those with the lowest incomes—have been priced out of the market and are worse off than they would have been if the exculpatory clause had been enforced. In addition, although those tenants remaining in the market are getting more favorable lease terms, they are paying higher rent. It is even possible that they preferred the old lease at the lower price to the new one at the higher price, so they too are worse off. Indeed, one might argue that had they wanted the newly provided protection, they could have purchased insurance.

There is another side of this story, though. First, as the graph illustrates, the increase in rent from P_1 to P_2 is not equal to the increase in the cost of supplying housing, which is the distance between a and b. It is possible that some of the increase is, therefore, actually absorbed by the lessors. As discussed in Chapter Two, whether the lessors absorb the cost will depend on market conditions. If the market is relatively competitive, lessors will have a difficult time passing the increased cost to tenants. On the other hand, if the market is not competitive, most of the increased cost will be passed along. This can be understood quite easily by supposing that the market has but one lessor—tenants must rent from that lessor or go without housing. In this instance, tenants will have little choice but to pay for nearly all of the cost increase. The phrase often used to describe contracts made when these are the market conditions is "contract of adhesion," which suggests that one of the parties was faced with a "take it or leave it" contract. In effect, there were no other parties with whom that person could have contracted on more favorable terms.

The rental apartment/exculpatory clause example calls for pushing the analysis one more step. So far, the discussion has been based on the assumption that a ruling that exculpatory provisions are unenforceable has an impact only on the supply side of the market. It is possible to view such a ruling as one that requires all apartments offered for lease to be of a higher quality. And, if all apartments were otherwise exactly as they were before, but now are of higher quality, demand may increase.

Figure 6 illustrates how this might work. The X axis shows numbers of apartments. From Chapter Two, we know that demand shows the amount people are willing and able to buy at each price. Conversely, it shows the price at which each quantity will be taken off the market. Thus, if the basic unit for sale increases in quality, one would expect the amount people are willing to pay to increase as well. This means that the demand curve would increase—shift upward and to the right. In the Figure this is depicted by a shift from D_1 to D_2. Precisely what this means in terms of the eventual price, quantity, and distributive effect depends on how much demand and supply shift and how elastic these curves are. In Figure 6, the eventual decrease in quantity, to Q_3, is less than if there had been no demand side reaction to the change in quality.

Figure 6

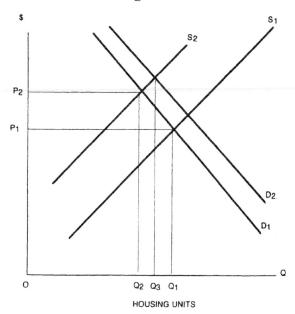

HOUSING UNITS

There is one more application of economic analysis that is relevant here. As already indicated, the supply curve will shift upward by the amount of increase in the cost of providing housing. The demand curve will shift upward by the amount of extra value tenants attribute to the "improved" housing. If the shift upward in demand exceeds the shift upward in supply, the change in the rule with respect to exculpatory clauses can be viewed as being allocatively efficient in that the increased value to buyers exceeds the cost of producing the improvement. In a smoothly working market, lessors would have recognized that the value of improvements exceeded their cost and exculpatory provisions would have disappeared without judicial or legislative help. There are many reasons why this might not happen. The primary one is the existence of transaction costs.

2. UNCONSCIONABILITY

Unconscionability is usually said to have a procedural and substantive component.[5] The notion of a procedural component means that there was something amiss in the contract-formation process. It could be something like fraud, but it could also be something as simple as overly aggressive sales practices or using small print or confusing language for terms that turn out to be especially disadvantageous to one of the parties. The substantive component has to do with the actual balance of the exchange.

The procedural element allows the court to examine whether the process of achieving mutual assent should, as a policy matter, be viewed as legitimate. The substantive element is a way of assessing whether any possible procedural problems really resulted in any "harm." Even though courts are quite reluctant to label a bargain unconscionable, it is likely that the theory is not just reserved for Pareto inferior outcomes. It seems also to be used when the bargain is so uneven that it violates norms of fairness.

5. Arthur A. Leff, "Unconscionability and the Code—The Emperor's New Clause," 115 *U. Pa. L. Rev.* 485 (1967).

Probably the most analyzed unconscionability case is *Williams v. Walker–Thomas Furniture* (D.C.Cir.1965). Williams made a series of purchases from Walker–Thomas. Her contract included what is called a cross-collaterization or add-on clause. In effect, when she made a purchase, all of the items that she had previously purchased on credit and that were not paid off became part of the collateral for the current purchase. When she defaulted, Walker–Thomas attempted to repossess a number of previously purchased items. The issue was whether the clause could be regarded as unconscionable.

A decision that an add-on clause like that in *Williams v. Walker–Thomas* is unconscionable can be seen as having a number of effects. The first and perhaps most obvious effect is to require the seller to be more forthcoming about what the buyer is giving up. If this occurs, Williams is in a better position to assess the full price and determine whether she is still willing to buy the item. In more technical terms, her information costs are lowered. In effect, Williams is in a better position to recognize more clearly what is being demanded of her and any surprises about the consequences of signing the contract are eliminated.

Other effects are not so favorable for Williams. The price paid, along with the add-on clause, are both part of the consideration package offered by Williams. It may be that she is better able to pay in the form of the add-on clause than in the form of its cash equivalent. If Williams is not permitted to pay with the "currency" of the add-on clause, she may not be able to afford the item at all.

At a more basic level, decisions about unconscionability can be seen as simply creating limits on the prices that can be charged by some merchants to some classes of buyers. As with exculpatory provisions, whether there is any long-run beneficial distributive effect is much debated. Those who oppose what amount to price ceilings seem to make two arguments. First, assume the high price really does permit the merchant to earn a very high profit. If the market system is working, the high profit will attract new sellers into the market. Supply will increase and prices will fall. The "problem" takes care of itself.

Second, it may be that the high price simply reflects the cost of doing business. In the case of *Walker–Thomas*, the argument might be that the store is in a crime-infested neighborhood and that a disproportionate number of its customers are bad credit risks. Consequently, the risk and, therefore, the cost of doing business is high. The add-on clause is necessary. This follows from the fact that a small down payment is all that is possible and the item sold immediately depreciates so that it is worth less than the amount owed. If the add-on clause reflects a cost of doing business and the firm is not making huge profits, the consequence of deeming the term unconscionable may be that the firm closes down. And, so the argument goes, the effort to achieve a different distributive outcome ends up leaving both buyers and sellers worse off.

These worst-case scenarios can be countered by other observations. First, take the case in which the firm is earning high or "economic" profits. There is no guarantee that these profits will lure new sellers into the market. Information costs and a general lack of responsiveness in investment resources may delay or prevent such a movement. Thus, whether today's high prices are necessary so that consumers will ultimately be better off is at least an empirical question. Moreover, the notion that it is somehow fair for today's buyers to take the brunt of high prices so that consumers in the future can have lower prices is subject to debate. Finally, there is the question of just how much the price ceiling will actually retard new entry. It is true that high profits are likely to attract new entrants. But what about lower profits and long lines of consumers willing to pay the lower price? Presumably, when the price ceiling is imposed, the quantity demanded will increase. The existing firm will either serve all those who want to buy at the lower price or it will find there are lines of consumers forming each day. Potential entrants, seeing the numbers of people who are willing to purchase at the lower price, may find entrance into the market quite attractive.

Aside from arguments that price ceilings will retard new entry, there are arguments that the ceiling will cause the existing seller to sell less. Put in more basic terms, if a price ceiling is imposed, sellers will move to a lower quantity supplied on their supply curves. Figure 7 illustrates the typical concerns. In the Figure, D is demand and S is supply. The equilibrium price is P_1 and the equilibrium quantity is Q_1. If the price ceiling is set at P_2, the quantity demanded will be Q_2 and the quantity supplied will be Q_3. Thus, sales in the market will drop from Q_1 to Q_3. Those who are able to purchase the good will get it at the regulated price and are presumably better off than they were at the original price. From the standpoint of economics, however, those who are now unable to buy the good are obviously not better off.

Figure 7

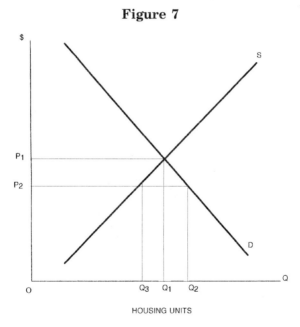

HOUSING UNITS

On the other hand, the analysis in Figure 7 holds only under special circumstances. Suppose instead that sellers have some market power and are not selling at prices equal to cost. In fact, what if the firm really is making a huge profit on each sale? As long as the price ceiling is high enough to cover the marginal cost of each sale, there seems to be little reason not to sell at least as much as was being sold before and perhaps even more.

To understand why, examine Figure 8, which is reproduced, with some additions, from the discussion of imperfect competition in Chapter 2. As will be recalled, the firm will select the quantity where marginal revenue (MR) and marginal cost (MC) intersect. Under ordinary circumstances, this will mean the quantity will be Q_1 and the price will be P_1. Suppose that a price ceiling is imposed at P_2. Obviously, everyone who was willing to pay above P_2 is still willing to purchase the item. From the firm's point of view, the relationship between its demand curve and marginal revenue curve is now beside the point. In other words, for all those people who were willing to pay above P_2, it will charge P_2. Since it does not have to lower the price to sell additional units to this group of buyers, the horizontal line at P_2 is really its new marginal revenue curve. This is true out to the intersection of the horizontal line at P_2 with the demand curve. At that point, the firm will have to lower the price to sell more and the original marginal revenue curve comes into play. This means the marginal revenue curve drops down, or is discontinuous, at point C.

Figure 8

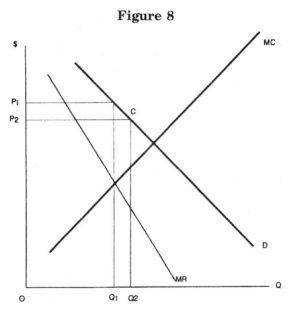

Now, following the standard of producing as long as marginal revenue exceeds marginal cost, the firm will produce out to Q_2. In effect, the price ceiling means that more is sold at a lower price. Here the distributive impact is that money that was once going to the seller is kept by the buyers. This is not to say there is increased efficiency. From a Paretian standpoint, even though buyers are better off, sellers are worse off and there is no way to gauge how things balance out. Still, the graph illustrates that, under some market conditions, efforts to redistribute in favor of buyers does not mean that they will necessarily be worse off after the effort.[6]

6. Discussions of inequities in contract law often focus on buyers who have been taken advantage of by sellers. It is good to

One final note is in order with respect to all efforts to use contract law for distributive goals. For the most part, conventional economic analysis has adopted a very narrow perspective and examined only whether those in the market are better or worse off. This is appealing and, perhaps, the most appropriate perspective to take. It misses, however, the impact of perceived market inequities on those who are not direct participants. In reality, if economists are to remain true to their own analysis, any discomfort outsiders feel about advantage-taking by others or any increased sense of well-being they experience when the perceived injustice is eliminated must be included in the calculation.

D. CONTRACT REMEDIES

One of the favorite areas of discussion for those applying economic analysis to contract law is remedies. All of the economic issues raised by contract remedies cannot be treated in an exhaustive manner here. Instead, several matters that are particularly susceptible to economic analysis are considered.

1. THE EFFICIENT BREACH

When economic analysis is brought to bear on contract remedies, the starting place is the so-called efficient breach. The idea is that contract remedies should be set so that a party will breach when it is

keep in mind that sellers too can be vulnerable. A good example is sellers of labor in certain labor markets.

"efficient" to do so. Efficiency in this context can refer to both Pareto superiority and wealth maximization, although Pareto superiority is more difficult to achieve.

The key to insuring that a breach will be efficient is to protect the expectancy of the non-breaching party. That is, the damages for breach must put the non-breaching party in the position, utility-wise, that he would have been in but for the breach. It is important that the damages do not improve the position of the non-breaching party.

A typical example goes like this. Suppose Bill has a rare set of tapes of Grateful Dead live performances, all signed by Jerry Garcia. He values the tapes at $3,000. Gennifer, a big fan of the Dead, values the tapes at $5,000. Bill agrees to sell the tapes to Gennifer for $4,000. This means Gennifer gets a consumer surplus or benefit of the bargain of $1,000. In economic terms, both parties are better off and, unless someone is worse off, this reallocation is Pareto superior.

Before Bill has delivered the tapes to Gennifer, suppose Hillary comes along and offers Bill $6,000 for the tapes. Thus, Hillary attributes more value to the tapes than either Gennifer or Bill. In fact, if Hillary had come along before Gennifer, a deal would have been stuck that would have meant that Hillary would have ended up with the tapes at some price between $4,000 and $6,000.

The key to the efficient breach is to set the remedy so that it just gives Gennifer her expectancy. In this example, it would mean that she gets the benefit of her bargain, which is $1,000. If Bill knows this when he meets Hillary, he will know that he should not breach unless Hillary is willing to pay something in excess of $5,000. For example, suppose Hillary and Bill arrive at a price of $5,500. This means that Hillary gets the tapes that she values at $6,000 for $5,500 and her position is improved. Gennifer will be paid $1,000 and be in a position that is the equivalent of what she expected. Bill, after paying Gennifer $1,000, receives $4,500, which improves his position.

In theory, the remedy that protects Gennifer's expectancy, but does no more than that, facilitates movement to a Pareto superior outcome. Contrast this with a policy that allows for punitive damages. For example, suppose the remedy is expectancy times three. Gennifer would be entitled to damages of $3000. The goal would be to discourage promise-breaking. As a consequence, Hillary would not end up with the tapes even though she values them at $6,000 and Gennifer only values them at $5,000. In fact, in the hypothetical, Hillary would have to pay Bill over $7,000 for it to be worthwhile for Bill to breach his contract with Gennifer. From this stand-point, the "efficient breach" would appear to be thwarted.

One should not take the notion of the efficient breach too seriously. First of all, the model assumes a very simple set of facts. If information costs were not prohibitive, an efficient reallocation could occur in the absence of a breach; for example, Bill sells to

Gennifer and then Gennifer sells to Hillary. Second, the model includes the assumption that one is able to determine the non-breaching party's expectancy or the monetary equivalent of performance. This is crucial because, if the expectancy is set at too low an amount, the breach will take place and the non-breaching party will be worse off. If the amount is too high, the breach may not take place even though everyone might have been better off if it had.

A related problem is that the model requires reliance on an objective standard for the determination of the non-breaching party's expectancy. This is fine unless the non-breaching party attributes value to the expected performance that is different from the market value. Thus, in the example, perhaps Gennifer values the collection at $7,000, and it is just the valuation of various collectors that puts the value at the lower figure. In short, the efficient breach model can subordinate the autonomy and preferences of the actual individuals involved. From the standpoint of efficiency, it may mean that Gennifer is worse off and the outcome, though possibly wealth maximizing, is not Pareto superior.

Finally, the efficient breach model seems to assume that the original contracting parties are unable to communicate with each other. For example, suppose the rule is that contract damages are triple expectancy. In the context of the Grateful Dead hypothetical, Gennifer values the tapes at $5,000 and would be entitled to $3,000 (3 x $1,000) if Bill breaches. We know that Gennifer was only expecting to be better off by $1,000 and that Hillary values the tapes at $6,000.

Using a Coasian analysis, Gennifer is entitled to the tapes or to $3,000 in damages. The question is whether Bill can, in effect, buy back the rights to the tapes from Gennifer. His leverage, if Gennifer insists on performance, would be to simply deliver the tapes, giving Gennifer only the $1,000 benefit of the bargain. Gennifer might decline Bill's offer of $1,000, but any amount he is willing to pay in excess of $1,000 will put her in a better position than his performance. Bill's top offer to Gennifer will be determined by what he thinks he can get from Hillary. The point is, as devoted Coasians have no doubt already noted, even if the legal rule about damages is "inefficient," the parties will have an opportunity to bargain around the rule to an efficient allocation. Of course, high transaction costs may impede this bargaining.

Those who are interested in the distributive implications of various legal rules may find the overprotection of Gennifer's expectancy through the triple expectancy rule attractive for other reasons. Under the conventional rule of protecting no more than expectancy, Gennifer is protected from being made worse off but she does not share in the gain from the sale to Hilary. When Hillary enters, there is an opportunity for a gain that, but for the fact that performance has not taken place, would have gone to Gennifer. The over-expectancy measure allows Gennifer to share in part of this gain. If you take the view that the collection was, effectively,

Gennifer's already, you may feel Gennifer deserves some part of the profit attributed to the breach. On the other hand, if it is the hard work of Bill that created the opportunity presented by Hillary, allowing Bill to keep the gain makes economic sense.

2.   SPECIFIC PERFORMANCE

Problems with expectancy as the baseline contract remedy lead naturally to considerations of specific performance. After all, specific performance can be regarded as "literal expectancy" in that it means that the non-breaching party does not run the risk of receiving an inadequate payment in the form of damages.

The primary drawback of specific performance is that it typically requires greater judicial resources to administer than a remedy that involves the payment of money. For example, the complexity of what is adequate performance may make it very difficult for a court to determine when the breaching party has adequately performed. Thus, specific performance is most attractive from an economic standpoint when judicial supervision is relatively easy and what constitutes "performance" can be defined.

One issue that arises is whether specific performance may stand in the way of the efficient breach. For example, if Bill is required by a court to turn over the Grateful Dead collection to Gennifer and the transaction costs associated with Gennifer and

Hillary finding each other are high, the efficient breach would appear to be thwarted.

Two very good cases that can be adapted to illustrate both the advantages of specific performance in terms of assuring the non-breaching party of receiving expectancy and the fact that specific performance may not retard an efficient reallocation are *Groves v. John Wunder* (Minn.1939) and *Peevyhouse v. Garland Coal & Min. Co.* (Okl.1962). One or both of these cases are in almost every contract law casebook because they are instances in which the cost of performing the contract greatly exceeds the objective value of that performance. The problem is one of determining which of these two possible measures of expectancy to use.

In *Garland Coal*, as part of its agreement to strip-mine coal from the Peevyhouse property, Garland agreed to restore the land to its original condition, which it failed to do. The cost of performance was $29,000. The performance would have enhanced the market value of the property by less than $300. From an objective market-based standpoint, the Peevyhouses could be given expectancy of less than $300. On the other hand, they may have subjectively valued having the land restored at a figure much higher than that—maybe $29,000 or more.

The problem is that, if the actual preferences of the Peevyhouses are to count, there is no way to accurately set a figure for damages that will assure an efficient breach. One approach is to actually test their subjective valuation by granting specific performance. In Coasian terms, they would be entitled to have the land restored. Of course, this entitlement could be transferred to Garland Coal.

Suppose, in fact, that it is worth $5,000 to the Peevyhouses to have the land restored. Obviously, it is worth up to $29,000 to Garland Coal to avoid restoring the land. The parties would agree on some figure between $5,000 and $29,000, and the land will not be restored. In fact, as long as the cost of restoration exceeds the value to the Peevyhouses of having the land restored, chances are they will settle the case and the land will not be restored. In short, specific performance, at least in theory, would seem to be a very effective way of making sure that expectancy is protected and an efficient resource allocation occurs.

The primary drawback to specific performance as a means to facilitating the efficient breach lies in the fact that it is dependent on an agreement between the parties. One complication is that the agreement must take place in the context of what is called bilateral monopoly. Bilateral monopoly is a structure under which there is only one buyer and one seller of a particular good—or in this case, a right. Since neither party can threaten to buy from or sell to a competitor, the parties have a strong incentive to engage in the types of strategic behavior that may impede and ultimately preclude a bargain.

The attraction of a judicially determined damage award is that it avoids the bilateral monopoly problem. In effect, the Peevyhouses are *forced* to sell their "right" to restoration at a price which may or may not fully protect their expectancy. Economists disagree about how important the bilateral monopoly problem is and, by implication, the merits of routinely granting specific performance.

3. LIQUIDATED DAMAGES

A fair amount of literature in law and economics and contract law is devoted to the issue of enforcement of liquidated damages clauses. The typical common law reluctance to enforce these clauses is generally viewed with disfavor. The consensus seems to be that a liquidated damage clause, even one in excess of what the likely damages may turn out to be, can be a useful way for one party to assure the other party of her dependability. Moreover, the liquidated damages clause is but one of the negotiated terms. Perhaps one party agreed to pay a higher price because the other agreed to what seems to be excessive liquidated damages. The point is that to not enforce the clause upsets the balance the parties have established.

At first glance, the common law position of disfavoring liquidated damage clauses because they may have the effect of a penalty seems to fit nicely with the theory of the efficient breach. Specifically, a clause setting damages at a level that would exceed the expectancy damages of the non-breaching party would deter the potentially breaching party.

The Grateful Dead example introduced above shows that this threat is not really very great. In that example, assume that the parties stipulated to damages of $4,000 should Bill not deliver the tapes to Gennifer. In this instance, Bill will not breach and sell the tapes unless he can avoid the liquidated damages. In effect, Gennifer is in the same position as someone who has been granted specific performance. She would prefer a payment of anything in excess of $1,000 to performance by Bill. Knowing that Hillary is willing to pay $6,000 for the tapes, Bill will be willing to offer Gennifer up to $3,000 to buy his way out of the liquidated damages provision.

It may be that Gennifer will simply hold out for the performance or for liquidated damages. But this seems unlikely. Bill's leverage, should Gennifer decide to hold out, would be the threat of performance. This would only make Gennifer $1,000 better off, while allowing Bill not to perform would be more valuable to her. In effect, Gennifer is likely to sell her "right" to liquidated damages for a price between $1,000 and $3,000, and the tapes will find their way into Hillary's hands. The point is that the so-called penalty will not lead to a different allocative outcome than would a proper determination of Gennifer's expectancy.

The liquidated damages example does reintroduce the problem of bilateral monopoly. In effect, Gennifer is the only one who can sell her right to liquidated damages, and Bill is the only one in the market for that right. On the other hand, liquidated damages and the process of bargaining around the "penalty" raise the probability that Gennifer will have an opportunity to share in the profit made by Bill when he sells the tapes to Hillary.

4. THE LOST VOLUME SELLER

An issue in contract damages that has been subject to economic analysis both in the literature and in judicial opinions is the matter of the "lost volume" seller. Typically, the issue arises in the sale of goods when the buyer breaches and the seller is able to resell the goods intended for the buyer at little or no loss. A good example of the problem and a sophisticated economically-based response is found in *R.E. Davis Chemical Corp. v. Diasonics, Inc.* (7th Cir.1987), in which the seller contracted to sell medical diagnostic equipment. When the buyer breached, the seller was able to sell the same equipment to another customer. From one point of view, the seller was not damaged by the breach since the resale was for the same price as the original sale. This might be the case if one applies section 2–706 of the Uniform Commercial Code. Or, even if there was not a resale, as long as the contract price and the market price were the same, one could argue that under section 2–708(1) of the Code, the seller was not damaged.

On the other hand, if the seller could have made the original sale as well as the second sale, the breach has resulted in lost volume. On first impression, the logical answer seems to be that in order to put the seller in the position it would have been in but for the breach, it is necessary to measure damages as the profit lost from the first sale. This appears to be what is permitted under section 2–708(2) of the Code.

A number of questions arise in determining whether a seller is actually a lost volume seller. These questions are derived from the basic price theory introduced in Chapter Two. In particular, according to economic theory, most firms select a unique level of output to sell. This is called the profit-maximizing level. Figure 9 illustrates this proposition. A firm will produce and sell units as long as the extra or marginal revenue (MR) from selling that item exceeds the marginal cost (MC). Thus, in the graph, the seller will produce seven units and sell them for $10.00.

Figure 9

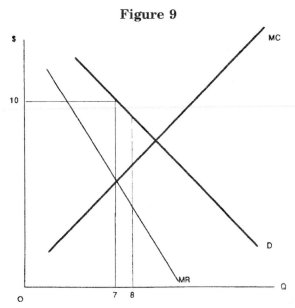

Under the lost volume analysis, the seventh unit is sold, the buyer breaches and then a new buyer agrees to buy unit seven. In order to claim that the breach has resulted in "lost volume," the seller would have to claim that even had the breach not occurred, he would have been willing to sell unit eight. The problem, as the graph indicates, is that unit eight would not have been produced and sold because the marginal cost of its production would have exceeded its marginal revenue.

In *Diasonics* the court responded to the problem by ruling that the seller making a lost volume claim would be required to show that it had the productive capacity to produce the extra unit and that the unit could have been sold at a profit. Even if the "lost volume" sale would have been possible and profitable, the question of *how* profitable should be examined. Since marginal revenue slopes downward and marginal cost upward, the profit lost due to the lost volume unit may be less than the profit resulting from the sale of other units.

E. BREACH AND EXCUSES FOR NON–PERFORMANCE

The issue of risk allocation in contract law is probably most starkly evident when the parties disagree about whether one of them has complied with the terms of the contract. In other words, has there been a breach? Closely related are the instances in which a party has admittedly not performed the contract but asks that its non-performance be excused as a result of mutual mistake, impossibility, frustration of purpose, or commercial impracticability.

1. BREACH

In many instances in which the issue of breach arises the analysis is straight-forward. In effect, the party who breaches has not shouldered all the risks that it had agreed to assume under the contract. Very often, however, the matter of how the risks and burdens were allocated by the parties is not clear. Here contract law is called on to interpret the contract and allocate these risks.

The range of ways this issue can present itself is enormous, but the basic economic approach tends to be one that assigns the risk of a lack of clarity to the party who might be viewed as having been in a better position to clarify things when the contract was formed. Take the casebook standard, *Frigaliment Importing Co. v. B.N.S. International Sales Corp.* (S.Dist. N.Y. 1960), in which Judge Friendly states the issue as "What is chicken?" The defendant argued for a broad definition that would permit it to fulfill the contract by shipping older, lower quality birds while the plaintiff claimed that the younger birds were intended. An economic approach to the issue would suggest that the party intending a narrower and more expensive definition of chicken should bear the burden of ensuring the that this point is clarified when the contract is made. And Judge Friendly's opinion is consistent with this approach.

Closely related is the reliance of the U.C.C. and the common law on gap-filler or contract default terms. For example, references to course of performance, course of dealing, or trade usage amount to the establishment of "norms," and the party wishing to deviate from the norm typically bears the risk of proving that the parties have agreed to that deviation. Similar in effect is the interpretation of the terms of requirement contracts and exclusive dealing arrangements. The problem, in the case of a requirements contract, for example, is that the quantity term is left open. Thus, the buyer may be tempted to vary the amount "required" by unexpectedly large amounts or for reasons the seller would find objectionable. Here the U.C.C. refers to "actual requirements as may occur in good faith" and sets norms equal to stated amounts or prior requirements. In essence, the party wishing to deviate from these norms assumes the risk of clarifying this in the contract. This approach has economic appeal because the party wishing to deviate from the norm is also the party most likely to possess the information about the need for deviation and is in the best position to avoid disagreement down the line.

One of the more intriguing interpretation problems arises when there is a shirking problem. Shirking can be an issue when the interests of the parties are aligned but not completely. Take the example of listing a house with a real estate agent. The agent may get a fixed percentage of the selling price. The realtor's net gain will be that fixed percentage minus any amount expended in his or her selling efforts. Obviously, the interests of the homeowner and the agent coincide with respect to the selling price. The problem is that the owner's preference is for the agent to expend maximum effort to sell the home while the agent must balance the selling costs against the income from the sale. The agent's reluctance to make as much effort as the owner would prefer can be interpreted as "shirking" and amount to a breach. The issue is complicated because, at the outset, both parties know that their interests do not exactly coincide. In many instances, they will specify exactly what is expected of the agent. When this does not occur, the courts are again left to fill in the gap with a default or norm-like position. This amounts to what the parties would have reasonably expected. The party wishing to deviate has the burden of establishing that both parties knew or should have known that the norm would not govern.

2. EXCUSES FOR NON–PERFORMANCE

The issue of excuse is very similar in theme to the question of how far the liability of a breaching party extends when the breach has resulted in special or consequential damages. In fact, the "lost profits" damages issue and all of the "excuse" doctrines are amenable to the same basic analysis.

When a party makes a contract, he naturally hopes that nothing will happen to make performance more difficult than planned or render the outcome valueless. It is clear that if events do spoil matters, the performing party is generally expected to perform nonetheless. For the courts to take any other view would undercut the basic risk allocation and insurance function of the contract.

It is clear that at some point, though, the party will be excused.[7] In other words, the party will not be viewed as assuming the risk of all events. In effect, these risks are the ones assumed by the other party. The real economic function of contract law in these instances is to allocate the risk in a manner that will signal which class of parties will be required to assume the risk in the future. In

7. In the context of damages this could be seen as being excused from paying for the full consequences of one's breach.

other words, the decision has little connection with "efficiency" with respect to the two parties currently in the dispute. (For them, the effects of the decision are distributive.) Instead, these cases can be viewed as tools through which courts can direct parties toward risk allocation in the future. This requires that the party assuming the risk be the party who is in the best position to avoid the harm from the event or to insure against it at the lowest cost.

In an important 1977 article, Richard Posner and Andrew Rosenfield[8] suggested a methodology for determining the proper risk allocation. They explain that the party who is better able to avoid the risk or insure against it is the one who would have assumed the risk at the time of contracting had the issue arisen. For example, suppose that Michael and Lisa Marie are preparing to sign a contract that will require Lisa Marie to use her boat to carry Michael's llamas from Costa Rica to Miami. Under the terms of the contract, Lisa Marie is to leave Costa Rica on June 15th and arrive in Miami on July 15th. Just before signing the contract, they both realize that it is hurricane season in the Caribbean and there is a 10% chance of a delay due to a hurricane. Lisa Marie asks to insert a clause that excuses her for delays due to hurricanes. Michael, of course, resists.

8. Richard Posner & Andrew Rosenfield, "Impossibility and Related Doctrines in Contract Law: An Economic Analysis," 6 *J. Leg. Stud.* 83 (1977).

The real issue is how much Michael will pay Lisa Marie if the clause is left out and what is the least Lisa Marie will take. Lisa Marie may realize that if the clause is left out, her only alternative will be to charter Sonny's airplane and have the llamas delivered at an extra cost of $1,000. Michael may calculate that the delay will cost him $2,000 and the best deal he can find on an air charter is $1,500. At this point, Lisa Marie will take no less than $100 to leave the clause out. This is the expected cost to her, calculated by multiplying the probability of a hurricane times the cost if the hurricane does materialize. Michael is willing to pay up to $150. In all likelihood, the clause will be left out and Michael will pay something between $100 and $150 to Lisa Marie.

Under the Posner/Rosenfield model, this means that had they not anticipated the hurricane problem and one did delay Lisa Marie's performance, she would be liable for Michael's losses. Lisa Marie's non-performance would not be excused. Posner and Rosenfield favor a rule that would only rarely excuse performance, apparently based on the notion that parties promising to do something are generally in the best position to anticipate what sorts of events might hamper performance or, in the case of frustration of purpose, render the received performance valueless.

Again, it should be noted that this model does not achieve any sort of efficiency between Michael and Lisa Marie. Only the most tenuous notions of consent and Pareto superiority would support a view that the parties had somehow agreed to this allocation. This "crystal ball" approach is best at providing some direction to parties in the future, who then allocate resources in such a way that the harm from the event is minimized. In a very real sense, it is comparable to allocating the risk of an accident to the party who could have avoided it or insured against it less expensively.

One important corollary of this approach is that there should be no effort to split the loss between the parties once the loss occurs. The argument is that dividing the extra cost would just lower the incentive for the party in the best position to assume the risk to actually take risk-avoidance steps. Once again, however, distributive concerns do come into play and some courts find ways of dividing the losses.

CHAPTER SIX

ECONOMICS OF TORT LAW

This Chapter focuses on unintentional torts.[1] As a general statement, an economic approach to tort law is one that seeks to minimize the costs of accidents. It does this by allocating the costs of accidents to the party or parties who are in the best position to avoid them or to minimize the losses. In theory, that person makes a decision about whether the benefits of the activity outweigh its costs.

By limiting its focus to "accidents," this Chapter does not consider the economics of intentional torts, including such torts as defamation or "tortious interference with business relationships." In addition, by emphasizing economics, this Chapter does not directly take on the weighty issues of what tort system is ultimately "just" and whether tort remedies should have as their main objective the "correction" of a "wrong."[2]

In terms of approach, there are good reasons for examining the economics of tort law from a different perspective than that applied in the case of contracts. Contract law is structured so that each

1. The organization of this Chapter is based on David Barnes and Lynn Stout, *Law and Economics: Cases and Materials*, Chapter 3 (1993).

2. See Jules Coleman, *Risks and Wrongs* (1992).

doctrine can be examined separately from the others and then combined to achieve an overall picture. An economic analysis of tort law requires a more integrated approach. In the pages that follow, the simple core elements will be discussed and then levels of complexity added.

This analysis begins with a description of the ideal outcome of tort law from the perspective of economic efficiency. The negligence standard is then considered, along with the Hand formula. Discussions of comparative negligence, strict liability, and damages follow. In all instances, the question is the extent to which economic goals are achieved.

A. THE COSTS OF ACCIDENTS AND THE ECONOMICS OF TORT LAW

When considering the economics of tort law, the touchstone scholarly work is Guido Calabresi's *The Costs of Accidents*[3]. Professor Calabresi identifies three types of costs that result from accidents. Primary costs are those associated with the harm to the injured party. This would include such things as the cost of medical care and lost earning capacity. Secondary costs, according to Calabresi, are "the societal costs resulting from accidents." Tertiary costs are those associated with administering the tort system.

Of these three categories, the second is the most difficult to understand. This category deals not with the absolute dollar losses associated with accidents,

3. Guido Calabresi, *The Costs of Accidents* (1970).

but as Jules Coleman puts it, with the "costs of bearing the costs of accidents."[4] For example, a $1,000 loss spread across 1000 individuals may result in less "dislocation" than if it were borne by a single person. Similarly, a wealthy person may suffer less utility from a $1000 loss that a poor person would.

Minimizing one cost may not be consistent with minimizing another cost. For example, a system that always accurately assigns the primary costs of accidents to those who cause accidents may be expensive to administer. Similarly, some efforts to reduce secondary accident costs may mean the party causing the accident does not feel the full impact of the harm done and may not take cost-justified steps to avoid the same accident in the future.

Although this list of costs is a useful way to envision the harms generated by accidents, the economic approach to tort law does not call for the minimization of these costs. For example, at some point the cost of avoiding accidents would be greater than the harm that would be caused by those accidents. Thus, the economic goal is to minimize the sum of the costs of accidents and the costs of efforts to prevent accidents. This is consistent with the notion of allocative efficiency discussed in Chapter Two. As long as the benefits of accident avoidance exceed the costs of prevention, it makes sense to invest in prevention. At some point, however, avoidance efforts will be more costly than the costs of the accident itself. The continued use of re-

4.   Jules Coleman, supra note 2, at 204.

sources to avoid accidents in these instances would be allocatively inefficient. The seemingly harsh conventional economic truth is that there may be an efficient level of accidents that results not just in property damage but in personal injury and death.

Also implicated in the economic goals of tort law is a factor similar to productive efficiency.[5] Not only is the economist interested in avoiding those accidents that result in more damage than the cost of avoiding them, but the avoidance steps, when warranted, should be the least costly available. Thus, the economic approach to accidents seeks to make certain that the right quantity of avoidance is "produced" at the lowest possible cost.

B. LIABILITY, THE ASSIGNMENT OF RIGHTS AND EXTERNALITIES

Production of the right amount of accident avoidance at the lowest possible cost fits within the basic construct of the Coase Theorem. As an example, suppose a common hazard is that shoppers in grocery stores slip and fall on milk that has been spilled around the dairy department. In the language of tort law, the question is whether the operator of the store has a "duty" to keep spills off the floor. This right can be viewed as an entitlement or property right and, from an economic perspective, it should wind up in the possession of the party who values it most.

5. See Chapter Three.

If the right in this example is "owned" by shoppers, the store will owe a duty to the shoppers and will be liable for "breaching" this duty if spills are allowed to occur and consumers slip on them. If the right is owned by the operators of grocery stores, they do not owe a duty to shoppers and are not liable in the typical "slip and fall" incident.

The question posed for determining the efficient assignment of this right or duty would be: Who would pay more for it? Presumably, rational consumers with perfect information would bid either an amount up to the probability that they will slip times the "damage" if the slip occurs or the cost of avoiding the slip, whichever is lower. For example, suppose the probability of a slip and damaging fall is 1 in 1,000 for each visit to the store and the resulting injury, on average, is valued at $1,000. Also assume that by renting slip-proof slippers at the grocery store door for fifty cents each shopper can avoid the harm. Given these options, the consumer would pay up to fifty cents to own the right to be free of slippery floors and have the duty assigned to the store operator. If there were 1,000 shoppers a day, a cooperative of shoppers, assuming no free-riding, would bid up to $500.

On the other hand, assume the store could completely avoid the spill hazard by posting a person with a mop at each end of the dairy department. The cost per day would be $100. Or, the average cost per shopper-visit would be ten cents per day.

Now if an auction could take place, it is clear that shoppers would outbid store operators for the right. The consumers would bid up to $500 per day to have the duty assigned to the store owner. The store operator would bid only up to $100 per day for the right that would permit him to ignore the milk spills and escape liability. In other words, if the right could be allocated through the market, it would end up being *owned* by consumers. And, the duty would be *owed* by the lowest cost avoider of the accident—store operators.

Of course, the ownership of the duty in this type of case will be determined by a court. The assignment of liability may be assigned to the shoppers or to store owners. Under the Coase Theorem, in the absence of transaction costs, this initial assignment will not affect the eventual ownership of the right. In the above example, suppose the court assigned rights so that grocery stores would not be liable for slips. Since stores value the right to milky floors at $100, and shoppers the right to milk-free floors at $500, the shoppers would buy the milk-free-floor right at something between $100 and $500. The store would then guarantee that there would be no milk spills on the floor. Avoidance would take place, and it would take place at the lowest cost.

Obviously, in this example transaction costs would probably make such an exchange impossible. One thousand shoppers who do not know each other would have to combine and enter into some kind of binding contract with the store owner. There would be huge coordination expenses as well as free-rider problems. In many other instances, the parties are simply unable to bargain over these "rights" because there is not enough time. All of these limitations on the ability of parties to private-ly establish "duties of care" mean that it is critical, from an economic perspective, for the court to make the "correct" assignment in the first place. This would be a classic example of what Calabresi and Melamed call a "liability rule."[6]

Determining the "correct" assignment is compli-cated by the many factors discussed in Chapter Four. In addition, as will be discussed in detail in the pages that follow, damages for violating the rights of another in a torts context are the "prices" one has to pay. In effect, an involuntary exchange takes place. In the context of contracts and volun-tary exchanges we can have some confidence that Pareto superior outcomes are achieved. The invol-untary exchanges of tort law, under liability rules, offer no such assurances. Although one can argue that the injurer is better off because he has consent-ed to the exchange by choosing the riskier course of action, this is stretching the limits of the type of consent that would be consistent with Pareto supe-riority. In addition, the compensation of the injured party may not put that party in a position, utility-wise, that is the equivalent of his pre-accident state. This compensation will be determined by objective indicators, not by the actual value attributed by the victim to the harm that is done. The danger from a Pareto standpoint is that the injured party will be

6.   See Chapter Four, Section E.

undercompensated.[7] Although the availability of punitive damages and damages for pain and suffering may offset this and provide for adequate compensation, the goal of punitive damages, in particular, is not compensation. Consequently, a match between damages and subjective losses will still be happenstance.

C. THE NEGLIGENCE STANDARD

1. THE HAND FORMULA

In order to achieve the goal of minimizing the sum of accident costs and their prevention, it is important that the right signal be sent to those who must make decisions about whether to invest in accident prevention. This "signaling" is captured at the most basic level by the Hand formula as explained in the well-known case, *United States v. Carroll Towing Co.* (2d Cir.1947). Judge Hand saw the issue of liability as being the function of three variables: the probability of the harm (P), the amount of harm should it occur (L) and the cost of prevention (B). P multiplied by L is the "expected harm." Thus, under the Hand formula, when PL exceeds B, a party is regarded as negligent. Conversely, if the expected harm is less than the cost of prevention, the party is not negligent.

Inherent in the Hand formula is a "pricing" effect that creates certain incentives. In theory, any actor has a choice of taking steps to avoid an

7. Over-compensation may also occur which raises problems discussed below in Section H.3.

accident or not. The Hand formula informs the actors of the price of each of those choices. When the prices are compared, presumably the rational actor will select the lower-priced option. For example, if the cost of avoidance is less than the expected harm, the choice would be to avoid the accident. The result of a "wrong" choice is that the injurer will be required to pay for the damages caused. Of course, it is also possible to make the wrong choice when PL is less than B. In these cases, the level of care is inefficiently high but there is no legal wrong. The overly cautious person does, however, internalize the cost of too much care.

At this basic level, the Hand formula focuses only on the behavior of the defendant. A finding that the defendant passed on an opportunity to take cost-justified preventive action does not mean that the defendant is the best cost avoider. Thus, a finding of liability under the negligence standard falls short of providing the proper signal if the other party can avoid the accident at a lower cost.

2.   DISTRIBUTIVE CONSEQUENCES

In virtually all instances of assigning rights, duties or entitlements, the effects are both allocative as well as distributive. To be more specific, the impact of the assignment of the right, even to the party that values it the most, is in no way "neutral." Thus, in the simple example of the potentially slippery dairy department, an assignment of the right to the shoppers to be free of the danger of spilled milk gives them something of value and has a distributive consequence. They become "richer," while the requirement that the store either pay for the accident or prevent it results in a decrease in the wealth of store owners. This is not to say, however, that some of this cost may not be shifted back to shoppers. The actual ultimate distributive effect can depend on a variety of factors in addition to the initial assignment.[8]

D. REFINING THE NEGLIGENCE MODEL: CONTRIBUTORY NEGLIGENCE

1. THE CONVENTIONAL DOCTRINE

Typically, the negligence standard is considered in the context of various defenses, including the possibility that the injured party has also acted negligently. The traditional approach in such instances could be to engage in the Hand formula calculation for the injured party. The question would be whether the injured party's accident-avoidance costs were lower than the expected harm of the accident.

In the slippery dairy department example, all shoppers could rent slip-proof slippers for fifty cents each time they visited the grocery store. The expected harm per shopper of $1.00 would exceed the shoppers' cost of avoidance and, from the standpoint of the Hand formula, the shoppers would be

8. For more on this see Chapter Three.

regarded as negligent. Thus, the conventional common law doctrine would allow what amounted to a defense if the injurer failed the Hand formula test as long as it was shown that PL exceeded B for the injured party also.

2.   RECONCILING CONTRIBUTORY NEGLIGENCE AND EFFICIENCY

The example of the slippery dairy section and the possibility of renting slip-proof slippers illustrates one of the economic problems of the standard contributory negligence formulation. Each shopper can avoid the expected harm of $1.00 for fifty cents. The store operators can avoid the harm for ten cents per shopper. Both parties could avoid the expected harm at a cost that is less than the expected harm. Consequently, adhering to the rule of contributory negligence will result in the harm being avoided by the parties—shoppers—who can efficiently do so but who are not the "best cost avoiders." In a sense, they are not the most productively efficient. Such an assignment would be inconsistent with the overall goal of minimizing the sum of the costs of accidents and their prevention.

Richard Posner makes the point that this inefficiency will not occur if the proper standard is applied. In the above example, he would say that, given that the store owners can avoid the care at ten cents per shopper, the shoppers will not be motivated to take care as long as the law defines due care as "the level of care that is optimal if the other party is taking due care."[9] A technical problem with Judge Posner's theory is that it defines due care in terms of due care. What he seems to mean is that each party is entitled to act as though the other party is acting in the matter that is most efficient from the standpoint of minimizing the primary cost of the accident. Thus, the shoppers, even though their B is less than PL, are permitted to act as though the store's B is also less than PL by an even greater margin and that the store has acted accordingly. According to Judge Posner, this is the way the courts define due care.[10]

This leads to the issue of whether a party who is likely to be harmed by the negligent conduct of another party must take steps to avoid the harm. First, it is useful to note that an injured party who has no basis to know of the injuring party's conduct will be able to recover even if he could have efficiently taken preventive action. In this situation, even though avoidance may be relatively inexpensive, the B in the Hand formula could be viewed as being quite high since the burden would involve not just the effort to avoid the harm but the costs of discovering that the other party has acted in a careless fashion.

9. Richard Posner, The Economic Analysis of Law 173 (6th ed. 2003) (emphasis deleted).

10. Judge Posner has been challenged on this. See David W. Barnes & Rosemary McCool, "Reasonable Care in Tort Law: The Duty to Take Corrective Precaution," 36 Ariz. L. Rev. 357 (1994).

On the other hand, if the victim knows or has reason to know of the other party's negligent conduct, the question is whether she can blithely bypass avoiding the accident confident that the injurer will be liable. In terms of the shoppers and the store, can the shoppers walk through obvious spilt milk and hold the store liable if they slip? Judge Posner evidently thinks that they can because they are permitted to act as though the store owners have acted efficiently.

From a common sense point of view, it seems clear that the victim should be required to take action to avoid the harm. This is consistent with the Hand formula if one views the issue in a compressed time frame because, once the hazard is known, the possibly large search costs are no longer part of the burden. This outcome is also consistent with section 466 of the *Restatement (Second) of Torts*, which states that a plaintiff is contributorily negligent when exposing himself "to danger created by the defendant's negligence, of which danger the plaintiff knows or has reason to know." The requirement that the victim react to the negligent behavior of the injuring party does not necessarily mean that the victim is the best cost avoider. Thus, the inconsistency of the negligence/contributory negligence standard with the cost minimization goal remains.

Another refinement of the negligence standard that seems designed to avoid inefficient outcomes resulting from strict adherence to contributory negligence is the doctrine of "last clear chance." Last clear chance is different from the possibilities discussed above in that it permits a negligent victim to shift liability back to the injurer by showing that the injurer was, *at the time of the accident*, able to avoid the accident at a cost that was lower than the expected harm. Again, the critical variable in terms of the Hand formula is B, the burden. At the time of the accident the burden on the victim may be quite high. Since P and L are the same for both parties, the proper risk allocation is to the injurer, who can efficiently avoid the harm.

E.   REFINING THE NEGLIGENCE STANDARD: COMPARATIVE NEGLIGENCE

The adoption of comparative negligence in one form or another by most states represents an effort to alter the perceived inequity resulting from the "all or nothing" outcomes of strict application of negligence and contributory negligence standards. Whatever the equities inherent in comparative negligence, it may or may not be an improvement over contributory negligence in terms of providing the best cost avoider with the maximum incentive to avoid the harm.

There are a variety of comparative negligence regimes. Under the most common, loss is apportioned among the parties according to how fault is allocated among them. Under this regime, the injured party's recovery is reduced, but not necessarily eliminated, because of negligence. In effect, it is apportioned. Under a less common approach, the negligent injured person may recover so long as the negligence of the injurer is gross when compared to that of the injured party. Under this approach, loss is not apportioned, so it has the all-or-nothing characteristic of traditional contributory negligence. These two forms of comparative negligence are discussed in turn.

1. APPORTIONED COMPARATIVE NEGLIGENCE

In order to illustrate the possible economic consequences of comparative negligence, it is useful to start with a simple example. In the case of the slippery dairy department, suppose the floor actually was wet from some recently spilled milk and that a shopper who was running through the department slipped and was injured to the extent of $200,000. A possible outcome in a comparative negligence state might be that the store is viewed as being 60 percent responsible, while the injured party is viewed as being 40 percent responsible. See *Scott v. Alpha Beta Company* (Cal.App.1980). The plaintiff would recover $120,000. In other words, the recovery is reduced by the portion of the plaintiff's contribution to the harm.

The obvious difference between contributory negligence and comparative negligence is that, under the former, one party *or* the other will be motivated to avoid the harm. Under comparative negligence, both parties will have some incentive to avoid the harm. The problem from an economic standpoint is that the parties may both attempt to avoid the harm when the efforts of either one would be sufficient. This may mean there is an over-investment in avoidance. Another possibility is that the incentive to avoid the harm is reduced to the point that neither party takes preventive action, even though the prevention of the accident is cost-justified.

For example, suppose an accident that will result in a $1,000 loss can be prevented by a $50 expenditure by the defendant or a $100 expenditure by the plaintiff.[11] Under an apportioned approach to comparative negligence, the defendant will be viewed as bearing two-thirds of the responsibility for the accident and the plaintiff's responsibility will be one-third. Each party's share is equal to the ratio of the other party's individual avoidance costs to the sum of the avoidance costs. Based on these numbers, the defendant would be responsible for $666.66 of the loss and the plaintiff $333.33. Thus, they would both be motivated to take the preventive steps for a total cost of $150, even though the accident could be avoided at a cost of only $50. On the other hand, each party may anticipate that the other will find it in his or her economic interest to avoid the accident. If so, neither party will avoid the accident, and the $1,000 loss will occur.

This is not to say that comparative negligence will always result in over-investment or under-investment in accident prevention. For example, sup-

11. This explanation is found in from *Golden v. McCurry* (Ala.1980), cited by Barnes and Stout, supra note 1.

pose an accident costs $15,000 and has a 1% chance of occurring.[12] Further suppose that the cost of avoidance to the injurer is $1.00 and the cost of avoidance to the victim is $100. In this case, the expected cost of the accident to the injurer would be the probability of the accident times the cost of the accident times the ratio of the victim's avoidance cost to the sum of the avoidance costs. This would be $148.51, and the injurer would be motivated to take the precautionary action at a cost of $1.00. Using the same calculation, the expected cost to the victim would be $1.49, and the victim would not be motivated to take precautionary action.

Using the same numbers, however, and applying a strict contributory negligence standard, the burden to the victim of avoidance—$100—would be less than PL, which would be $150, and the victim would be motivated to spend $100 to avoid an accident that the injurer could have avoided at just $1.00.

Whether comparative negligence is inefficient depends on the numbers. The critical factor seems to be the avoidance costs of both parties relative to the risk. David Barnes and Lynn Stout divide the possibilities into three groups.[13] When avoidance costs for both parties are high relative to the risk, neither party is as likely to avoid the accident. On the other hand, when both parties' avoidance costs are relatively low as compared to the loss, both parties are

12. This example is from David Barnes and Lynn Stout, *supra* note 1, at 122.

13. See David Barnes and Lynn Stout, *supra* note 1, at 123.

likely to take action. These are the instances in which comparative negligence may lead to inefficient outcomes. On the other hand, as the numerical illustration shows, when one party's avoidance costs are high and the other's low relative to the loss, the lower cost avoider—whether injurer or victim—will be motivated to take precautionary action.

2. UNAPPORTIONED COMPARATIVE NEGLIGENCE

Although both contributory negligence and comparative negligence can lead to inefficient outcomes, there are variations that increase the likelihood that the best cost avoider will take preventive steps. Although not applicable currently in any state, a rule that would consistently incorporate the equitable considerations of comparative negligence with the goal of motivating the best cost avoider to take the precautions necessary to avoid an accident is called the *Galena* rule.[14]

Under *Galena,* the injuring party is fully liable even though the victim is also negligent as long as the injuring party's negligence is gross relative to the victim's negligence. As long as comparative costs of accident avoidance are used to determine the relative negligence of the parties, the proper economic signal should be sent to motivate the best cost avoider to take the precautionary action. The key feature of the rule, when compared to compara-

14. See Id., at 123–124.

tive negligence, is that liability is not split and whichever party is the lower cost avoider will have the maximum incentive to avoid the accident.

Another effort to steer a path between contributory negligence and comparative negligence is the South Dakota Comparative Negligence Statute which does not bar recovery by a contributorily negligent plaintiff as long as the plaintiff's negligence was "slight in comparison with the negligence of the defendant." Although recovery is not barred, it is reduced by the amount of the plaintiff's negligence. The economic effect of the rule should be that a defendant, who is the best cost avoider, will not escape liability when the plaintiff has also been negligent. Conversely, by barring a plaintiff's recovery whose negligence is more than "slight" when compared to that of the defendant, the efficient economic message should be sent to plaintiffs.

F. ASSUMPTION OF THE RISK

Assumption of the risk bars the recovery of a plaintiff in much the same manner as contributory negligence. In one form, "primary assumption of the risk," the injurer is engaged in a possibly dangerous activity, but the costs of eliminating the risk may be quite high. For example, there is a danger that spectators at a golf tournament will be bonked on the head by stray golf balls. Completely avoiding the risk, B, is probably higher than PL; the injurer is not negligent. The victim can be said to have assumed the risk.

In another form, "secondary assumption of the risk," the plaintiff's actions are dangerous because of a situation created by the injurer. In the slippery floor example, it could mean that the plaintiff walked across the floor knowing that it was slick with spilled milk. Secondary assumption of the risk can be evaluated in the same manner as contributory negligence in that it may operate as a complete bar to a plaintiff even though the defendant was the best cost avoider. The idea is that, having witnessed the negligence of the defendant, the plaintiff cannot ignore an easy and inexpensive opportunity to avoid the harm.

G. STRICT LIABILITY

Strict liability means that a party is liable for damage caused by her activity even if there is no showing of negligence. Although this may seem to undermine efforts to achieve economic efficiency, presumably those parties who are more likely to be in control of the activity will be the ones held strictly liable. Furthermore, streamlining the fault-finding process can reduce the tertiary costs of accidents.

The decision that a party will be strictly liable for the damages resulting from an activity amounts to an assignment of a right to others to be free of the consequences of the activity or to be compensated. In effect, the harm to the others is treated as an externality that the liable party is forced to "internalize."[15] Either the harm to the injured party from the activity or the investment the injuring party makes to avoid the harm becomes a cost of production whether or not the injuring party has acted negligently.

It is important to note that the fact that a party is strictly liable does not mean that she will take steps to avoid the harm. The party has a choice and presumably will choose the lower of the cost to avoid the harm and the cost of the harm itself. In making this decision, the liable party can be seen as applying the Hand formula on an individualized basis in that she will be likely to take preventive action when PL exceeds B.

1. EFFICIENCY AND STRICT LIABILITY

One of the obvious dangers of strict liability in terms of efficiency is that the liable party may not be the best cost avoider. There are two versions of this possibility. The first occurs when an accident that should be prevented from the standpoint of the Hand formula will not be prevented. In these instances, the liable party will find that PL does not exceed B and, therefore, will not take preventive action. It may be that the opposite is true for the victim and that PL will exceed B, but since the victim will be compensated by the injuring party, there will be insufficient motivation to take the cost-justified preventive action. Of course, this would not be the case if contributory negligence

15. For an extended discussion see Chapter Three.

were a defense to strict liability. Such a defense makes sense except that it then undermines one of the attractions of strict liability, the reduction of tertiary or administrative expenses.

The second possibility is that the accident will be avoided, but not by the best cost avoider. This will occur when the B exceeds the PL for both the injurer and the victim, but the B to the victim is less than the B to the injurer. In such a case, the injurer will act to avoid the accident, although it would have been less costly for the victim to do so. This inefficiency, like those described in the preceding paragraph, can be overcome by the proper application of defenses to strict liability, some of which are discussed below. In any case, if these inefficiencies are relatively rare, or relatively low-cost, the savings in tertiary costs of strict liability may still lower the overall cost of accidents.

One major consequence of applying strict liability that has important efficiency implications is that it forces the party who will be liable to consider not only the standard of care but the *level of activity.*[16] For example, under a negligence system, a person who engages in a certain activity, like blasting, only has to be concerned with damages as a result of negligent blasting. Thus, the number of times blasting takes place would only be influenced by the likelihood that increased numbers mean increased probability that negligence will occur. On the other hand, since under strict liability all damage caused

16. Steve Shavell, *"Strict Liability Verses Negligence,"* 9 J. *Legal. Stud.* 1 (1980).

is chargeable to the blasting party, those damages will be treated like any other cost of blasting. They will increase with the amount of blasting, whether carefully or negligently conducted. Thus, the party is concerned not just with the level of care but with the level of the activity.

This distinction has particularly important implications from the standpoint of allocative efficiency. It will be recalled from Chapter Two that production is at an allocatively efficient level when the amount people are willing to pay for a product is equal to its marginal cost of production. Imagine a situation in which there is some damage to a nearby residential neighborhood every time a potential defendant engages in blasting. Under a negligence standard, the blaster would not be liable, no matter how much blasting was done and no matter how much damage accumulated unless it could be shown that the cost of prevention was less than the expected accident costs. This produces an allocative inefficiency because the cost of blasting will not be recognized as a cost of production. This is depicted in Figure 1 which shows the demand and supply for a good. S_1 is the supply under the negligence standard. The quantity produced would be Q_1 and the price would be P_1.

Figure 1

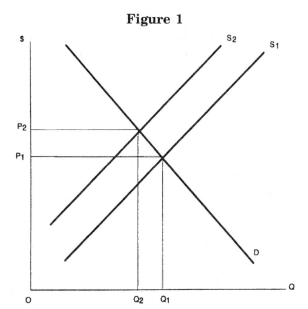

On the other hand, if the blaster pays for all damage whether the result of negligence or not, the amount of blasting becomes critical and the damage caused by the activity itself—not just when it is conducted in a negligent manner—is treated like any other cost of production. In Figure 1, S_2 represents the supply of the product under strict liability. It is lower than S_1 by the amount of the damage caused by blasting. The quantity now is reduced to Q_2 and the new price is P_2. This is a price that reflects the cost of production including the external costs of blasting and is, therefore, consistent with allocative efficiency.

Much the same analysis can be applied in the case of products liability. The harm resulting from the use of a product is tantamount to an external cost of production that the manufacturer is required to internalize. The effect of this internalization, as Figure 1 illustrates, would be to increase the cost of production and the price of the item while lowering output.

As in other instances of strict liability, there is no guarantee that the products actually will be safer than they would be under a negligence standard. The manufacturer will presumably engage in the same cost-benefit analysis implicit in the Hand formula and take those measures that are less expensive than the expected costs to those who are injured by the product. Similarly, there is nothing to insure that the manufacturer is the best cost avoider. It is true, however, that when the dangerousness is a result of design or manufacturing defects, the manufacturer seems likely to be in a better position to discover most problems and may enjoy significant economies of scale in correcting those problems. In other words, although it is ultimately an empirical question, it probably makes sense to begin with the assumption that in most instances manufacturers are in the best position to minimize primary accident costs resulting from product defects.

2. RISK–AVERSION AND LOSS SPREADING

Strict liability is also often seen as a method of minimizing secondary accident costs. It will be recalled that secondary accident costs are the actual burdens felt by society as a result of accidents. The notion of secondary accident costs can be linked to the view that people are generally risk-averse in that they would pay more to avoid a loss than the amount of the actual expected loss. For example, a risk-averse individual would pay $1.01 to avoid a one in a thousand chance of incurring a $1,000 loss. A risk neutral person would be willing to pay only $1.00.

One can translate this to the question of products liability by asking whether consumers would prefer to pay a dollar to avoid the loss resulting from the use of a product with a possibly dangerous characteristic or pay a dollar less and know there is a one in a thousand chance that they will suffer a $1,000 injury due to the product. If they prefer the former, then secondary accident costs can be lowered through the use of strict products liability. This would be the case even if primary accident costs were not minimized. In other words, even if the manufacturer were not the best cost avoider, secondary and tertiary accident costs may be reduced by holding the manufacturer strictly liable.

The logic supporting the position that individuals are generally risk-averse and that secondary accident costs can be reduced by spreading losses through the use of strict liability is based on the belief that money has diminishing marginal utility. This means that, as a person has additional money, the utility derived from each additional dollar eventually declines. Thus, a person "values" his 1000th dollar more than his 5000th dollar. Of course, in this context, the important issue is reactions to losses. If money is subject to declining marginal utility, people will be less willing to give up their last few dollars of income or wealth than a few dollars when they are relatively flush. Thus, it may be less costly for 5000 people to suffer $1 losses than for one person to suffer a $5,000 loss.

The diminishing marginal utility possibility means that wealthier or "deeper pocket" parties should feel the sting of the cost of an accident less than any individual customers. Thus, the argument can be made that secondary accident costs can be reduced by holding the wealthier party—perhaps a corporation—liable for product defects. It is important to note that this theory is built on the supposition that overall preferences for money are about the same. Suppose instead that wealthy people value small sums more than people who are not wealthy. For example, it is possible that a person earning $50,000 per year finds it easier to part with $5.00 than a person earning $300,000 per year. Both parties may be subject to the diminishing marginal utility for money. On the other hand, the wealthier party's generalized preference for money may be higher than that of the middle-class person. If so, the basis for believing that the secondary costs of accidents can be lowered by loss spreading is weakened.

There are other concerns about the consequence of assigning liability to manufacturers as a means of either spreading the loss or assigning it to the wealthier party. The problem is that it is not clear who ends up ultimately paying for the accident costs. In addition, assigning it to the firm may have undesired effects. Figure 2 can be used to illustrate the problem. The demand curve for the product is D. The supply curve before strict products liability is S_1. The price is P_1 and the quantity produced is equal to Q_1.

Figure 2

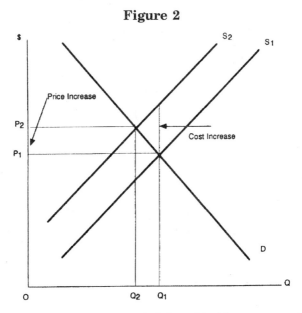

After strict products liability, the firm internalizes the cost of either accidents or preventive measures and the new supply curve is S_2. The actual cost per unit has increased by the vertical distance between S_1 and S_2. The price increase, however, is from P_1 to P_2. In other words, the price increase is less than the increase in production costs. This means that the cost increase is shared between consumers and the firm.

How the extra cost is divided between buyers and the firm is determined by the elasticities of demand and supply. The concept of elasticity is discussed in detail in Chapter Two, but for the purposes at hand it is enough to recall that elasticity measures the degree of responsiveness of buyers or sellers to changes in price. As a simple example, consider Figures 3 and 4. In Figure 3, demand is very inelastic, meaning that buyers are not very responsive to price changes. In Figure 4 on the other hand, consumers are relatively responsive to price.

Figure 3

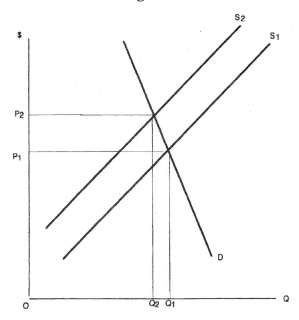

In the graphs, the initial supply curves (S_1) are identical, and the price for the item is P_1. The supply curves (S_2) after strict products liability are also identical. In other words, they have shifted up by the same vertical distance. In both instances, there is a new price (P_2). In Figure 3, however, the new price is higher than the new price in Figure 4. This makes sense because the consumers in the market illustrated in Figure 3 are not very responsive to price and are, therefore, willing to absorb most of the cost increase. The Figure 4 consumers, on the other hand, are responsive to price and the

firm finds that it is unable to pass along most of the
cost increase in the form of higher prices.

Figure 4

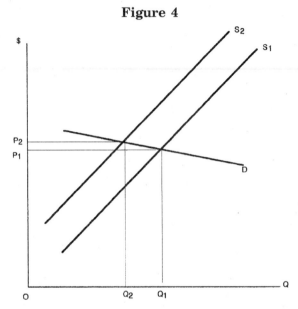

What this suggests is that strict products liability
may have an impact on the costs and ultimately the
profitability of firms. Of course, profitability is important to shareholders. Furthermore, a firm that is
less profitable than others may not be able to attract investors as readily as more profitable firms.
At the extreme, the solvency of the firm may be
threatened. Consequently, the employment of those
working for the firm will also be affected. The point
is that the issue of strict products liability is more
complex than simply spreading losses or assigning
losses to the deepest pocket.

3. DUTY TO RESCUE

The "duty to rescue" is discussed here because the general rule that individuals are not liable for declining to undertake even relatively easy rescues can be seen as applying strict liability to those who are imperiled. Even seen in this light, it is difficult to square the absence of a duty to rescue with economic efficiency. The problem can be seen by thinking in terms of the Hand Formula again. In the case of the easy rescue, B is going to be quite small when compared to PL. Thus, it would seem to be efficient, at least from the standpoint of primary accident costs, to hold those liable who do not offer assistance when the burden would be small.

Arguments can be made that appear to reconcile the lack of a duty with economic efficiency. There are valid points to be made, but, even so, some of the arguments have a make-weight feel to them. For example, Richard Posner makes the point that a duty to rescue would impose a cost on being in a position in which a rescue might be necessary and, therefore, reduce the number of would-be rescuers.[17] Similarly, he argues that a duty to rescue would eliminate the psychic income received by altruists who are likely to engage in rescues. Again the result may be fewer rescues.

Although all these arguments may be valid, it is still hard to understand how a duty to engage in

17. Richard Posner, *Economic Analysis of Law* 190–191 (6th ed. 2003).

easy rescues would actually decrease the number of rescues and, therefore, increase primary accident costs. The costs that may well increase if there were a duty to rescue are tertiary costs. Determining when the duty arises and when it has been abided by would be difficult and inexact.

Although the lack of a duty to rescue can probably best be explained by reference to something other than a purely economic rationale, the policy does make some economic sense. The absence of a duty to rescue is like holding parties who find themselves in need of a rescue strictly liable. For example, if you swim in deep water you are, in a sense, liable for any misfortune not caused by others. This forces you to internalize the full cost of your decision so that it is more efficient. The opposite possibility would be one in which people standing on the shore would all be liable if they did not come to your rescue. This enables you to shift some of the cost of your decision to others. In effect, your swimming would create an externality.

4. DEFENSES TO STRICT LIABILITY

As with negligence, there are defenses available to those defendants who would otherwise be strictly liable. From an economic standpoint, the use of these defenses can be a problem. Their introduction may lower primary accident costs, but cause tertiary costs to increase and offset any gains. This possible offsetting effect can be lowered if the defense is clear in terms of its applicability. In the case of all defenses, the important economic question is whether the availability of the defense will increase the probability that the best cost avoider will take preventive action.

a. Unforeseeable Misuse

Although there are good economic arguments for holding manufacturers strictly liable for the sale of defective products, a problem arises when the product is used in a manner that is not reasonably anticipated by the manufacturer. In terms of the Hand Formula, one could say that the probability of the accident is extremely low or that the burden to the manufacturer of attempting to anticipate and respond to all the possible ways in which a product might be misused is quite high. The party who misuses the product would find it less burdensome and is, therefore, more likely to be the best cost avoider.

The focus in the "unforeseeable" misuse cases is not so much on misuse as it is on whether manufacturers could have reasonably anticipated the misuse and designed the product in such a way that the resulting harm could have been avoided. For example, crashing a car into another car can be viewed as a misuse of the car, but it is also something manufacturers can readily anticipate and respond to by designing and manufacturing crash-worthy cars. On the other hand, the use of the car's radiator as a food processor is not a misuse that a manufacturer would be expected to anticipate. It is important to keep in mind that even finding a manufacturer liable for "foreseeable" misuses does not mean that preventive action will be taken. As in all instances of strict liability, the firm will decide whether the burdens of making the modifications are justified by the expected liability.

b. Unreasonable Assumption of Risk

The defense of "assumption of the risk" arises when the plaintiff knows of a particular danger associated with using the product but chooses to use it anyway. Timing appears to be a factor in these cases; the product may actually be defective, but the manufacturer escapes liability because, at the time of the use of the product, the plaintiff was the best cost avoider. This approach makes economic sense when the product is not generally defective but may be dangerous for a specific use and the plaintiff is both aware of that shortcoming and chooses to use the product in a manner that tests its limitations.

Any defense may decrease a manufacturer's incentive to redesign the product. This may not be of great consequence for a couple of reasons. First, even holding the manufacturer liable may not mean that accidents are avoided in instances in which the costs of redesign are high. Second, the cost of redesign, even if justified by the expected accident costs, may not be the least expensive method of avoiding the accident. In other words, the manufacturer may not be the best cost avoider.

c. Contributory and Comparative Negligence

A possible defense to strict liability would be to permit the defendant to show the plaintiff was negligent. If this were a complete bar to the plaintiff's recovery, there is no guarantee that primary accident costs would be minimized. The problem is that, even though the plaintiff might be negligent, the defendant may be the best cost avoider. By allowing this defense, the defendant would not receive the proper economic signal and would not have the incentive to avoid the accident.

Another possibility is to apportion the damages between the parties with the plaintiff's recovery reduced by the extent to which he contributed to the accident. Such an approach has appeal since, if the plaintiff's actions contributed to the harm, it may be incorrect to regard the full amount of the harm as an externality of the manufacturer's activity. On the other hand, as demonstrated in the context of comparative negligence, dividing the losses between the parties may lead to over or under investment in prevention. Thus, if the objective is to minimize primary accident costs, it makes sense to treat the party who is the best cost avoider as liable for the full amount of the loss even if the other party could have also avoided or decreased the harm.

H. DAMAGES

As suggested throughout this Chapter, the tort system can be viewed as an effort to minimize accident costs and efforts to prevent them by providing the proper market incentives. Like any market, the critical link to achieving efficient outcomes is that the price charged—in this case the price for negligent behavior—be accurate. Accuracy in this instance means that the damages paid by the defendant actually reflect the costs of the behavior to the plaintiff. Four specific issues that arise to complicate the pricing problem are the collateral source rule, future losses, and punitive damages.

1.   THE COLLATERAL SOURCE RULE

Under the collateral source rule, a plaintiff who recovers from a source collateral to the injurer, like a medical insurer, can still recover in full from the injurer. This creates the possibility that the plaintiff will be over-compensated. On the other hand, one solution to over-compensation is to not require the defendant to compensate the plaintiff when the plaintiff recovers from another source. The question from the point of view of economics is which is less desirable: over-compensation for plaintiffs or under-internalization by defendants which may result inefficient levels of care by defendants.

In the case of insurance, these possibilities are unlikely if the insurer has the benefit of a subrogation clause. This means that the plaintiff will collect only once and the insurance company will be reimbursed for any payment it has made. The market signal sent to the defendant should be the correct one from the point of view of minimizing primary accident costs.

2. FUTURE LOSSES

One of the most common problems that arises in arriving at the right pricing signal is the calculation of future losses. For example, if the harm reduces the earning power of the injured party, how are these future losses to be expressed in current dollar damages? One possibility, of course, is simply to add up all the lost future income. Thus, if the injured party's earning power is reduced by $100 per year for 10 years, one could award $1,000 in damages. There are, however, a number of complicating factors.

First, although it is possible for the earning power of the plaintiff to be reduced by a constant level of $100 per year, in a more typical case we would expect someone to become more productive as she becomes more experienced. Thus, estimates of future earnings need to be adjusted for increases in income resulting from increases in productivity.

Second, even if the losses are constant at $100 per year for 10 years, awarding the plaintiff $1,000 will result in over-compensation. The plaintiff would have earned the $100 in the *future*, so the award should take this into account. Unless it is, the plaintiff could invest the $1,000 awarded and end up with more compensation than $100 a year. From the point of view of the proper "pricing," the price of the activity determined to be negligent would be too high.

Third, income may also be higher in the future due to inflation. If the injured party really is to live as well after the injury as before, then the dollars received today as damages must not lose their buying power as time passes. In the absence of an accident, it is likely that the plaintiff would receive something like "cost of living" wage increases in order to at least hold her real buying power at some constant level. This suggests that the damages must also be adjusted up to allow for inflation.

Of these complications, the first is probably the least controversial. Pretty clearly, if the plaintiff were likely to experience higher income due to increases in productivity, then the loss of this potential is a legitimate part of the damage. This does not mean that showing these losses will be easy as a practical matter.

The second and third problems are related and here there is some controversy. In theory, the plaintiff should be given just enough in damages to compensate for the losses in income. Thus, rather than simply add up the losses, the goal is to give the plaintiff enough as a single payment that, when invested, will produce the desired future income stream. This means that the actual loss in the future is discounted or lowered to an amount that will result in the appropriate level of income. Technically, the future income is discounted to a present value. For example, if the going interest rate is 10%, the present value of a $100 installment due at the end of the first year would be approximately $90. This is because the $90 would grow to $100 by the end of the year.

The actual formula for the discounting process and calculating present value is:

Future income in year $n/(1 + r)^n$

where r is the interest rate and n is the year in which the income would have been received. Since the denominator of this fraction becomes larger as n increases, it is logical and obvious that income to be received in the more distant future is discounted more heavily.

In the context of discounting to present value, a number of issues arise. The first is whether the discounting should take place at all. One of the arguments for bypassing discounting is that the process is speculative with respect to the interest rate. In addition, if one first adjusts the future income stream up in order to allow for inflation and then discounts to present value, the two steps just offset each other. Matters are simplified by assuming that the two effects cancel each other out. If the assumption that the discount rate and the rate of inflation offset each other is wrong, it is almost certainly because the discount rate exceeds the rate of inflation. This means that plaintiffs would be over-compensated. Although the "price" is then inaccurate with respect to primary accident costs, the approach has some appeal due to the fact that it can lower tertiary costs.

If one does not subscribe to the offset approach, then the issue becomes what discount rate to use and how to account for inflation. To understand why these issues are related, it is useful to examine the components of the interest rate. Part of the reason people charge interest is because the dollars they will be paid back in the future may be worth less than today's dollars due to inflation. The rest of the interest rate, calculated by subtracting the rate of inflation from the interest rate, is called the "real interest rate."

This means that, in theory, to adjust expected future income upward to allow for inflation and then to discount it by the full interest rate is a partially offsetting process. One approach to the discounting issue is to bypass any inflation adjustment and then discount by the real interest rate. This does not mean that there is a real interest rate that everyone can agree upon. While the real interest rate cannot be pinned down with precision, it is probably in the range of 1.5 to 3 percent.

Another issue is what to use as the discount rate. It is popular to say the discount rate should be the amount that could be earned in a safe investment, like long-term government securities. The theory is that the victim should be put in a position to take the damage award and invest it at a very low risk and receive income that would have been received but for the accident. The problem here is that the plaintiff's future income stream was probably not as risk-free as the payment from a government security. For example, the income of a jockey, or even a physician in an era of health care reform, can be quite unpredictable. Thus the argument has been made that the discount rate must be adjusted upward to allow for the risk associated with the expected future income streams.

3.   HEDONIC LOSSES

Hedonic losses are those associated with losing the pleasures of life. These losses are not linked to actual expenses or lost income. For example, if you like fishing but an accident renders you unable to fish, the loss is hedonic. The idea of hedonic losses can be extended to victims who are killed. In theory, all harm caused by an accident should be internalized by the injuring party and the loss of enjoyment in life should be part of the calculation. The matter gets complicated and controversial when it involves the determination of what a victim's life was worth to him or her.

Economists can approach the issue by reasoning that goes like this. Suppose you have an option of buying a side air bag for your car and it costs $200. You buy the airbag. The chances you will be killed in a car wreck if you have the air bag is .00003. If you do not have the airbag, the chance is .00004. A way of looking at this is that .00001 of your life is worth at least $200. If .00001 is worth at least $200, then your entire life is worth at least ($200 times 100,000) $20 million. The methodology is questionable because it relies on decisions that may not have been fully informed and treats the value of an entire life as though it is divisible.

4.   PUNITIVE DAMAGES

In some torts cases, plaintiffs are awarded punitive damages or damages above those that would compensate them for the harm suffered. From the standpoint of minimizing accident costs and implementation of the Hand Formula, punitive damages appear to introduce the possibility that potential injurers will take inefficiently high levels of care. For example, suppose the burden of avoiding an accident is $100 and the expected harm (PL) is $90. In this instance, the efficient course of action would be to forego steps designed to avoid the accident.

On the other hand, if there is some likelihood that punitive damages will be awarded, the injurer must compare the avoidance costs with the total award including punitive damages. Suppose this is $150. Now it becomes rational for the injurer to spend up to $150 to avoid the accident. The problem, of course, is that the harm to be avoided at a cost of $100 is still only $90 and accident costs are not minimized.

It is important to note that the over-investment danger is not present if it already makes economic sense for the injurer to take precautionary action. Thus, if the burden of avoiding the accident is less than the expected harm, the injurer will take steps to avoid the harm. Adding more to the expected recovery would not change this outcome. Consequently, the effect of punitive damages will only be to encourage investment in avoidance efforts that are not justified by the harm to be avoided.

In this latter case, over-investment still may not occur. The basic model employed here includes the assumption that everyone harmed will bring an action against the injurer. If the injuries to the injured parties are relatively small compared to the costs to bring suit, the injured persons may just internalize the cost of the injuries by not bringing suit. This may be the case even though several people are similarly injured and, from an economic perspective, it would be efficient for the injurer to take precautionary action.

In these instances, the effect of punitive damages may be to make plaintiffs more interested in bringing an action than they otherwise would be. To the extent that the expected award, inclusive of the punitive damages, approaches the harm to all victims by the defendant's conduct, punitive damages may encourage more efficient behavior and lower primary accident costs. This is not, however, an outcome that can be depended upon. It is more likely a result of coincidence.

CHAPTER SEVEN

ECONOMIC ANALYSIS OF CRIMINAL LAW

A variety of issues can be raised when applying economic analysis to criminal law[1]—even more if one extends the analysis to criminal procedure. In fact, a comprehensive application of economic analysis to criminal law issues would require consideration of substantive criminal law and criminal procedure together with mental health law and moral philosophy. The goal in this Chapter is much more modest. It addresses two basic questions. First, what are the economic bases for criminal law? Second, what factors are to be considered in determining the "right" level of punishment?

More than any other area of law addressed in this book, the application of conventional economics to criminal law will seem strained. First, and at a practical level, some of the conclusions that economic analysis presents with respect to why criminal law exists and why it is administered the way it is will simply not be consistent with common under-

1. For a look at the variety of topics see Richard Posner, *Economic Analysis of Law*, Chapter 7 (5th ed. 1998). Judge Posner addresses general criminal law matters as well as criminal intent, the war on drugs, organized crime, and various defenses.

standings of criminal law. For example, one is unlikely to treat seriously or even hear an argument that a shorter prison sentence for, let's say, car theft is warranted because current prison sentences create too much deterrence and inefficiently low levels of car theft. Yet this is the nature of the analysis when economics is applied to criminal law.

Second, criminal law seems influenced by moral considerations and the possibility that not all values in life can be reduced to the type of cost-benefit analysis favored by conventional economic analysis of law. Despite this, a great deal of the economic analysis of criminal law involves an assumption that those involved in criminal activities are not motivated by a sense of obligation to obey the law. Instead they are "rational maximizers of self-interest" and basically amoral. In fact, in the analysis of efficiency, general social welfare can be a function of a great many values that can change from era to era and which may seem irrational to some. Third, because what conduct is punishable is a political question to be answered by legislatures and there are theories suggesting that markets exist for legislation, it is useful to look at criminal law from the perspective of "public choice," a topic taken up in Chapter Eleven.

A. WHY HAVE CRIMINAL LAW?

Chapter Six briefly addressed the issue of whether it makes economic sense to award punitive damages in the context of negligence. The answer there was that the use of punitive damages can mean that potential harmers of others would take inefficiently high levels of care to avoid accidents. Thus, when the goal is to minimize accident costs, the use of punitive damages is questionable. On the other hand, as noted in that Chapter, punitive damages may make sense when the harm to each person is so small as to mean that no one person will take legal action even though the total harm exceeds the cost of avoiding the harm.

Other than the possibility that no one person would be motivated to bring an action that would create an incentive for those causing harm to take preventative actions, what other bases exist for the use of penalties? At a fundamental level there are probably three. First, there are instances in which we would prefer exchanges to take place in the market, and criminal law can play a role in channeling them in that direction. Second, there are actions that we would like to avoid because we believe that the conduct, even if it is not against the will of the parties involved, may create external costs. Closely related to this is the possibility that the conduct will lead to external harms that offend our moral sensibilities. Finally, it is possible that criminal law, by stigmatizing some conduct, may actually have a preference-shaping capacity.

1.   CREATING AN INCENTIVE FOR MARKET EXCHANGES

One of the economic functions of criminal law is to channel behavior that results in a transfer of property or rights into the market. In order to understand this connection it is useful to review the work of Calabresi and Melamed in connection with liability rules and property rules.[2] Calabresi and Melamed distinguish between liability rules and property rules as methods of protecting rights. Under a liability rule, individuals are permitted to make involuntary transfers from others but compensation at market value is required. This type of "protection" is appropriate when transaction costs are high and a voluntary exchange, even if the parties were, in theory, willing is very difficult or impossible. The danger of relying on liability rules is that the involuntary exchange may not actually be efficient. In other words compensation equal to the fair market value may not be equal to the value attributed by the losing party to the item taken.

Property rules, the authors suggest, make sense when transaction costs are low. In these instances, the transfer must be consensual. The idea is that when consensual exchanges are practical, the danger of an inefficient exchange can be reduced by requiring the parties to interact. An example may be useful. Suppose you have a mint condition 1966 Austin Mini with a market value of $5,000. Because of your attachment to the car you have turned down offers for it in excess of $5,000. In fact, you would not accept less that $7,000 for the car. Strict adherence to a liability rule would permit someone to

2. Guido Calabresi & A. Douglas Melamed, "Property Rules, Liability Rules and Inalienability: One View of the Cathedral," 85 *Harv. L. Rev.* 1086 (1972).

take the car without your permission and compensate you at the market value. And that person may only attribute a value of $5500 to the car. The liability rule would mean that an exchange could take place which would result in the car being owned by someone who actually values it less. The new allocation would be inefficient.

On the other hand, if car ownership were protected by a property rule, the car could not be transferred without your consent. In essence, the buyer would have to show you, by the amount offered, that he or she actually values the car more than you do. Criminal law is often seen as a means to assuring that the exchange is, in fact, efficient. Thus, the person who takes the car without permission runs the risk of being punished. In this context, it means the thief will be required to pay more than the market value of the item taken. In the criminal law and economics literature this is sometimes called a "kicker." The size of the kicker—the amount of punishment—is another question and is discussed in the second section of this Chapter. Suffice it to say at this point that a low level of punishment may not be enough to encourage the market exchange. For example, if there is a $10.00 fine for stealing a car, the thief is unlikely to find the market transaction preferable even if the likelihood of discovery is 100%.[3] Obviously, the penalty must be set high enough to make the market transaction preferable.

3. As explained later, the probability of detection is an important element in determining the proper level of punishment.

Put differently, with an inadequate kicker, property rules can be made into liability rules.[4]

The notion of criminal sanctions as means of channeling transfers into markets are relatively simple to grasp when one considers protecting one's property. It may seem somewhat artificial, but one can stretch the analysis to bodily harm as well. For example, a person who harms another or commits rape could be viewed as a thief of a sort. The question then becomes whether he should be permitted to harm others as long as he pays the fair market value of the sex or harm. In other words, should a liability rule be applied? Here, though, objective market valuations are difficult to arrive at and seem even less reliable in terms of encouraging efficient transfers than in the case of property. The silliness of such notions is suggested by asking what would be the compensation in the case of rape. It could not be simply the price of sex in some area in which prostitution is illegal—like looking up the Blue Book value of a stolen car. For one thing, as Richard Posner points out, the rapist is not simply a thief of sex but may gain utility from the fact that it is coercive.[5] The same problems probably apply in other instances of those who get pleasure from harming others.[6] A liability rule is obviously ill-suited.

4. See Calabresi & Melamed, *supra* note 2, at 1125.

5. Richard Posner Economic Analysis of Law, *supra* note 1, at 238.

6. Unlike the case of rape in which the act is, by definition, nonconsensual, there are instances of people who do get pleasure from being harmed by others.

The fact that transaction costs are low may mean that a property rule is more attractive in instances of rape or other assaults. This would seem to go a long way toward discouraging rape. First, the price is likely to be quite high. Second, if the rapist wants coercive sex, this is probably not available in the market at any price. The reason is that as soon as a price is agreed upon, the utility derived from the coercive nature of the act would disappear. Nevertheless, even though a property rule seems to achieve the desired outcomes in cases involving bodily harm, it is seems unlikely that the law is motivated by a desire to achieve an "efficient" level of rape or assault.

The property rule/liability rule distinction has logical appeal and can be reconciled with much of criminal law even if it is not the actual explanation for why the law is what it is. But there are many instances in which the coincidence of criminal law with the system of property and liability rules breaks down. First, there are instances in which transaction costs are low and property rules would seem to apply, but the law does not permit exchange to freely take place. This is especially true in the case of so-called victimless crimes. For example, there are laws prohibiting the sale of human organs and sex. Second, there are instances in which transactions costs are high and a liability rule would seem to apply, but the law requires more than compensation of the victim. Thus, drunk drivers are not allowed merely to compensate those who they harm. Third, as illustrated above, only a very

strained interpretation of economic interests can
explain the existence of laws prohibiting rape and
similar crimes. In all of these instances, broader
moral concepts of right and wrong come into play.
In effect, consent may have independent and high
value so that it is the violation of one's autonomy
that is protected rather than the fair market value
of sex. Finally, some of the activities we label as
criminal are not property rules at all but are rules
of inalienability. In other words, they do not permit
certain types of transactions. In these instances, the
law itself can be seen as the transaction cost, and it
is purposely high in order to eliminate such exchanges that might otherwise take place, not simply
to make sure they are done efficiently. This category includes instances in which the criminal law is
designed to prevent people from turning liability
rules into property rules. As Jules Coleman notes,
we might subject a polluter to tort liability but not
permit the polluter to buy the right to pollute ahead
of time.[7]

2.   CRIMINAL LAW AND EXTERNALITIES

As already noted, one would be hard pressed to
reconcile all of criminal law with the simple notion
of forcing exchanges to be consensual when transaction costs are low. For example, in many instances
transaction costs are high, but the activity is a
crime nonetheless. Generally, the law seems de-

7. Jules L. Coleman, "Crime, Kickers, and Transactional
Structures", *Nomos XVII: Criminal Justice* 313 (J. Panache & J.
Chipman, eds. 1985).

signed to prohibit activity that is likely to create externalities. Speeding, double-parking and flag burning would seem to fit in this category. A special case of this is when the real or imagined externality flows from conduct that is consensual with respect to the primary participants. Crimes like consensual sodomy, prostitution, the selling and buying of some drugs, and the selling of human organs and babies seem to fall in this category.

a.   Externalities Generally

As the discussion in Chapter Six indicates, the central economic focus of tort law is on externalities. When a party does not take into consideration the harms to others of her activities, she is more likely to engage in activities that are inefficient. The tort system is designed to ensure that these external effects are internalized. In some instances, however, rather that channel harmful activities into market transactions through the use of a property rule or to rely exclusively on *ex post* compensation as a pricing mechanism, criminal sanctions are imposed. Thus, the speeding motorist cannot buy the right to speed from those who feel endangered by the speeding nor is it sufficient for the speeder simply to pay the damages of those who are actually injured by speeding. Similarly, the double-parker cannot negotiate in advance with those likely to be inconvenienced nor simply pay those whose trip across town was actually delayed by the congestion resulting from parking in the street.

The question from an economic point of view is why these types of activities having third party effects are treated any differently from garden variety torts. Specifically, why not rely on something as basic as the Hand formula to identify when speeding is negligent? When the probability of an accident occasioned by the speeding is multiplied by the loss and compared with the cost of prevention, the speeder will almost always be the negligent party. On the other hand, there may also be instances in which speeding would not be negligent, even though leading to an accident. For example, it might not be deemed negligent to speed across town to reach a hospital with an injured person. Basic tort law seems to have flexibility to respond to both these possibilities.

One way to understand these laws is to place them in the context of the Coase Theorem. As discussed in Chapter Three, a simple version of the Theorem is that, in a transaction-costs-free environment, rights will end up in the hands of those who value them the most. One corollary mentioned in Chapter Three and typically attributed to Judge Posner is that when transaction costs are high it makes economic sense for a court or a legislature to allocate the right initially to those who value it the most. In the case of speeding, consider two laws. One permits speeding and requires payment only of actual damages if the driver injures another and is successfully sued in a civil action. The counter-law is that speeding is penalized whether or not the speeder is involved in an accident. At one level this can be seen as a determination of whether drivers who speed from time to time value the right to do so more than other drivers, bike-riders, and pedestrians value the extra security of less speeding. There is another way to frame the choice, however, that may be more important. The choice is whether people who choose to speed may harm others *without their consent*. Here the issue is whether people value being free of the threat of non-consensual harm to property or person more than they value a rule permitting non-consensual harm. If people generally place a high value on personal autonomy and the right to choose, a rule penalizing those who harm others without their consent can be squared with efficiency.

This explanation of some criminal laws is also consistent with other aspects of criminal law. While people may value a rule that protects them from involuntary transfers, they are not likely to oppose all such transfers. Thus, they may be willing to accept the risk of a non-consensual transfer if the motorist has a compelling reason to create that risk. The punishment for speeding is not, therefore, life in prison but is set at a level high enough to discourage those who might speed simply as a matter of convenience. Thus, the father speeding to the hospital with his injured son in the car would not be deterred. In effect, while the penalty is a cost of creating a risk of non-consensual transfer, it is not set so high as to deter all transfers.

In fact, variations in "price" do make economic sense in a great many instances. For example, the speeding father may pay the basic fine for speeding. On the other hand, the penalty for drunk driving is much higher because there are few compelling reasons to drink and drive. In keeping with this theme, double-parking is at most an inconvenience for other motorists and the reason to inconvenience others need not be as compelling as the reason for speeding. The price is set low so as to discourage only the habitual double-parker. More generally what this suggests is that there are efficient levels of activities that technically are "against the law." It is fairly simple to understand this in the context of minor violations. But the rule also applies in all but the most serious crimes. Clearly, there are instances in which it is efficient to steal a car or even break into a house. The price of these crimes, however, is high because the harm is high as is the value the injured party is likely to attribute to being given an opportunity to choose to consent or decline.

b. Externalities and "Victimless Crimes"

The view that there are low transaction costs involved in the exchange of sex or drugs for money would seem to lead to the conclusion that criminal law should have nothing further to say about those who do make voluntary exchanges. There are three economic rationales for prohibiting these sales. The first goes back to the basic teaching of contract law. The efficient exchange is that which takes place between people who are competent. In some instances of victimless crimes, there is a sense that both participants are not fully competent. For example, is it meaningful to say that the drug addicted prostitute is really engaged in a voluntary exchange? Obviously, in a great many instances the decision about competence is a political one—what is viewed as competent seems to change with society's views of privacy and paternalism. Still, a voluntary exchange that takes place in the context of duress or a lack of clear understanding by one of the parties can be prohibited by reasoning that they do not produce allocatively efficient outcomes.

Probably more important than the efficiency implications of these exchanges are the distributive outcomes. Although economists are not comfortable, while acting within the constraints of the discipline, making decisions about the relative merits of various distributive outcomes, the information provided by economics is of value to those willing to consider distributive matters. Some of the so-called victimless crimes may be objected to on the basis of a perception that there is undue advantage-taking by one of the parties. This is, of course, bound up in the notion of competency as well, but the basic idea is one of prohibiting exchanges that are viewed as exploitative.[8]

It is an unnecessary simplification to equate concerns about the possible prohibition of transactions that seem to systematically disadvantage one of the parties as exclusively reflecting distributive interests. In fact, the concern that one or the collective

---

8. Economists have a technical definition of exploitation. Here it is in the more generic sense of taking advantage of someone to further one's own ends.

feels about the way in which some bargains are struck may be also stated in terms of utility. For example, I may oppose baby-selling because I believe low-income mothers will be taken advantage of by well-to-do childless couples.[9] The existence of such bargains lowers my utility and perhaps that of others. From the standpoint of Pareto optimality, these exchanges are not efficient because some parties are worse off, even if the exchanging parties feel that they are better off. Even the more liberal Kaldor–Hicks standard would suggest that these exchanges are only efficient if the transacting parties could compensate those who are honestly offended by the outcome of the exchange. Two points are suggested by this analysis. The first is that the high tax rates associated with some exchanges that are not illegal may reflect a societal sense that the exchanges are somehow inappropriate and those who engage in those transactions should compensate the rest of us. Second, the complete prohibition of some of these exchanges may also be seen as indicating a government assessment that, whatever the gain to the parties from the exchange, it is unlikely to be sufficient to compensate those made uncomfortable by it.

This efficiency-based analysis of distributive effects is one way of saying that victimless crimes are not always victimless. A more direct and conventional analysis is one that recognizes that some transactions do have the capacity to harm those who are not parties to the transaction. For example,

9. *See In the Matter of Baby M (N.J. 1988).*

prostitution may contribute to the spread of AIDs, meaning that third parties are required to expend energy and money to avoid contracting AIDs. Similarly, because drug transactions may involve large sums of money, those people who engage in the transactions may carry weapons. Concentrations of weapons create risks even for passers-by. These are relatively concrete externalities. In other instances they are harder to describe. For example, in the *Baby M* case, in addition to the distributive issues discussed above, the decision also cites the "potential degradation of some women" resulting from enforcement of a surrogacy contract.[10]

As with the economic analysis of tort law, the issue becomes one of how to respond to these externalities. Like the channeling function of criminal law, the objective can be seen as encouraging efficient conduct. The standard liability rule/property rule analysis is, however, somewhat complex. In the case of the sale of drugs, babies, organs and sex, the agreement between the principle parties creates the harm. The property rule/liability rule model would then ask whether these consenting parties face high or low transaction costs. If transaction costs are low, criminals sanctions would apply in order to require those engaged in the activity to get the consent of third-party victims. And, if the transaction costs are high, the activity would be permitted with compensation to come later. Obviously, in the case of drug and baby sellers and the like, a liability rule would seem to follow. In fact, the law imposes

10. Id. at 537 A.2d at 1250.

what looks like a property rule but which is in actuality a rule of inalienability.

Is there an economic basis for leaving high transaction cost exchanges in the realm of property rules? One possibility is that there is no meaningful likelihood that those harmed could be compensated by the consenting parties if a liability rule were used. For example, how does one compensate those who find market transactions for human organs morally repugnant? How does one locate and assess the damages to those offended? The law seems to signify any one of a number of possibilities here. One is that the costs of operating a system of compensation is much too high to justify what gains might be had from the "exchanges." Second, it is possible to reconcile the law with the view that the amount those willing to pay for the right to offend will almost never be more than the lowest victims are willing to take. Thus, what amounts to a per se rule against even attempting these transactions makes sense economically. Finally, to some extent the externality here is based on a view that certain things should not be bought and sold at all. The rule applied in these cases simply reflects the sense that if certain market transactions are offensive then so too are market transactions for the permission of those who are offended by the initial transaction.

3.   CRIMINAL LAW AND BEHAVIOR

As the above discussion suggests, it is possible to explain criminal law in terms that are obviously related to tort law. Much of the analysis focuses on the issue of externalities and forcing actors to internalize those externalities. Also at the heart of this analysis is the notion of an efficient level of crime which means that it includes the supposition that some criminal behavior is beneficial to society. At least one commentator writing from an economics perspective rejects these explanations for the existence of criminal law. Kenneth Dau–Schmidt rejects the view that society values criminal conduct. He argues that such a view is inconsistent with common sense and some aspects of our criminal law system.[11] For example, we increase punishment for repeat offenders yet the harm caused is the same for each offense.

If criminal law cannot be explained in terms of the traditional view that recognizes social benefits, it may be possible to explain it in terms of efforts to change preferences. That is, the goal is not to achieve some kind of balance in order to maximize social well-being. Instead criminal law may be viewed as an effort to change the things from which people derive utility. It is important to note the type of behavioral change this suggests. In its simplest form, criminal law and the penalties that are involved raise the prices of some choices with the likely consequence that those choices will me made less often.[12] For example, in a world in which speed-

11. Kenneth G. Dau–Schmidt, "And Economic Analysis of the Criminal Law as a Preference–Shaping Policy," 1990 *Duke L. J.* 1.

12. This is not to say that this is necessarily the case. Government action that creates a penalty or the appearance of a

ing is penalized, drivers are more likely to choose the substitute of leaving for their destinations earlier. And, if criminal prosecution is likely, those who would like the property of another and experience no moral qualms about stealing still may be more likely to buy the property. As economic theory would predict, when the price of one activity is raised, individuals tend to move to substitutes.

The preference-shaping view is quite different and can be understood by recalling what a demand curve represents. The curve shows the amounts that will be purchased at various prices. An assumption underlying all demand curves is that tastes and preferences are constant. For example, when prices increase and people demand less it is not because they find the item they are buying less satisfying. Their preference does not change. What has changed is relative prices, and an increase in the price of one item is likely to mean that substitutes now are more attractive.

Within the context of demand curves, a change in taste or preference means a shift in the entire demand curve. An increase in demand in response to a change in tastes means that individuals are willing and able to purchase more of the item at each price. A fundamental economic teaching is that

taboo actually may make the activity more glamorous and attractive to some. For example, penalties associated with flag burning may encourage flag burning because the penalties actually may make the meaning conveyed by the action of flag burning more powerful and the audience broader. Still, even though the exact impact is difficult to quantify, the direction of the impact is likely to be predictable.

a change in the price of an item does not mean that tastes or preferences change. Whether that teaching is true in the context of criminal law is not clear. When an activity is criminalized it may affect the amount of the activity in two ways. First, the cost of the activity will go up and the amount "purchased" will decline. In Figure 1, if the sanction increased from S_1 to S_2, there would be a movement from point A to B on demand curve D_1. Suppose criminalization also causes the activity to become less attractive. This would be represented by a shift in the demand curve from D_1 to D_2. More importantly, consider the impact on quantity of the activity. As Figure 1 indicates, the level of the activity before it is criminalized is Q_1. After sanctions are imposed the quantity is Q_2 if there is no change in preferences. If the sanctions also affect preferences, the quantity is Q_3. The point is that the stigmas associated with criminal conduct, including revocation of voting rights and efforts to rehabilitate and condition violators, may be more consistent with demand shifting than they are with efforts to move people to different points on existing demand curves.

Figure 1

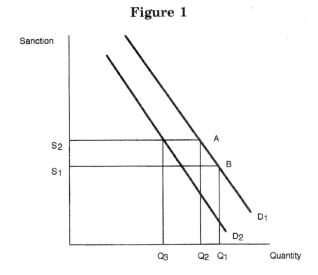

B. ADMINISTERING CRIMINAL SANCTIONS

If one adopts the preference-shaping role of criminal law, the amount invested in that effort could be determined by comparing the costs of various forms of preference-shaping measures with the benefits derived from changing what amounts to personalities. This approach gives rise to a great many philosophical questions that are difficult to answer. The more conventional approach to criminal law—the one that recognizes that some criminal behavior is part of overall social welfare—typically involves efforts to determine the optimal sanction. In other words, what price should society "charge" those who engage in prohibited activity in order to ensure that the benefits exceed the costs? The analysis has an allocative efficiency and a productive efficiency component. Thus, one objective is to find the right price to encourage the allocatively efficient level of criminal conduct. A related objective is to create a system that charges that price at the lowest cost.

1.   THE OPTIMAL LEVEL OF CRIMINAL CONDUCT

The first issue of encouraging the optimal level of criminal conduct can be depicted graphically. The underlying assumption of the presentation is that the actor is not influenced by the fact that it is labeled illegal. Put differently, the violator feels no moral obligations to obey the law simply because it is the law. In Figure 2, the Y axis measures benefits and the X axis measures the level of an activity. The downward sloping line, MB, represents the extra benefit of an additional unit of the activity in question. Suppose the curve relates to speeding. What it suggests is that there are a few instances in which the benefits of exceeding the speed limit are quite high. This might be consistent with the notion that there truly are emergencies in which speed can make a difference between relatively large or small gains. It also suggests that as more and more speeding takes place, the benefit decreases. In effect, people may be speeding simply to avoid being late for a movie or for class.

Figure 2

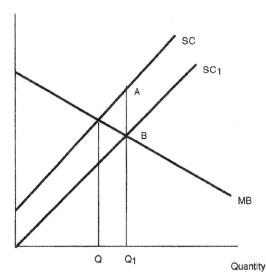

The other line on the graph represents marginal social cost. This is the cost to society of speeding. When the frequency of speeding is low the cost is low. As speeding becomes commonplace, the harm increases. The harm can be visualized as the probability the harm will occur times the severity of the harm. At low levels of speeding, the probability is low. It increases as more and more people drive in a riskier fashion. Returning to a familiar theme, the objective would be to permit speeding as long as the benefit of another incident of speeding exceeds the cost of that additional incident. This can be seen as an issue of involuntary transfers. MB represents what is taken by the speeder. SC is the value of what is taken. Based on the analysis presented above, the social cost function would include not just the harm times the probability of harm but would also include any aversion people feel about involuntary takings. As long as the marginal benefit exceeds the marginal social cost, net social welfare is increased by speeding.

As is typical in this analysis, the critical question is whether the speeder will react to the appropriate signal. For example, in the graph, the optimal level of speeding is Q. On the other hand, if speeders do not react to this actual social cost, they may act as though the social cost function were SC_1. The amount of speeding will be Q_1 which is inefficiently high. As Figure 2 indicates, the marginal benefit from speeding at Q_1 is below the social cost. There are a number of reasons the speeder may react to an inaccurate sense of social cost. First, although all speeders contribute to the risk of harm, only some are detected. Thus, the speeder does not react to the cost of speeding but to the cost multiplied by some probability that he or she will actually have to make a payment. Second, speeders may not factor in the aversion others have to involuntary transfers.

The role of the criminal law in this context is to add sufficiently to the perceived cost of speeding. A fine and a possible loss of one's driver's license are the typical measures employed here. Graphically, the result is a shift upward of the social cost curve from SC_1 to SC by an amount equal to the vertical distance between the curves or AB. In theory, the level of speeding would then be reduced to the socially optimal level of Q.

Obviously there is a high degree of artificiality in the model. On the other hand, if one accepts the basic rationale, the model is rather flexible. For example, rather than speeding, one could substitute one of the so-called victimless crimes. Suppose that crime is buying and selling marijuana. Again, if marijuana has therapeutic values, the benefits from a market in marijuana may be quite high for some. As one moves to more and more transactions the marginal benefit is likely to decline to the point that its use is entirely recreational. This is not to say that there are not positive benefits but that the level of benefit declines. On the social cost side, a few marijuana sales for medical purposes are unlikely to give rise to a great deal of social cost. On the other hand, if wide spread marijuana use is associated with poor driving, drug addiction, and expensive publicly-supported drug rehabilitation efforts, the marginal social cost curve will generally be upward-sloping as in Figure 2. In addition, since economic analysis validates all forms of disutility, the social cost curve would also factor in any moral objections to drug use. This latter point is important because in the case of some victimless crimes it is possible that the only social cost is the moral repugnancy experienced by those who object because the activity just seems to be "wrong."

While it can accommodate a fair amount of what is observable, the model cannot account for all criminal law. In the case of a great many offenses, it is hard to see any level as being efficient. For example, it is difficult to think in terms of an efficient level of baby selling, rape, or arson. In the case of baby and organ selling, it is hard to distinguish one sale from another. Either they are all objectionable or they all aren't. One might respond by saying that all baby and organ selling is equally costly. The marginal social cost in Figure 2 would be a horizontal line. And one could also argue the marginal benefits from buying a baby or a kidney do actually decline like the marginal benefits curve in Figure 2. Some people desperately want to be parents while others might just think it would be a neat idea. The conclusion one would draw from the model is that criminal law should accommodate those with particularly strong preferences.

This might be a palatable explanation in the context of baby and organ selling, but it seems far less acceptable in the context of rape and arson. While it is hard to imagine a situation in which any level other than zero would be efficient in the case of rape or arson, the economic model allows for that possibility. The model would seem to suggest the possibility that a person who gets tremendous utility from the act of rape may conceivably engage in efficient rape, and the pyromaniac may engage in efficient arson. One answer is that the punishment for rape and arson are high because it is so unlikely that the efficient levels are anything but zero. The problem with this argument is that it leaves open the possibility of the efficient rape and arson, and the individuals who the possibility is "open" for are the same people whose preferences are the most socially unacceptable. In other words, the model suggests that as a matter of public policy we want to permit some rape and arson if undertaken by the truly depraved.

Obviously, this undercuts the model in those cases in which efficient criminal activity is likely only to occur when abnormal preferences are at work. It also raises more general doubt about the accuracy of the model. If the model fails to square with basic and intuitive notions of fairness in the context of crimes for which there appear to be no value, the question becomes whether it is any more accurate with respect to the policy—even intuitive—behind other aspects of criminal law. More specifically, is it really likely that laws about baby, organ, and marijuana selling are designed to permit certain levels of those activities because they create a net benefit for society?

2.   DETERRENCE OPTIONS

As noted above, the idea of creating disincentives for criminal conduct involves not just determining the level of punishment but how to most efficiently create the required disincentive. To understand the issue go back to Figure 2. In that figure the optimal punishment was equal to the distance AB. But what is this punishment? It could be, as that illustration suggests, a fine. Or it could be imprisonment, caning or pillorying. The critical matter is that it be seen as a cost of engaging in the activity. In addition, the usual analysis stresses that the cost is an expected cost. Assuming that the violator is risk-neutral this means, for example, that a one percent chance of a $100 fine packs the same wallop as a twenty percent chance of a $5 fine. Thus the expected sanction can take the form of a high probability of a relative low level of punishment or a very low probability of severe punishment. In effect the package of punishment (POP) is a combination of probabilities and various sorts of sanctions. The key in terms of economic analysis is to find the lowest-cost way of creating the POP.

The first impression one is likely to have is that the lowest-cost method of creating the proper incentive is to apply severe punishment in a low probability of instances. The reasoning is that the low probability is associated with lower costs of detection and lower budgets for law enforcement agencies. In addition, the POP should be in terms of fines or physical punishment because these forms of punishment are less costly than extended imprisonment.

Although this may be a valid starting point, several complexities arise. For example, if those who commit crimes are risk-averse then the same level of expected punishment in an absolute sense may not translate into identical POPs with respect to behavioral reactions. For example, in absolute terms a certain one year prison sentence if one sells marijuana is the same as a five percent chance of a twenty year sentence. On the other hand, if risk itself is a source of disutility, then the POP which includes the 5 percent likelihood of a twenty year sentence will be perceived and responded to as if it is a higher cost than the certain one year sentence. What this means in terms of the optimal level of punishment is that one may over-deter law-breaking if the disutility of the risk is not factored in. In addition, as Mitchell Polinsky points out, the disutility associated with risk which is experienced by the individual whose law-breaking is efficient is a cost. He suggests that the cost to the law-breaker should be weighed against the sums saved by lowering investments in law enforcement.[13]

Another complicating factor to be considered is that almost any POP is likely to involve price discrimination. In effect, different people will experience a different cost. This is exacerbated if the POP is composed of expected sanctions—a fixed fine or prison term multiplied by the probability of conviction. In these instances part of the disutility will be a function of risk, but this cost will vary from person to person depending on levels of risk averseness. In addition, if money is subject to diminishing marginal utility, relatively wealthy individuals may view the POP as being less expensive than poor people. Finally, some people may be more sensitive to the stigmatizing effect of a criminal sanction than others, and the level of stigma may vary depending on whether the POP is composed of fines or imprisonment. The more general point is that all of these factors make it impossible to charge each person the same price. People who are risk-averse and have strong reputational interests may

13.   A. Mitchell Polinsky, *An Introduction to Law and Economics* 82 (2d ed. 1989).

be less inclined to commit a crime. On the other hand, changing and lowering the POP in recognition of this may mean that less risk-averse people and people with little to preserve in the form of reputation may undertake criminal activity when it is not efficient for them to do so.

The complexity of discovering the right level of deterrence and the POP that delivers it may also be systematically understated. Usually, the sanction for criminal violations is viewed in terms of fine or imprisonment or some combination. The stigmatizing effect of a conviction is also frequently noted. Less frequently noted in the formulation of the POP is the fact that those convicted of felonies may lose voting rights and the right to participate in certain professions. Consideration of these and other negative consequences may seem like fine tuning an already shaky model. These seem unlikely to be the sorts of things even the rational, cost-benefit sensitive criminal might consider. This, however, may be a function of imperfect information, and a comprehensive POP would seem to include greater information for the individual contemplating an illegal act.

When one adopts a broader perspective with respect to the purposes of punishment an additional problem arises. The textbook analysis of criminal law usually lists deterrence as but one of a variety of purposes of punishment. Additional purposes are rehabilitation and retribution. Although in recent years the association of criminal punishment with rehabilitation has weakened, the issue of the efficient level of punishment seems to miss the point that punishment or some other response from law enforcement agencies may have a therapeutic effect. This "therapeutic effect" could take the form of reshaping preferences or more ordinary forms of behavior modification. For example, the modern trend toward requiring law-breakers to engage in community service may make them more empathic and less likely to break the law again. Whatever beneficial effects might be associated with personal reactions to punishment, they seem less likely to occur when the sanction is a fine only.

Finally a factor that is left out of most economic considerations of criminal law is the value of retribution. In economic terms, retribution can be said to be a source of utility to law-abiders. That is, the sense that people are punished simply because they deserve to be punished when they have committed a wrong is, to some, a value inherent in a system of criminal sanctions. Obviously this is a very different matter than punishing in order to deter or to make sure potential violators fully account for the social costs in their decision-making. In the usual economic model the sanction only produces disutility for those who violate the law. A comprehensive economic model of criminal law would recognize the utility-producing capacity of punishment as well. Such a consideration will influence the POP and support some types of punishment that are not necessarily the least expensive to administer.

C. CRIMINAL PROCEDURE

It may seem odd to think about applying the implicit cost-benefit analysis of economics to safeguards for criminal defendants. You may regard these rights as "absolutes" that cannot be weighed against other interests. What this suggests is that the decision about whether or not to apply economic analysis is itself a philosophical one. In addition, the weighing, if it did take place, would be tricky owing to the nature of our system. To understand why, you must realize that in our criminal justice system there are two types of mistakes that can occur: an innocent party may be convicted, or a guilty party may be acquitted. On balance, it seems pretty clear that the system is set up to reflect the view that the second error is preferred to the first. Thus, an evaluation of procedure is not one that begins by assuming we are equally interested in minimizing all mistakes.

In fact, economic considerations enter the picture at a number of levels. For example, Professor William Stuntz makes a convincing argument that privacy rights and protection from surveillance under the Fourth Amendment vary from group to group depending on their relative economic conditions.[14] For example, poorer people are more likely than the affluent to use public transportation, live in smaller houses closer to public areas, and transact business in the open. In other words, like it or not, privacy

14. See William J. Stuntz, "The Distribution of Fourth Amendment Privacy," 67 George Wash. L. Rev. 1265 (1999).

and the avoidance of snooping can be bought on the open market.

Beyond this broad perspective, there are economic aspects of more specific criminal procedure issues. Some of these possibilities are obvious, as in the case of cruel and unusual punishment. If one views criminal law as about creating incentives for the efficient level of crime, the idea of cruel and unusual punishment can be easily connected. For example, a level of punishment that would deter all double parking would probably be cruel and unusual and inefficient. One of the more interesting issues arises with the exclusionary rule. As you know, the rule prohibits the use of evidence obtained by an unreasonable search or seizure in a criminal trial. The benefits of the rule are that it provides freedom for all people from government intrusion, selective enforcement, and arbitrary uses of power. On the other hand, one of the costs of the rule is that guilty defendants may not be convicted if the crucial evidence either cannot be obtained or is obtained improperly.

An improper search can be viewed as a violation of a property rule. Typically the violation of a property rule means the party at fault is forced to pay damages or even penalized. In other words, the party who has acted improperly must internalize the costs of that conduct. The exclusionary rule may deter unlawful searches and seizures, but it does not, at least directly, involve internalization by those who have violated someone else's rights. In fact, it can be argued that the illegal search produces an externality in the form of an acquitted guilty party who is ultimately shouldered by society generally. In some sense, citizens may react to that cost by calling for the employment of people who are more careful about the Fourth Amendment, but it seems illogical to expect people to react to more crime by calling for fewer searches.

Richard Posner has made a case for replacing the exclusionary rule with more conventional tort remedies.[15] The idea is that the Fourth Amendment does not offer protection to criminals from prosecution. Instead, it provides a right for all people to avoid unreasonable searches. The damages from an illegal search may be fairly slight. Perhaps a door or door lock is broken and the victims distressed. As long as victims are adequately compensated for their loss by those guilty of the violation—one of which is not the loss of liberty if a victim is sent to jail—the economically proper level of internalization occurs. This leads to the question of what the compensation would be. If it is fair market value, the tort solution makes the Fourth Amendment into a liability rule. That might seem fine, but think about whether you would agree to a search and seizure at any time by public officials as long as they paid for whatever was broken. Issues obviously arise with respect to the price to be set for illegal searches. On the other hand, a property rule requires permission or punishment of those who attempt to change the property rule into a liability rule.

15. Richard A. Posner, "Rethinking the Fourth Amendment," 1981 Supreme Court Review 49 (1981).

Although the Fourth Amendment and the exclusionary rule are amenable to economic analysis, albeit difficult economic analysis, other procedural issues are even more difficult to fit into an economic framework. In these difficult cases, it is possible to see the debate as existing at two levels. One level is whether a cost-benefit or economic analysis should take place at all. The other is what the relevant factors are if such an analysis is undertaken. Take, for instance, *Maryland v. Craig* (1990), a case in which the Supreme Court considered the right of criminal defendants to confront witnesses as required by the Sixth Amendment when the witness is a child. The majority opinion amounts to an analysis of the costs and benefits of confrontation in the context of a right that the dissent views as absolute.

Whatever the implicit economic analyses of procedural issues, they can hardly be said to apply consistently. In the case of testimony by a minor, a weighing process is used that may reduce defendants' rights and, arguably, increase the likelihood of a mistaken conviction. The testimony is like evidence that the Court evidently views as so critical that it should not be excluded. On the other hand, rock-solid evidence of guilt that is gathered illegally is completely barred. If the implied economic analysis of Craig were applied to search and seizure cases, the outcome could very well be a different rule than that which exists.

CHAPTER EIGHT

THE ECONOMICS OF ANTITRUST

Economic analysis has long been an important element of antitrust law. Even very early antitrust opinions used economic analysis to determine market share and the impact on competition of agreements among competitors. In addition, the calculation of damages is often based on economic projections.

Economic analysis became even more central to antitrust in the 1970's when the philosophy of the Supreme Court with respect to the antitrust laws took a decided turn. Prior to that time, purely economic concerns were often balanced against other social goals. In the 1970's, however, the Court adopted the view that the antitrust laws were designed solely to further economic objectives. These economic ends are efficiency and competition; they do not directly involve distributive issues.

Entire texts have been devoted to industrial organization and to the economic analysis specifically applied to antitrust law. The pages that follow, by necessity, have a narrower focus. The basic price theory that explains the advantage of competitive conditions over the absence of competition is presented first. The determinants of "market power" are explained next. The presence or absence of market power has become the cornerstone of modern antitrust analysis.

A. THE COMPETITIVE EXTREMES OF PERFECT COMPETITION AND MONOPOLY

The standard economic analysis applied to antitrust law involves a comparison of prices and output in an industry that is highly or perfectly competitive with prices and output in the same industry operating under monopoly conditions. In order to make this comparison, it is necessary to review some of the basic economic theory introduced in Chapter Two.

1. DEMAND AND SUPPLY

Perfect competition means that the industry is characterized by many small firms selling a homogeneous product, that there is easy entry into and exit from the industry, and that there is complete and inexpensive information for sellers and buyers. Basically, this means that all the firms are "price-takers." In other words, firms are powerless to raise prices above their costs without quickly losing all sales to competing firms. It is important to remember that "costs" in this context includes a "normal profit." A normal profit is the minimum necessary to keep investors from withdrawing their capital from the industry.

In perfect competition, the price in the market is set by the interaction of demand and supply. Demand for an individual buyer is a schedule of prices and the quantities that buyer would be willing and able to buy in that market at each price. Demand is usually illustrated graphically as a demand curve which plots the possible prices and quantities. For example, the demand of a single law student for ball point pens might look like Figure 1. At a price of $1, the student would be willing and able to purchase 10 pens. At a price of $2, the quantity would be 8 pens and so on.

Figure 1

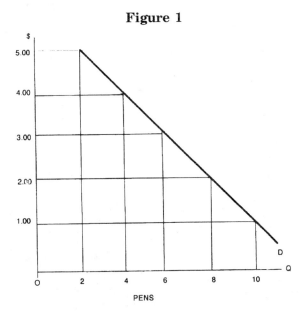

Total demand would be determined by "horizontally summing" the demand curves for all the possi-

ble buyers in the market. Suppose the market consisted of all 1,000 citizens of Lawtown. To derive
the horizontal summation, one would take a price
and add the total quantity that would be purchased
at that price by all buyers. The same process would
be repeated for each price. The result might look
like Figure 2. Now, for the market, the quantity
demanded at $1 would be 10,000. The quantity
demanded at $2 is 8,000 and so on.

Figure 2

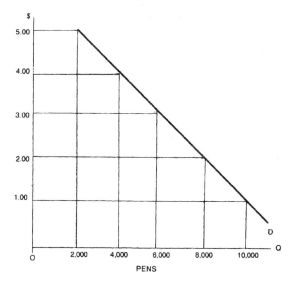

Of course, to get the price in the market, it is
necessary to have a supply curve. As indicated in
Chapter Two, an individual firm's supply is a series
of prices and the quantities that would be offered
for sale at each price. Figure 3 shows the prices that

might exist in a market and the quantities of ball point pens that would be offered for sale by a single supplier at each price.

Figure 3

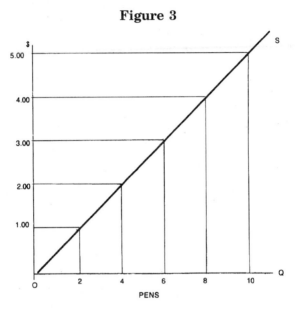

It is important for the analysis that follows to note that the individual firm's supply curve is the same as its marginal cost curve. Marginal cost is the additional cost of producing one more unit of output, and the curve simply shows the marginal cost at several levels of output. Thus, in order to derive the supply curve, one might ask the supplier how much it would offer to sell at a specified price. The supplier would presumably offer units for sale as long as the additional cost of producing each unit is less than or perhaps just equal to the price offered.

In other words, as long as the marginal cost of producing the unit was not in excess of the price offered, that unit would be offered for sale.

As with demand, the supply for the entire market can be determined by horizontally summing the supply curves of all the individual producers. Figure 4 illustrates the supply for the industry. The graph represents something of a simplification, as it is unlikely that supply would extend all the way down to a price of zero. In other words, the quantity supplied would probably reach zero (intersect with the y axis) at a price above zero.

Figure 4

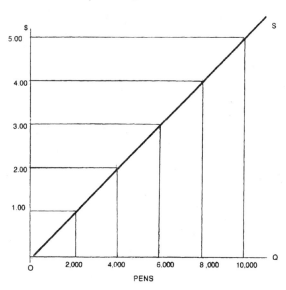

2.　MARKET EQUILIBRIUM, PRODUCER AND CONSUMER SURPLUS

Figure 5 combines the industry demand curve from Figure 2 with the industry supply curve from Figure 4. In the graph, the curves intersect at a price of $3 and a quantity of 6,000. This is the equilibrium price and quantity. When price exceeds $3 it will tend to fall, and when it is below $3 it will tend to increase. The reasons are fairly obvious. Take, for example, a price of $4. At that price the quantity demanded is 4000 and the quantity supplied is 8000. There is a surplus of ball point pens in the market, and the tendency will be for sellers to lower their prices.

Figure 5

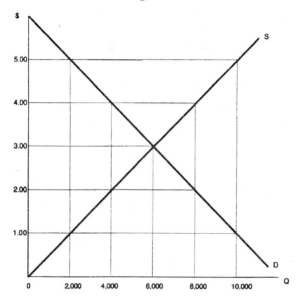

At a price of $2, on the other hand, the quantity demanded is 8000 and the quantity supplied is only 4000. Here buyers will begin to bid against each other for the pens, and the effect will be for prices to increase. Only at a price of $3, at which the quantity demanded and the quantity supplied are both 6000, will there not be a tendency for prices to increase or decrease.

Figure 5 is also useful to illustrate what is meant by the important concepts of "consumer surplus" and "producer surplus." In the market for ball point pens, the price was $3, but in actuality, some people were willing to pay more than $3 for the pens. For example, the demand curve tells us that even at a price of $5, 2,000 pens would have been demanded. In effect, some people have paid only $3 for something they would have paid up to $5 to have. When a person is able to obtain something for less than the most they would have paid for it, they have received consumer surplus. If 10 people received $2 worth of consumer surplus, the total consumer surplus would be $20.

Similarly, in the Figure, even though the price is $3, there are some units that would be offered for sale at prices less than $3. For example, as the graph shows, even at a price of $1, 2,000 units would be offered for sale. When a producer receives more for a unit of output than the least it would take, it receives producer surplus.

Figure 6 illustrates total consumer surplus and producer surplus. The equilibrium price is P. The total consumer surplus is the area of the triangle PAC. In the graph, the total amount of producer surplus is equal to the area of the triangle P0C.

Figure 6

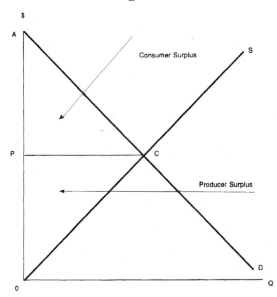

One can combine the surplus received by consumers with the surplus received by producers to determine the total surplus created by exchanges that take place in this market. This would be the area 0AC. As the graph shows, the process of determining the price also determines how the surplus created by the exchange is to be divided between consumers and producers.

3.   THE INDIVIDUAL FIRM UNDER PERFECT COMPETITION: THE MARGINAL COST = MARGINAL REVENUE RULE

By combining demands of individual consumers and supplies of individual producers, the discussion so far has focused on the competitive industry as a whole. In order to fully understand the critical differences between competitive markets and monopoly markets, it is important to examine the decision-making of the individual firm.

Under conditions of perfect competition, the individual firm cannot control price. It responds passively to the price that is set in the market and sells as much as it would like in that market. Thus, if we assume that the competitively determined price in the ball point pen market is $3, the individual firm faces a demand curve that looks like curve d in Figure 7. The curve is really a horizontal line at the competitively determined price. This is because the firm will sell no units of output if it attempts to raise price to higher than competitive levels. It is not relevant to think of a price below $3 since the firm can sell all it wants at that price and would not, therefore, sell any for less.

Figure 7

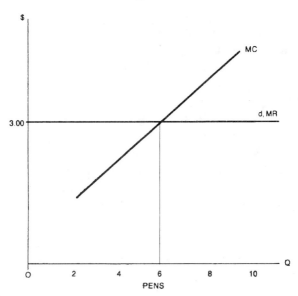

The demand curve also plots what is know as marginal revenue (MR). Marginal revenue is the additional revenue obtained from selling one more unit of output. For a firm operating under perfectly competitive conditions, the marginal revenue curve and the demand curve are the same. The significance of this will become evident shortly when conditions of monopoly are examined.

Figure 7 also illustrates the firm's supply curve. As explained above, the supply curve is the same as the firm's marginal cost curve. Just as in the industry as a whole, the firm's output will be determined by the intersection of the demand it faces and the supply curve. In the graph, this intersection takes place at 6 units.

For analytical purposes, it is more important to focus on the marginal revenue and marginal cost curves. The quantity sold by the firm is determined by the intersection of these curves. This makes sense when one considers the information provided by the marginal revenue and marginal cost curves: marginal revenue is the extra revenue from selling one more unit of output, and marginal cost is the additional cost of producing the unit. The rational producer will produce and sell any unit for which the additional revenue generated by its sale exceeds or is equal[1] to the additional cost of production. On the graph, if one starts at the origin and moves outward, it is evident that up until unit 6 marginal revenue exceeds marginal cost. At unit 6, they are just equal, and the firm would not produce additional units. The idea that a firm will produce until marginal revenue and marginal cost are equal is fundamental to price theory.

4. COST CURVES

In order to further understand the general economic preference for competitive conditions over monopoly conditions, it is necessary to become familiar with an assortment of production costs in addition to marginal cost. Typically, production costs are classified as fixed or variable. Fixed costs

1. Actually, the firm may be indifferent to producing the unit at which marginal revenue and marginal cost are equal.

do not vary as production increases. An example might be the rent paid for a factory. Variable costs increase as production increases. An example would be the raw materials used in producing a good. Total cost is fixed cost plus variable cost.

In most economics books, these costs are expressed as averages per unit of output. For example, if fixed costs were $200 and 4 units were produced, the average fixed cost would be $50 per unit. Average fixed cost will steadily decline as the level of output increases. This is because the same fixed cost is being divided by higher and higher levels of output. In Figure 8, the curve labelled AFC illustrates average fixed costs.

Figure 8

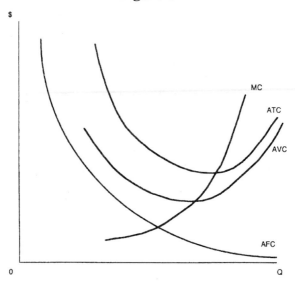

Variable cost is also typically divided by the level of output to get average variable cost. Here, though, higher and higher levels of output are divided into higher and higher levels of variable costs. As it turns out, average variable cost is likely to take on a U shape as illustrated by curve AVC in Figure 8. As production increases, the firm is likely to become more efficient. That is, its output will increase more rapidly than the increase in inputs used. This will cause average variable cost to fall. After some point, however, efficiency will no longer increase and, on the average, units will become more costly to produce.

ATC in the Figure illustrates average total cost. It is calculated by dividing total cost by the level of output. Or it can be seen as the sum of average fixed cost and average variable cost. Since it is the total of average fixed cost and average variable cost, it lies above average variable cost. The influence of average variable cost is reflected in its U shape. The average total cost curve draws closer to the average variable cost curve as output increases. This is because the difference between the curves is average fixed cost which steadily declines as output increases.

Figure 8 also illustrates the firm's marginal cost (MC) curve. It is drawn to intersect both average total cost and average variable cost at their lowest points. It is easy to understand why as long as one keeps in mind the information contained in the two types of curves. Marginal cost is the extra cost of producing a unit of output. As long as it is less than the average cost of the units being produced, it will have the effect of lowering the average. For example, if the average variable cost of 10 units is $10 and then an eleventh unit is added that has a marginal cost of $8, the average variable cost will decrease to approximately $9.80. On the other hand, if the marginal cost is above the average cost curve, it will tend to pull up average cost.

It may be useful to view the relationship of the curves in a slightly more technical way. When average variable cost or average total cost "bottom out," or reach their minimums, they are neither increasing or decreasing. For a very short span they are flat. At this point, and only at this point, marginal cost exerts no upward or downward influence on these curves. The only way for marginal cost to exert no influence is for it to be equal to the average at that point. And, as the graph illustrates, marginal cost intersects the curves only at the point where they are neither rising nor falling.

5. EQUILIBRIUM AND PERFECT COMPETITION

Figure 9 includes all the cost curves from Figure 8 except average fixed cost which has limited usefulness. To those curves has been added the demand curve faced by the firm under competitive conditions. In the graph, the horizontal demand curve (d), which represents the market-determined price, has been drawn so that it intersects with the average total cost curve at that curve's lowest point. The firm will produce Q_c units. It is drawn this way because there is a tendency for this to be the long-term relationship between price and average total cost under competitive conditions. More directly, firms in perfectly competitive markets tend to charge prices that are equal to minimum average total cost.

Figure 9

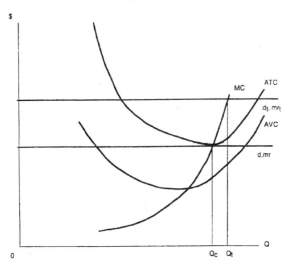

In order to understand why, focus again on Figure 9. In addition to demand curve d, another higher demand curve has been drawn at d_t. The firm might find that it is faced with this higher demand if there is an increase in industry demand that drives prices up. At this price, the firm would expand output to Q_t and, since price would be in excess of average total cost, it would be earning an economic profit.

In a perfectly competitive market, this can only be temporary. By definition, there is easy entry into the industry, and information is readily available. Thus, the presence of economic profits will quickly lure new firms into the market. The effect will be to increase supply and cause price to decrease back to levels that are equal to average total cost. Thus, under perfectly competitive conditions, consumers will tend to be charged a price equal to average total cost and average total cost will tend to be at its minimum.

An additional and important characteristic of perfect competition is that the industry price and output will be consistent with "allocative efficiency."[2] An allocatively efficient outcome is one in which resources are drawn into the production of a good or services in quantities that are justified by the value attributed by buyers to those goods or services. In order to understand why allocative efficiency is achieved, it must be recalled that the price and quantity in the competitive market are determined by the intersection of market demand and supply. Demand indicates the value attributed to units of output by potential buyers. The supply curve indicates the cost, in terms of resources used, of making the good available. Thus, as long as the value attributed to a particular unit of output, as indicated by the demand curve, exceeds the extra cost of producing the unit, as indicated by the supply curve, it is allocatively efficient to produce that unit. As Figure 5 illustrates, the competitive market encourages production of all the units that are valued more than their marginal cost of production. Production beyond that point, at least in theory, does not occur.

2. For a more detailed discussion see Chapter Two.

6. MONOPOLY

It is easiest to understand the objections to monopoly by comparing price and output under monopoly conditions with price and output under conditions of perfect competition. In order to do so, assume that through some unlikely merger, the ball point pen market that we started with is now served by a single firm. This means two critical things. First, the industry demand curve is now *the* demand curve facing the monopolist. Second, instead of reacting passively to the market-determined price, the monopolist will actually set the price. In fact, it is no longer meaningful to speak in terms of an industry supply curve showing prices and the quantities that would be offered for sale at each price. Instead, there will simply be one price—the price that maximizes the monopolist's profits.

In determining this price, the monopolist will follow the basic rule of finding the level of output where marginal revenue is equal to marginal cost. Things are different for the monopolist, however, in that the demand curve it faces is downward-sloping. This means that it must lower price in order to sell additional units. Moreover, it will have to lower the price for all units. Thus, in order to determine the marginal revenue from selling an additional unit of output, the firm must subtract the decrease in price for the other units from the price received for selling the additional units.

For example, suppose the firm is selling 5 units at a price of $10 per unit. If it wishes to sell 6 units, it may have to lower price to $9 per unit. Its marginal revenue from selling the sixth unit will be $4. This is a price of $9, which it gets for the sixth unit, reduced by a $1 per unit price reduction on the five units it was selling at $10. As a consequence, the marginal revenue curve for the monopolist is not the same as the demand curve but lies below the demand curve. This relationship is depicted in Figure 10.

Figure 10

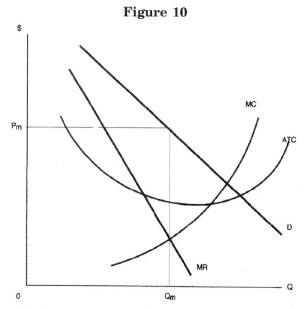

Figure 10 also includes the monopolist's marginal cost curve. In order to simplify the comparison with perfect competition, it is assumed that the marginal cost curve is the summation of all the marginal cost curves of the firms that previously existed in the industry.

To determine the profit-maximizing level of output, the monopolist goes through the same basic analysis as the firm in the competitive market. It will want to produce and sell as long as the additional revenue generated by selling an additional unit (MR) exceeds the extra cost of producing an additional unit (MC). In Figure 10, marginal revenue exceeds marginal cost for all units produced until the firm reaches unit Q_m. Thus, the monopolist will produce Q_m units of output.

The monopolist must also determine the profit-maximizing price. Obviously, the monopolist will charge the highest price that is consistent with selling Q_m units of output. One can find this by simply using the demand curve. Not only does it indicate the amounts that will be sold at each price, it also indicates the maximum price that could be charged and still sell any specified quantity. In Figure 10, the highest price that is consistent with selling Q_m units is P_m.

7.   PERFECT COMPETITION AND MONOPOLY COMPARED

With this background, one can understand the general preference for competitive markets over those that are imperfect or have monopolistic tendencies. Figure 11 is useful in this comparison. The intersection of demand (D) and supply (S) in the graph determines the price (P_c) and output (Q_c) under competitive conditions. The intersection of the marginal revenue curve (MR) and the marginal cost curve (MC) determines the monopoly level of production (Q_m). The monopoly price is P_m. Thus, one of the obvious distinctions between the competitive model and the monopoly model is that price will tend to be higher and output lower under monopoly conditions than under competitive conditions.

Figure 11

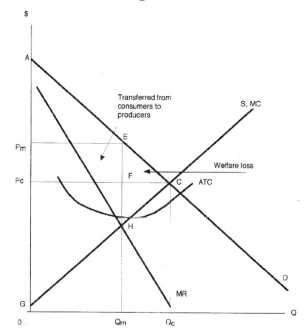

Another important distinction lies in the impact on consumer and producer surplus. Under competitive conditions, the consumer surplus is equal to the area of triangle P_cAC. Under monopoly conditions, consumer surplus is equal to the area P_mAE. Consumer surplus is, therefore, smaller under monopoly conditions.

The critical question is: what has happened to the portion of consumer surplus that is no longer enjoyed by consumers? First, a portion of it is captured by the monopolist in the form of producer surplus. In other words, under competitive conditions, the producer surplus was equal to area P_cCG. Under monopoly, this has been expanded to P_m GHE. Part of this new expanded producer surplus, area P_mP_cEF, was originally part of consumer surplus and now has been transferred to producers. Another portion of what was consumer surplus, area EFC, is not captured by the monopolist. This is called the "welfare loss" or "deadweight loss."

In other words, part of what was consumer surplus under competitive conditions remains consumer surplus under monopoly conditions. A portion has been captured by the monopolist. This represents, in effect, a redistribution from consumers to the producer. Whether it is "right" or "wrong" or *ought* to happen is not a question that economics as a field of study is equipped to answer. A final portion of consumer surplus is lost and not captured by the monopolist. There is little controversy that this is a real loss in welfare. It was a measure of well-being or utility that has vanished.

Closely tied to this welfare loss is the impact monopoly has on allocative efficiency. It will be recalled that allocative efficiency is achieved when production is carried out to the point where demand and supply intersect. Under conditions of monopoly, production stops short of this level. The economic importance of this can be seen by focusing on the units between Q_m and Q_c. These are units that will be produced under competitive conditions and are not produced under monopoly conditions. Yet, for all of these units, the value attributed to them by consumers exceeds the value of the resources that would be used in their production. Under monopolistic conditions, the allocatively efficient level of output is not achieved.

Another cost of monopoly that has been identified lies in the lure it represents to those who would like to achieve monopoly status and maintain it. In theory, the increased financial gains associated with the possibility of capturing a portion of consumer surplus can be regarded as a return to the investments devoted to gaining a competitive edge. Some of the means used, however, may be wasteful and not really result in the production of new or better products. Perhaps they are designed simply to hurt other competitors without making consumers any better off. If so, this expenditure is a waste as far as furthering consumer interests.

8.   SOME LIMITS ON THE COMPARISON

The models presented here and the discussion of the advantages of competition over monopoly in terms of price, quantity, and allocative efficiency represent a kind of first-level analysis. When one pushes the analysis a bit further the overall picture of monopoly versus competition becomes cloudier. One such complication arises from the fact that perfect competition requires a large number of firms. On the other hand, each firm may be too small to operate very efficiently. Figure 12 illustrates the problem. The average total cost curve is drawn so that the most efficient level of output is 10,000 units. The average cost of production would then be $1. This level of output may only be possible if one large firm buys an expensive but very efficient piece of machinery.

Figure 12

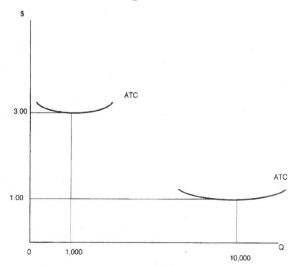

The graph also indicates that if 10 firms existed, each of which produced 1,000 units, the average total cost would be $3. Thus, while a market with 10 producers may be very attractive from the point of view of competitive pressure, the simple fact is that no matter how hard they compete, the price will remain close to $3. The problem is that the one large firm is able to take advantage of efficiency in production—productive efficiencies—that the smaller firms cannot. While the large firm, if left unregulated, may charge a higher price than the 10 competing firms, it is actually using resources in a more efficient manner.

This is not to say that the tension between competition and productive efficiency exists in every instance. In many cases, it may be that relatively small firms are able to take advantage of all the efficiencies in production. In other words, in some industries, the "minimum optimal size" for firms may be small enough that many firms can occupy the same industry, vigorously compete, and produce efficiently.

Another complicating factor for the simple model of antitrust is the "theory of second best." The problem can be envisioned by reexamining the notion of "allocative efficiency." A key requirement in achieving allocative efficiency is that marginal cost reflect the value of the resources used to produce the output and that the price paid be equal to marginal cost. As already demonstrated, this is the case in equilibrium under conditions of perfect competition. If, however, a firm is buying resources that are not supplied by perfectly competitive firms, the "signal" that drives output to the allocatively efficient level will be distorted. The point is that perfect competition as a means of achieving allocative efficiency really only works when all other related firms are also perfectly competitive. If they are not, one might more closely approach allocative efficiency in an economy of firms that are equally imperfectly competitive. This would be the "second best" solution. The theory of second best has not really influenced antitrust policy, but it suggests that policy implications of simply comparing monopoly to perfect competition can be misleading.

B. MARKET POWER AND MARKET DEFINITION

1. MARKET POWER

The second critical economic element of modern antitrust analysis is the determination of market power. It is important because the vast amount of antitrust litigation under the Sherman and Clayton Acts requires plaintiffs to demonstrate that the defendant possessed market power.

Market power can be simply defined as the ability to raise prices above competitive levels and profitably keep them there. In effect, any firm, including one that is in a very competitive industry, can raise prices. The issue is whether it can keep them there or whether buyers will turn relatively quickly to other products or whether suppliers will enter the market and begin selling the product in question. In either case, the price increase will not be sustainable.

Market power was traditionally assessed by determining the firm's market share. Market share is the firm's sales in the market divided by total sales in the market. Although market share is still the mainstay of market power analysis for antitrust purposes, it has given way to somewhat more sophisticated analyses that focus more on the actual factors that determine whether prices can be profitably raised above competitive levels.

2.   THE LERNER INDEX

The Lerner Index is a tool for measuring market power that captures more of the substance of market power than simple reliance on market share.[3] It is expressed as follows:

$$L = (P-C)/P$$

In the equation, L is the index, P is the firm's profit-maximizing price, and C is the firm's marginal cost at the profit-maximizing level of output. If the firm were operating under highly competitive conditions, P would approach C and the index would be very low. When the firm has market power, P can exceed C and the ratio will be higher.

Another way of expressing market power is to focus on the elasticity of the demand faced by the firm. Elasticity of demand is a measure of how responsive buyers are to changes in price. It is determined by comparing a certain percentage change in price to the resulting percentage change

3.   Abba Lerner, "The Concept of Monopoly and the Measurement of Monopoly Power," 1 *Rev. Econ. Stud.* 157 (1934).

in quantity demanded. If the percentage change in quantity demanded is less than the percentage change in price, demand is regarded as "inelastic." A firm has greater market power—it is more likely to be able to raise prices above its marginal costs— the more inelastic the demand it faces. In fact, the Lerner Index is also equal to the reciprocal of the elasticity of the demand faced by the firm or 1/Ed, where Ed is the elasticity of demand. Obviously, the lower the elasticity, the higher the index.

3. THE DETERMINANTS OF MARKET POWER

The Lerner Index can be reformulated to illustrate that the elasticity of demand faced by the firm and market power are determined by three factors.[4] The first factor is the elasticity of demand for the industry of which the firm is a part. The reasons are fairly straight forward. If the industry produces a good for which there are available substitutes, it is less likely that an individual firm in that industry will have market power.

A second critical factor is the elasticity of supply. Elasticity of supply, as the term implies, is a measure of responsiveness to price changes by actual or potential producers of the good. In other words, it is a measure of how quickly producers can respond to price increases for a product by increasing the amount of it they make available. An increase in

4. See Richard Posner & William Landes, "Market Power in Antitrust Cases," 94 *Harv. L. Rev.* 937 (1981).

supply may come from firms already in the industry that have excess capacity. It also may come in the form of firms that are able to switch their productive capacity from one product to the one that now has the higher price. It might even come from firms entering production from scratch. If firms are very responsive in terms of increasing output—supply elasticity is high—it will be very difficult for an individual firm to increase price and keep it high.

Finally, market share also plays a role in determining market power and, if all other things are equal, firms with high market shares will tend to have higher market power. For example, a firm with a 90% market share may find that it can increase prices and actually lose substantial numbers of customers without suffering a large decrease in its overall share of the market. On the other hand, a firm in the same market with only a 10% share will not be able to sustain as much in the way of losses in volume of sales.

4.   MARKET DEFINITION AND CROSS–ELASTICITY

Much of the foregoing discussion suggests a neat mathematical solution to the problem of market power. This is not, however, a real possibility. The problem is that the calculation requires a determination of the firm's market; for example, which products can be regarded as a part of the firm's market? Similarly, in order to determine the elasticity of demand for the industry, one would have to determine which firms are part of that industry.

Unfortunately, markets can rarely be defined with precision. Thus, market definition and the determination of market power remain activities that are "art" as much as "science." A useful, albeit imperfect, tool is the cross-elasticity of demand. Cross-elasticity is a measure of the responsiveness of the sale of one product to price changes of another. When an increase in the price of one product leads to increases in the sales of another, the products are substitutes. The greater this reaction, the more substitutable the products. There is no bright line test for when cross-elasticity is high enough for the products to be regarded as occupying the same market.

Furthermore, there are a number of pitfalls associated with a simplistic reliance on cross-elasticity. First, cross-elasticity may change and become higher as the period of time allowed for the reaction is increased. For example, if the price of coal as a home heating fuel goes up, people may not respond immediately by switching to natural gas because they are committed to furnaces that use only coal. When these furnaces wear out, though, they may switch to gas-burning furnaces and the cross-elasticity between gas and coal will appear higher.

Another problem is that the base upon which the calculations are made may cause a distortion. A firm that raises prices may find that it loses all of its customers. If, however, it loses them to a very large firm with a much higher volume of sales, the percentage increase in sales for that firm may be low, implying that the cross-elasticity is very low.

A final problem results from the fact that cross-elasticity may vary with the price at which it is measured. For example, a firm that is charging a relatively low price when compared to sellers of competing products may find that it can increase its prices without losing sales to those competitors. On the other hand, if it is charging a high price, it may be just at the point where consumers would abandon the product if prices were increased any further. Measuring cross-elasticity at the higher price will indicate a higher cross-elasticity than measuring it at the lower price.

5. GEOGRAPHIC MARKETS

Antitrust market analysis focuses not only on products that are reasonably interchangeable but on the geographic boundaries of the market. The geographic market contains all those producers who, in the eyes of buyers, compete with the firm in question. In a sense, product market analysis concentrates on the products that are interchangeable and geographic market analysis concentrates on actual suppliers who are reasonably interchangeable. To fully account for all those firms that may limit the ability of the seller to raise price, both dimensions of the market must be considered.

The geographic market question can be approached with the same methodology as product market definition. The question is how responsive buyers will be to price increases in terms of buying from remote sellers. If they quickly move to remote sellers when local prices go up, the distant sellers are part of the market. If not, they are not part of the market. Again, there is no bright line test for including a firm in the geographic market. It is a matter of judgement and ultimately leads to the use of expert opinion at trial.

The primary determinant of the ease with which buyers will turn to distant sellers is transportation costs. Obviously, the more expensive it is to ship goods from distant locations, the less willing buyers will be to rely on those sellers. This can be refined a bit in the sense that the importance of transportation costs can probably best be judged in light of the cost of the product. Thus, one would expect the concrete block industry to be local because the cost of shipment as a percentage of the cost of the product is relatively high. The market for diamonds, on the other hand, may be international in scope.

6. SUPPLY ELASTICITY

As the expanded discussion of the Lerner Index indicated, one of the factors that affects the elasticity of demand faced by a firm is the quickness with which other firms can respond to price increases by making output available to customers. If there are no such firms, then no matter how willing buyers may be to switch to alternative suppliers, it will not make a difference in terms of limiting the ability of a firm to raise price. As already noted, the increase in supply can come from three sources: existing producers of the product who have excess capacity, firms that can switch existing capacity from the production of another good to the production of the good in question, and firms that enter the industry *de novo*.

One can best visualize the problem by thinking in terms of determining the firm's market share. If the market is defined to include only the production that exists in the market at the time of the evaluation, it may overstate the importance of the firm. In other words, the denominator in the market share calculation will be artificially low. This would be especially true if there were firms in the industry that could switch into the production of the good in question with very little effort. Once again there are no bright line tests for deciding when a firm should be included in a market even though it may not currently be producing the product in question.

The main determinant of supply elasticity is how fast production costs increase as output increases. The connection is obvious. If price goes up, firms will increase output as long as they can produce additional output at a cost that is less than the new price. If production costs rise very slowly as production increases, then suppliers are likely to play more of a role in limiting another firm's efforts to exercise market power.

In summary, market power varies inversely with industry elasticity of demand and elasticity of supply. It varies directly with market share.

7. A CLASSIC AND A CONTEMPORARY EXAMPLE

The complexities of market analysis can best be illustrated by reference to two important cases: one an antitrust classic and one a recent headline grabber.

a. United States v. Aluminum Company of America (Alcoa)

Judge Learned Hand's market analysis in the 1945 Alcoa case is probably the most closely studied market analysis. Judge Hand reasoned that Alcoa was a monopoly by virtue of its possession of 90% of the market for virgin aluminum ingot. The 10% that was not sold by Alcoa consisted of imports. In effect, Judge Hand made decisions about what was to be included in the numerator and the denominator of the market share fraction. In doing so, Judge Hand did not have the benefit of the technical language found in today's judicial market analyses, but his reasoning, though possibly flawed, considered a number of the factors discussed above.

In coming to the decision about Alcoa's market share, Judge Hand took a series of steps. First, he excluded secondary or recycled aluminum from the market or the denominator of the market share fraction. He reasoned that secondary aluminum was not reasonably interchangeable because for some users it was not acceptable. In today's terminology, the cross-elasticity was too low. In addition, he was concerned that Alcoa had control over the production of aluminum that would be recycled. In effect, this type of competition was, in part, under the control of Alcoa. To include it in the market would, in his view, be misleading as to the potential for secondary aluminum to act as a limiting factor on Alcoa's control of price. Most scholars now feel that complete exclusion of secondary aluminum resulted in too narrow a market and an inflated market share for Alcoa.

In a second step, Judge Hand included in the denominator only foreign-produced aluminum that was already sold in the United States. The other possibility would have been to include all foreign-produced ingot. The issue was one of elasticity of supply. In other words, how sensitive would foreign producers be to price increases in the United States? It was probably incorrect for Judge Hand to include only the ingot currently imported, since additional imports would likely have occurred if Alcoa's prices increased. In fact, Judge Hand seemed to recognize this in some of his reasoning. As with secondary aluminum, most scholars now feel that the impact was to artificially narrow the market and inflate Alcoa's market share.

A third step taken by Judge Hand dealt with ingot that was fabricated by Alcoa. In effect, this was virgin ingot that Alcoa processed itself rather than selling to others. The question was whether ingot Alcoa processed should be included in the numerator. If it were included, Alcoa's market share would be higher, and if excluded, it would be lower. Hand elected to include the processed ingot.

His reasoning was that the decision of whether to process or sell was one that had an impact on prices. To exclude fabricated ingot from the numerator would lower Alcoa's share and understate its power over price.

b. *Unites States v. Microsoft*

In the heralded 2001 Microsoft case, the Court of Appeals for the District of Columbia assessed Microsoft's market power in the market for operating systems. As in *Alcoa*, much of the controversy concerned what would be included in the relevant market or in the denominator of the market share fraction. Microsoft sought to include in the market the Apple operating system as well as operating systems for non-PCS devices, including middleware. The court rejected all of these as failing the reasonably interchangeable test.

More interesting are two additional and less conventional arguments made by Microsoft. The first one was that a high market share overstated Microsoft's control over price because of the ease of entering the market. The court rejected this argument, reasoning that as long as most software was written for the Microsoft operating system, there was little likelihood of serious competition through new entry.

Microsoft also argued that whatever dominance it possessed was the result of the popularity of its system. This line of argument ties into the concept of network effects. Network effects occur when the desirability of a product increases as the manufacturer has greater market share. In the context of computers, the argument would be that the greater Microsoft's market share the better its product because it means a greater number of computer users have compatible systems. In effect, monopoly becomes consistent rather than inconsistent with consumer welfare. The court did not find the network effects argument compelling, but this particular type of reasoning may eventually lead to changes in conventional market analysis.

CHAPTER NINE

THE ECONOMICS OF GOVERNMENT REGULATION

With the exception of Chapter Eight, much of the material in the preceding chapters deals with the ways in which private law influences resource allocation or income and wealth distribution. There is, of course, a huge body of public law that is also specifically designed to achieve particular allocative or distributive outcomes. In law school, this material is covered in courses ranging from regulated industries to securities regulation and environmental law. This Chapter, by necessity, adopts a more basic perspective than any of those courses. The focus is on the economic rationales offered as bases for regulatory intervention.[1] The critical question in the cases of all these rationales is whether the regulation produces a result that is more desirable than that which would be produced in an unregulated market.

1. The structure of this Chapter is based on Jeffrey Harrison, Tom Morgan & Paul Verkuil, *Regulation and Deregulation* (1995).

A. THE NATURAL MONOPOLY RATIONALE

1. THE THEORY OF NATURAL MONOPOLY

The bedrock justification for government regulation is the existence of natural monopoly.[2] A natural monopoly is said to exist when a market can be served most efficiently by a single firm. Table 1 illustrates how the costs of a natural monopoly may vary as output increases. The column for fixed costs shows total fixed costs of $10,000 for all levels of output. On the other hand, variable cost (VC) steadily increases with output. Thus, total cost (TC) also increases as output increases. The key column to examine, however, is the average total cost column (ATC). For every level of output on the chart, average total cost decreases. For example, at an output of 10 units, the average total cost has decreased to $1,000.64.

Table 1

Output	Fixed Cost	Variable Cost	TC	ATC
1	$10,000	$1.00	$10,001	$10,001.00
2	10,000	1.90	10,001.90	5,000.95
3	10,000	2.70	10,002.70	3,333.90
4	10,000	3.40	10,003.40	2,500.85
5	10,000	4.00	10,004	2,000.80
6	10,000	4.50	10,004.50	1,667.40
7	10,000	4.90	10,004.90	1,429.27
8	10,000	5.30	10,005.30	1,250.66
9	10,000	5.80	10,005.80	1,111.75
10	10,000	6.40	10,006.40	1,000.64

2. See Kenneth E. Train, *Optimal Regulation: The Economic Theory of Natural Monopoly* (1991).

This steady decline in average total cost will occur when the firm's costs of production include a relatively large component of fixed costs. Fixed costs are those that do not change as the level of production increases. The typical example of a firm with large fixed costs is a utility. Since fixed costs are relatively large when compared to variable costs (those that do increase with the level of production) and do not increase as output increases, the average cost of production will fall even though some of the other costs of production are increasing.

Figure 1 illustrates the natural monopoly phenomenon graphically. The average total cost for the firm is depicted by ATC in the graph. The curve is drawn so as to steadily decline over most of the production levels graphed along the X axis. Curve D represents demand in the industry. As the graph shows, the average cost of production is falling throughout all levels of demand. In effect, from the point of view of production costs, the most efficient way to organize this industry is to have the total demand "served" by a single firm. The structure is called a natural monopoly, because if the market were unregulated it would evolve to the point at which only one firm survived.

Figure 1

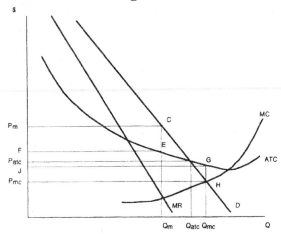

For example, suppose two producers of electricity were attempting to serve the same market. Given that they both would have high fixed costs, they would each need to serve most of the market in order to avoid losses. The ensuing competition could take the form of fierce price competition with each firm pricing below average total cost. Eventually, one firm would abandon the market, leaving it to the other firm.

The relationship of costs and demand resulting in natural monopoly conditions creates a dilemma. If the firms are left unregulated, prices will fall until one of them leaves the market. At that point, the remaining firm is a monopolist and will have the capacity to raise price. Following basic pricing principles discussed in Chapters Two and Eight, the firm would produce out to the point at which marginal cost (MC in Figure 1) and marginal revenue

(MR) are equal and charge the price that is consistent with selling that level of output. In Figure 1, this results in the quantity Q_m and a price equal to P_m. The monopolist will earn a profit equal to the area of rectangle FP_mCE. Given the high costs of entering the industry, the likelihood is that the firm can keep its prices at supracompetitive levels.

A reaction to the threat of monopoly pricing is to regulate prices. If prices are regulated, the question then becomes: what is the appropriate rate? This question has both a general and a specific version. The specific questions are discussed below. At a more general level, there are two leading standards for the regulated price. The first is to choose the price that achieves allocative efficiency—marginal cost. For example, in Figure 1, if the allocatively efficient rate is chosen, the price would be set at P_{mc}. As was discussed in Chapter Two, this is because marginal cost reflects the cost to society of producing an additional unit of output, and the demand curve shows the value attributed to those units of output by buyers. From the point of view of overall welfare, it makes sense to produce as long as the demand curve is above the marginal cost curve.

The problem with this, as the graph illustrates, is that the price of P_{mc} is below the average total cost of production for the firm. In fact, the total loss to the firm is equal to the loss per unit times the number of units sold or the area of rectangle $JGHP_{mc}$ in the Figure. Thus, the firm cannot survive in the long run without some kind of outside source of funding, possibly a government subsidy.

Because of this, there is invariably pressure to allow the firm to recover its full costs of production including a normal profit. On the graph, this would mean charging a price equal to average total cost or P_{atc}.

2.   AGENCY REGULATION

a.   Revenue Requirement

Often the response to natural monopolies is to regulate prices through the use of a regulatory body. This actually involves two steps. One is the determination of the total revenue the firm will be permitted to raise through its pricing structure. As noted above, the typical approach is to permit the firm to collect revenue equal to its costs including a normal profit. The amount of revenue can be expressed as a formula:

$$R = C + Ir$$

where R is the total revenue, C is the operating expense or the costs of goods and services consumed during the relevant time period, I is the rate base or the assets that are not consumed during the relevant time period, and r is the rate of return.

In a rate hearing, each of the above components will be at issue, ranging from whether the executives of the utility are paid too much to calculating the utility's cost of capital. The issue is usually not whether the utility may incur a certain expense, but whether that expense may be fairly passed on to ratepayers. For example, a utility may choose to pay its president a salary of $200,000. A regulatory commission may determine that a fair salary is $150,000 and only permit that amount of the president's salary to be included in the charges that are passed on to customers. It has, in effect, "disallowed" part of the expense in determining the utility's revenue requirement.

If the regulatory mechanism is working ideally, the total revenue collected by the utility will be equal to its total reasonable costs including an acceptable level of profit. In other words, the total revenue would approximate the revenue collected if the firm were operating under competitive conditions. The problems of approaching this goal are well documented and fairly obvious. One key question is how to properly provide incentives for the firm to operate as efficiently as possible. If the firm is assured of recovering its cost and is restricted in terms of the profit it can make, many of the normal incentives found in an unregulated market are lost. To some extent, this problem is offset by the possibility that time will pass between rate hearings, during which time costs increase yet the firm must abide by the agency's decision about allowable costs. This "regulatory lag" can force management to be concerned about costs, but whatever impact it may have will only coincidentally match the pressure in an unregulated market.

Two problems associated with attempting to regulate the firm's rates and revenues in order to simulate an unregulated outcome are especially noteworthy. The first is the circularity in any effort to encourage efficient operation. For example, suppose the utility chose to pay its president an extravagant salary and to make large contributions to a local charity. At a rate hearing, the administrative body may determine not to allow the utility to pass these charges on to ratepayers. Since the expenses are already incurred by the utility, the net effect will be no different than had an unregulated firm been unable to charge a price at least equal to its costs— profit will decrease. Low or uncertain profits make it more difficult for the firm to attract new investors. The effect of this will be to make the cost of capital in the formula increase. Thus, disallowing a particular expense may not mean that ratepayers do not eventually pay for that expense in some other form.

Another widely discussed consequence of rate regulation is called the Averch–Johnson effect. Typically, the regulated firm is permitted to earn a "fair" rate of return on its invested assets. The money used for acquisition of these assets is the capital contributed by investors. If the fair rate of return is higher than the firm's actual cost of capital, the firm will have an incentive to invest in capital and substitute it when possible for other inputs like labor. The basic Averch–Johnson effect is that the regulated firm will be encouraged to use a different and less efficient mix of inputs than an unregulated firm.

b.   Rate Regulation

The formula presented above only indicates the amount of revenue the firm is permitted to collect.

Another step in the process involves the determination of actual rates to be charged. There are two basic methodologies. One is to attempt to match users up with the actual cost of serving them. This "cost of service" approach can be based on the average cost of service or on the marginal cost of service. A second approach is sometimes referred to as being based on the "value of service." Typically, "value of service" pricing means that prices for different customer groups will vary inversely with the elasticity of the demand for that group. All of these approaches have complexities and shortcomings, some of which are discussed here. In addition, the two basic philosophies can be combined.

The problems with adopting one pricing strategy or another stem primarily from the tension between the need to raise revenue equal to the total cost of operating the firm and the desire to send the right pricing signal to consumers as a means of achieving allocative efficiency. Thus, as noted above, a price equal to marginal cost may mean that a firm is unable to meet all of its expenses. A response may be to try to allocate to each user the "full cost" of production. In other words, all of the fixed costs of the firm would be allocated so that each unit is priced in a way that the consumer pays some portion of the total costs of production. Of course, this means losing the advantages of marginal cost pricing in that the pricing signal sent to consumers will no longer encourage the socially optimal level of consumption.

A related possibility is called two-part or multi-part pricing. In this case the consumer is charged some price for simply being able to consume at all and then a price per unit actually purchased. The fixed part of the charge could be designed to insure that the firm recovers the fixed costs of production. It might be allocated to customers on the basis of how much they demand at the highest period of demand. The per unit charge could then be set to reflect marginal cost. This approach to rate-setting is something of a hybrid in that the objective is to enable the firm to collect its revenue requirement while providing consumers information about marginal cost.

In the form described here, the two-part price is also a type of peak load pricing. Peak load pricing involves charging different prices depending on the time of consumption. To the extent a consumer's demand coincides with the time of overall peak demand on the system, one could say that she is responsible for the costs associated with the firm's acquisition of the fixed plant necessary to serve all customers at the peak period of demand. In a sense, she is charged in a way that matches her responsibility for marginal investment costs.

"Value of service" pricing involves a different perspective than "cost of service" pricing. Instead of attempting to match consumers up with the costs they cause the producer to incur, the focus is on the elasticity of demand of the consumers. Those consumers with relatively inelastic demand are charged a higher price than those with relatively elastic demands. This is not to say that the consumers with inelastic demands actually "value" the service any more than others; other factors may influence their responsiveness. For example, the shipper of a relatively valuable commodity may be willing to pay a higher freight rate than the shipper of a less expensive commodity because the cost of shipping is an insignificant element of the total cost of the commodity.

One advantage of the value of service approach over the cost of service approach is that it provides a way for the seller to charge a rate in excess of average total cost to some consumers—those with relatively inelastic demands—in order to offset charging a price which is below average total cost to other consumers—those with relatively elastic demands. Under an approach called "Ramsey pricing,"[3] the goal is to charge different prices depending upon elasticity of demand in order to just meet the total cost of production.

Figures 2 and 3 illustrate this possibility. In Figure 2, the demand curve for one group of consumers is drawn to be relatively flat, indicating that demand is relatively elastic. The firm's average total cost and marginal cost curves are also on the graph. The price (P_1) is set at the intersection of the demand curve and the marginal cost curve. This group of consumers is making no contribution toward the firm's fixed costs, and the "loss" associated with serving this group of consumers alone is equal to the area of rectangle P_1ABC.

3. See Kenneth E. Train, *supra* note 2, at 117–125.

Figure 2

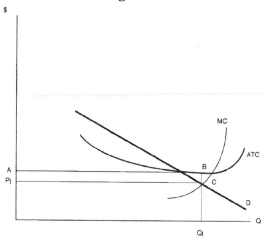

Figure 3

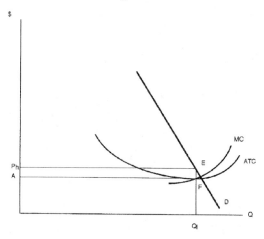

In Figure 3, the demand curve of a second class of consumers is relatively steep in order to illustrate a relatively inelastic demand. In this case, the price charged is equal to P_h, which is in excess of average total cost. The area of rectangle P_hEFA is the total "profit" recovered from this group of consumers. As long as the area of P_lABC in Figure 2 is equal to the area of P_hEFA in Figure 3, the firm is able to cover its total costs of production.

c. Cross–Subsidization

The possibility of charging different prices to different groups of customers brings up the issue of cross-subsidization or, as Richard Posner calls it, "taxation by regulation."[4] As a general matter, the subsidization occurs when one group is charged above-cost rates so that another group can be charged below-cost rates. There is an obvious relationship to value of service pricing since the subsidizing group will typically have the relatively inelastic demand for the service.

Even at this simple level, two things should be clarified. First, it is not just relative rates that determine whether one group is subsidizing another. Thus, one group, to which it is very expensive to provide service, may be charged a higher price than a group that is less expensive to serve. The group paying the higher rate could still be the subsidized group if the rate charged is lower than cost.

4. Richard Posner, "Taxation by Regulation," 2 *Bell J.* 22 (1971).

A second point is that it is sometimes difficult to determine which group is being subsidized and which group is subsidizing. For example, suppose group one pays a rate below average cost but above marginal cost and group two pays a rate in excess of average cost. In a sense, group two appears to be subsidizing group one. On the other hand, if it were not for the contribution that group one is making towards fixed costs by paying a rate that is in excess of marginal cost, the rates paid by group two would have to be raised even further. Indeed, if group one had a very elastic demand for the good or service because there were many good substitutes available and would stop purchasing altogether if rates were any higher, one might conclude that its members were actually subsidizing the members of the higher-paying group.

A better example of cross-subsidization is when one customer or a group of customers is not paying a charge equal to marginal cost. The classic example is a remote purchaser of electricity or telephone service who pays the same rate as customers living in concentrated areas. Unless the remote purchaser has paid the full cost of constructing the necessary cables or lines to the remote location, that cost must be accounted for elsewhere in the system, most likely in the rates of others. Another prominent example is the effort to provide electricity to the needy through what are called "life-line" rates. Again, unless the life-line rate is equal to or above marginal cost, the "loss" must be made up in the form of higher rates elsewhere in the system.

True cross-subsidization, where the customer pays a rate that is lower than marginal cost, is hard to defend on traditional economic grounds. The most obvious problem is that below marginal cost rates send the "wrong" signal to consumers in the subsidized group and encourage an allocatively inefficient level of consumption. This is because marginal cost reflects the actual cost to society of producing the output. Consumers who purchase at a price that is less than marginal cost cannot be said to "value" the output at a high enough level to justify its production over the production of other goods or services for which those inputs might be used.

Although narrow conventional economic reasoning does not support true subsidization, there may still be economic or perfectly sound moral reasons for subsidizing the consumption of a product. For example, there may be sufficient positive externalities associated with the use of electricity by the needy for warmth that the demand they express in the market actually understates the "value" associated with their consumption of electricity. Similarly, the fact that traditional economics defines demand as a willingness and ability to pay may give one pause about allocating necessary goods and services to only those who "demand" them.

Another problem has less to do with allocative efficiency than with the taxation character of cross-subsidization. It is hard to distinguish cross-subsidization in the regulatory context from any other policy-based decision to subsidize one group at the expense of another. Thus, subsidizing the purchase of electricity is really no different from issuing food stamps or providing subsidies to tobacco farmers. Any system of widespread subsidization should at least strive for some semblance of coherence and consistency. Whether participation by a regulated firm and its regulating agency detracts from or assists in achieving this coherence is highly questionable.

3.   CONTESTABLE MARKETS

Another approach to natural monopolies is one that does not so readily give up on the use of the market as an allocative mechanism. The basic idea here is that the condition of natural monopoly does not mean that prices must be regulated in order to avoid monopoly pricing. Instead, the focus is on *which* firm will be the single supplier. This can be determined by competition.[5] The competition is not, however, for individual customers; it is for the market itself.

One version of this approach is to make the determination of which firm will operate in the market by auctioning the right to operate. For example, a local government might auction off the right to be the exclusive supplier to the firm that bids for that right by offering the lowest pricing schedule and the highest quality of service. The local government might own the fixed resources

5. Harold Demsetz, "Why Regulate Utilities," 11 *J. L. & Econ.* 55 (1968).

required to operate in the market and, in effect, auction off the right to use these resources to a single firm.

This alternative is not without complications.[6] For example, the auctioning agency would presumably have a contract with the winning bidder for a substantial duration. Most likely, the contract will provide for price adjustments. The process of deciding when an adjustment is called for can begin to resemble a more typical rate-making process.

Another more theoretical view is that under certain conditions, it will be impossible for a monopolist to charge prices at which it earns above a normal profit. The key here is that entry into and exit from the industry by a newcomer must not be more expensive than for an incumbent. Under these conditions, if an incumbent monopolist attempted to charge a price that resulted in a profit that was higher than the minimum necessary, another monopolist could enter and charge a lower price and completely take away the incumbent's market. Presumably, this constant threat would be sufficient to force the incumbent monopolist to hold prices down. It is not clear just how often monopoly producers are as fungible as this theory requires.

B. EXCESSIVE COMPETITION

At times, regulations have been enacted in response to what is termed excessive or "destructive" competition. These regulations typically take the

6. See Kenneth Train, supra note 2, at 297–315.

form of restrictions on entry into the market or on minimum prices that can be charged. In general, the destructive competition rationale has been invoked in four different types of cases. The first is related to the value of the service pricing approach discussed above and to a policy of cross-subsidization. In these instances the "losses" incurred by serving one group are made by the extra revenue generated from serving another group—typically the group with a relatively inelastic demand. It would be profitable if a new firm could enter the market and serve only the group with the inelastic demand. The name that has been attached to this practice is "cream-skimming." As the label implies, the cream-skimming firm enters the market and takes only the very "best" customers, leaving those who are willing and able to pay a price below average total cost to the remaining firm. The obvious response to cream-skimming is to protect the incumbent firm from new entry.

A second reason for regulating entry or setting minimum prices arises when cream-skimming is an issue but involves a more direct response to the types of costs a firm has. It must be recalled that fixed costs are those that do not vary with the level of output. The firm must pay even if it produces nothing. If the firm has a high level of fixed costs, it is especially vulnerable to competition. Increases in competition, including competition for the most desirable customers, may mean that the firm cannot charge a price equal to average total cost. Moreover, since most of its costs are fixed, it cannot escape these losses by simply closing.

This predicament can be visualized by referring back to Figure 1. The firm will sell output as long as its price is no less than marginal cost. This is because that price at least covers the costs that are incurred by deciding to produce and allows for some contribution towards fixed costs. A price below average total cost cannot, however, go on indefinitely. Eventually, a firm that cannot cover all of its costs, including fixed costs, will go out of business. Thus, in order to avoid the risk of chronic losses and the possibility of a general hesitancy to enter the market in the first place, cream-skimming may be prevented by regulating new entry and setting minimum rates.

A third basic category of "destructive" competition is of a totally different character than the high fixed costs case. Sometimes rates and entry have been regulated simply because the firms in the market are inherently unstable. In other words, entry and exit from the market are relatively easy, price-cutting is the predominant method of competing, and there can be widespread business failures. Of course, this is not a pleasant prospect for the actual participants in the market, and there is likely to be political pressure brought to bear in order to protect them from the rigors of the market. This appears to have been the impetus behind the Motor Carriers Act of 1935, which provided this type of protection to the trucking industry. That protection was motivated more by Depression-era concerns about the general welfare of the individual trucker than by concern that the industry would either cease to exist or become highly concentrated.

A final justification for reducing competitive pressure in an industry is based on the possibility that intense competition results in a decrease in the quality of service. Sometimes the argument, when made in the context of something like the airline industry, preys on the fears of customers and relates specifically to safety. Although the quality of service argument has some appeal, there are a series of responses, based on conventional economic thinking, that tend to undermine it as a basis for regulating competition. The first starts from the assumption that every profit-maximizing firm is constantly on the lookout for ways to increase profit, including ways that involve reducing costs of production and possibly quality. Unless this quest for higher profits is somehow different or more relentless during periods of intense competition, it is not clear that quality will be any different than under normal market conditions.

In addition, the argument that quality will suffer seems based on the belief that consumers either do not value higher quality or are unable to assess differences in quality. If the former is the case, the reduction in quality is actually desirable. The second possibility has a little more appeal, although it once again suggests that firms have not taken full advantage of profitable strategies until faced with competitive pressure. But suppose that market imperfections relating to information costs really do render the consumers unable to effectively express preferences for higher quality and that it is only during periods of intense competition that quality suffers. Even here it is not clear that the most effective method of assuring higher quality is to decrease competitive pressure; directly regulating minimum quality standards may make more sense.

C.   THE ALLOCATION OF INHERENTLY SCARCE RESOURCES

A rationale that is sometimes offered for regulation is the allocation of inherently scarce resources. This general justification probably stands for two more basic concerns. Broadcast frequency regulation illustrates these two concerns. The justification for the regulation of broadcast frequencies was that unrestricted and unregulated use would mean that competing broadcasters would interfere with each other and thereby severely limit the usefulness of the broadcast spectrum. This particular problem could have been solved simply by creating a system of exclusive broadcast rights, a step which would have been sufficient to overcome the "tragedy of the broadcast commons." This is probably the strongest basis for regulation since a system of property rights and means of enforcing those rights is basic to an efficiently operating system.

The second concern is about how the limited resources are to be allocated. Thus, in the case of broadcasting, auctioning the broadcast/property rights would have been one possible solution. The market would determine eventual ownership. Alternatively, the rights could be, and were, assigned on the basis of factors other than the willingness and ability to pay. In all likelihood, the "allocation of scarce resources" rationale reflects concerns about distribution as much as it does concerns about setting up a system of property rights.

This is not meant to imply that economic factors are only at work when rights are sold on the open market. In fact, there are often sound economic reasons for deviating from market solutions. In the case of broadcasting, there is an economic justification based on the presence of positive externalities. In other words, the benefits of having a broad range of views heard over the broadcast spectrum may accrue to people other than those vying for broadcast rights. This is one of the economic gains from favoring racial diversity in the allocation of broadcast rights.

In recent years, the allocation of scarce resources problem has been played out in the context of the geosynchronous zone. The geosynchronous zone is 22,300 miles out in space. Satellites placed there travel at roughly the same speed as the rotation of the earth and are, therefore, "stationary" with respect to the earth's surface. The zone is the primary location for communications satellites. The geosynchronous zone is inherently limited in that only so much of it exists. In addition, much of the zone is over oceans and, therefore, less valuable than other spaces. Finally, satellites in the zone are capable of crowding one another.

These problems are like those encountered in early broadcast regulation. One option is a massive "land rush," with the first parties successfully launching satellites, in effect, laying claim to the space occupied. This is comparable to a market solution in that the parties or countries that are willing and able to pay the most and take the risk are like the high bidders in an auction. The problem that has been recognized and treated, if not absolutely solved, by international treaty, is that many Third World countries are not as able to join in the "auction" as are more affluent countries. Here again, the decision has been made to deviate from a simplistic market solution.

A question that arises in virtually all decisions to allocate rights in a way different from the market allocation is whether the recipients of the rights can then resell the rights to the highest bidders. If they can, the eventual outcome in terms of ownership is unlikely to be much different from that resulting from an auction. And whatever positive externalities were behind the initial assignment will be lost. Of course, there are important distributive consequences in that the original recipient of the right will experience an increase in wealth.

D. REACTIONS TO TRANSACTION COSTS AND EXTERNALITIES

A great deal of the regulation encountered on a day by day basis concerns government efforts to respond to transaction costs and externalities. Transaction costs, as discussed in Chapter Three, are the costs of actually making an exchange happen. Transaction costs are not the actual consideration flowing from one party to another, but the costs associated with such things as locating each other, gathering information, negotiating, and drafting the terms of the exchange. High transaction costs may cause otherwise beneficial exchanges not to take place. Sometimes regulations are designed to make transactions smoother or less costly to those involved.

In general, there are three broad areas of responses to transaction costs. The first amounts to setting standards that "rationalize" an industry. The most basic of these rules relates to the assignment and definition of property rights or entitlements. The second general response is to require that information is made available. Third, a great deal of regulation is a direct response to externalities. In each instance, it is important to ask whether the market, left alone, could work around the transaction costs problem and reach an efficient outcome.

This is not to suggest that these responses are found in neat self-contained regulatory compartments. Take, for example, the regulation of drugs. Some drugs are sold without a prescription, some are sold only with a prescription, and some cannot be legally sold at all. From one perspective this classification system creates the standards for drug manufacturers to use in the development of new drugs. They amount to rules or rationalizing devices that indicate what it takes to acquire different levels of marketing rights. The different classifications are valuable sources of information for manufactures, as well as consumers. In addition, consumers benefit from the requirement that certain warnings and information be provided. Finally, a policy designed to keep some drugs off the market entirely can be explained by possible negative externalities.

1. RATIONALIZING AN INDUSTRY

One can garner an understanding of the importance of government regulation as a means of setting up the basic format of a market or an industry by recalling the initial justification for broadcast regulation discussed above. Without an initial assignment of broadcast rights, it is unlikely that anyone could claim the exclusivity that would then permit them to exchange or even use a broadcast frequency successfully. Although there may be a theoretical possibility that all people interested in broadcasting could somehow buy out the claims of other potential broadcasters and set up a system of privately determined property rights, such an effort would be incredibly costly and is subject to major problems of extortion, hold-outs, and enforcement. The industry is made rational or predictable by government intervention which defines the rights involved.

The same sort of thing happens when the government defines what it means to own a patent, copyright, or trademark. Similarly, decisions concerning water rights or whether one has a right to collect damages from a polluting factory establish entitlements that the parties can then exchange. Without this initial entitlement, however, it would be difficult for meaningful exchange to take place.

The rationalizing function can also be seen at work in the context of professional licensing. Imagine, for example, a situation in which an individual needs medical care but lives in a state in which there are no formal licensing procedures. Perhaps anyone could hang out a sign advertising that he or she is offering medical care and use the "M.D." label. In this instance, "M.D." would be a fairly valueless piece of information for the consumer. By permitting only those with a certain level of training or expertise to use the label "M.D." and offer medical care, the government promotes standardization in labeling and makes comparisons more feasible.

2. INCREASING THE AVAILABILITY OF INFORMATION

In the example described above, the regulated use of the label "M.D." rationalized the industry by encouraging standardization. The standardization also carries with it the information that all those calling themselves medical doctors are of a certain quality. Without this standardization and the information about minimum quality standards implicit in the permitted use of the label, consumers concerned about the quality of the training and expertise of potential medical care providers would face incredibly high information costs. These high costs may mean that, in some instances, the consumer makes no choice at all and does not participate in the market. In other instances, the consumer runs the risk of making a poor choice.

The requirement that sellers provide certain types of information—whether it is the nutritional content of foods, the health hazards associated with smoking or drinking, the gas mileage of a new car, or the "plain language" disclosure of credit terms— is no more than a requirement that sellers produce and provide a "product" in the form of information to consumers. The requirement that this service be provided is almost uniformly a reaction to the belief that information would be expensive for the individual consumer to discover and that it enables consumers to make better choices.

As an economic matter, it is important that this requirement have either a desired distributive or allocative consequence. The possible distributive objectives associated with requiring that information be provided are fairly obvious. To the extent the information makes consumers better able to compare producers, market power may be lowered and sellers forced to price more competitively. For example, by reading the label on a can of tuna, a consumer may find that the generic or house brand has the same nutritional qualities as the higher-priced, nationally-advertised brand. When prices are more competitive than they otherwise would be, the distributive impact is in favor of consumers. This is why sellers resist making information available even if it is relatively inexpensive to produce.

This is not to say that the distributive consequences of information requirements exist apart from allocative consequences. In fact, as discussed in Chapter Eight, the elimination of market power has very important allocative effects as well as distributive effects. The fact that the labeling of the cans of tuna means that the market is more competitive also means that prices will be lower, output higher, and the outcome more allocatively efficient. The same reasoning is behind the requirement that the terms of loans be explained fully and in some detail; borrowers are better able to shop for better deals and lenders less able to conceal the fact that money is essentially fungible.

Still, from the standpoint of traditional notions of efficiency, a different focus is useful. The requirement that information be made available really is a requirement that sellers produce and sell information to consumers as a condition of selling the product. In addition, no one should suffer from the illusion that the cost of supplying information will not be treated as a cost of production. Since consumers end up making what amounts to a forced purchase, it is important that the "exchange" be one that might take place if the market for information were perfectly fluid.

This leads to the question of why the information is not viewed as being produced in sufficient quantities without regulation. After all, unlike the distributive justification, the allocative justification lies in the belief that the information is more valuable to buyers than it is to potential sellers. Provision of the information and the resulting adjustments in demand will not happen, however, if there are transaction costs that impede the smooth working of the information market.

An obvious type of transaction cost that impedes the free flow of information is that potential consumers of the information to not know it exists or are unable assess its value. In these instances, the actual demand for the information will understate its value. A good example might be the warnings about the health or safety hazards of various products ranging from cigarettes to athletic equipment. In order to demand the information in efficient quantities, consumers would first have to be "educated" about the existence of the information and its relevance. Having been enlightened about the existence of hypothetically useful information, demand for the information would appear. Of course, this intermediate step would alone require the production of information that consumers may mistakenly undervalue, possibly by discounting the eventual benefits of having access to the information.

But even if they were entirely enlightened about the existence of such information and were willing to pay for it, there may be free-rider problems. For example, if one person bought the information, there is little guarantee that the information could be kept secret. Thus, each potential consumer may simply wait in hopes that the demand of others will result in the production of the information.

The free-riding problem also plays out on the supply side of the market in a different context. Suppose the problem is not one of danger, but of the important properties of a product. Suppose further that, in order to understand these properties, consumers require some basic education. This was the case with respect to R-values on insulation materials.[7] While R-value was a useful way to compare materials, its use required that some basic information be provided. The problem is that any supplier of the information would be unable to capture all the benefits of providing the information; consumers might well use the information and then buy from other producers. The problem is similar to that which would be faced by a composer of music in the absence of copyright protection. The outcome is that it may not be rational for any individual producer to supply information which

7. See Trade Regulation Rules: Labeling and Advertising of Home Insulation, F.T.C., 1979, 44 Fed. Reg. 50218.

actually is of sufficient value to consumers to warrant its production. Required production by all is one solution to this problem.

3. REACTIONS TO EXTERNALITIES

As discussed in Chapter Three, externalities can be either positive or negative. Positive externalities exist when the producer is unable to "internalize" all the benefits of what has been produced. The classic example is that of an inventor who has no control over the use of his invention after it is put into use. Goods or services that are likely to result in positive externalities tend to be produced in inefficiently small quantities because much of the motivation to produce is siphoned off by those who enjoy the benefits without paying. Some possible reactions are to require users to pay for their use through a regime of copyright or patent law or to subsidize the production of the good. As just illustrated in the context of information, another reaction is to require some producers to provide the underproduced good as a condition of operating at all.

Most government regulation, as opposed to subsidization, concerns negative externalites. These are costs of production or consumption that are not borne by the producer or user. The polluting factory and the person smoking a cigarette in a crowded room are good examples. It should be noted that defining something as an externality raises one of the issues addressed here: the factory that emits smoke is only creating an "externality" if the people surrounding the factory have a right to clean air.

A decision that an activity produces an externality sets up a framework in which the "offending" party can buy the right to continue his activity. It also creates a situation in which the injured parties can vindicate their property rights by seeking compensation or injunctive relief. In these situations, which are discussed in Chapters Three and Four, the private party is permitted to sell her right or entitlement.

In this section, the focus is on action that not only assigns the right, but preemptively protects the right by banning activity that may interfere with it. In effect, the right cannot be sold—voluntarily or involuntarily—by the owner. A good example of this is the requirement that certain safety features be incorporated into new cars. The buyer has, in a sense, the right to buy a car that complies with certain safety standards. On the other hand, she is not permitted to sell that right back to the manufacturer and buy a less safe car at a lower price. Other examples include workplace safety, meat inspection, and prescription drug effectiveness.

Before examining some specifics, it is useful to note that in these situations, two less restrictive regulatory possibilities are passed up. The first, as already noted, is to permit the buyer to sell her "right" to the safe car or safe workplace. The second is to provide information about the product or service to the consumer and allow the consumer to adjust demand accordingly.

The important question is why go further than defining the rights, making information available, and allowing the parties to express their preferences in the market? Perhaps some people would prefer automobiles without air bags and seat belts at lower prices than they must pay for automobiles equipped with these features. Perhaps some people are also willing to take their chances with drugs that have not been proven to be "safe and effective." From the standpoint of economics, regulations that go further than these alternatives make sense only if they result in a better allocative or distributive outcome.

One strong possibility is that owners are prevented from selling rights that they may tend to undervalue. This may be the justification for safety standards in the workplace and in the manufacture of automobiles as well as in the case of the application of building codes. For example, suppose workers were assigned the right to safe working conditions and these rights could be sold; employers could offer higher wages for working in hazardous conditions. It is possible that these "rights" are actually more valuable than the potential sellers realize, so much so that it would be allocatively inefficient for the rights to be sold. One might argue that workers with accurate information will not tend to undervalue these rights. Technically this may be correct, but efforts to inform workers so thoroughly that they will make the right valuation may be more expensive than simply preventing the sale of these rights in the first place.

In other instances, like automobile safety features, there may be important benefits to third parties associated with the regulation. For example, potential victims of accidents may benefit from better braking systems and better visibility. The features may be undervalued by buyers because the benefits of the features do not accrue to buyers alone. At the same time, huge transaction costs preclude translating these third party benefits into market demand.

While potential mistakes in valuation explain some regulations, distributive goals are also relevant. General requirements about minimum product quality or workplace safety standards can be seen as ways of favoring purchasers or workers with respect to the terms of the exchange. In other words, they are presumably made better off at the expense of the other party. Just how effectively distributive goals can be achieved through regulations forcing one party to internalize a cost is open to question.

For example, in Figure 4, the Y axis is the cost of labor and the X axis is units of labor. D_1 is the demand for labor before a factory is required to install an air filter and other safety devices. It is important to remember that the demand curve shows the most the firm is willing to pay for each quantity of labor. S is the supply of labor. The cost of labor and the wage paid is equal to W_1. The installation of the equipment is viewed by the owners of the factory as another cost of using labor and in that regard this cost is indistinguishable from the payment of wages. The fact that some labor cost is now used to improve working conditions does not alter the amount the firm is willing to pay for each quantity of labor.

Figure 4

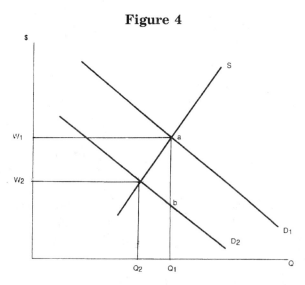

There is a difference between the amount the firm is willing to pay for each quantity of labor and what it is willing to pay in the form of wages. This means there is a new demand curve that shows the maximum wage the firm is willing to offer for each quantity of labor. This is D_2 in the graph. The vertical distance between D_1 and D_2 (ab in the graph) is the cost of the safety measures.

The new wage is determined by the intersection of D_2 and S and indicates that wages will fall from the initial level to W_2. In addition, the quantity of labor employed has dropped from Q_1 to Q_2. Thus, although the workers still employed may enjoy a safer workplace, it has come at a price to them in terms of wages and employment opportunities. Clearly, the distributive impact is not as simple as adding better working conditions to the value of existing wages.

This does not mean that this effort to achieve distributive ends through the control of externalities must fail. First, although wages fall, they do not fall by as much as the total cost of the safety measures. One can see this by comparing the difference between W_1 and W_2—the wage decrease—with the vertical distance between D_1 and D_2—the cost of the safety measures. The amount of the cost of the safety measures that will be passed on to workers in the form of lower wages will vary depending on the relative elasticities of demand and supply.

Second, the simplistic model used here and favored by conventional economists does not allow for the fact that workers may become more productive with safer working conditions. Consequently, demand may not change at all. Third, demand and supply models like that in Figure 4 are not representative of labor markets in which employers have monopsony power (power on the buying side of the market). In these markets, the forced increase in compensation may not lead to lower wages or lower levels of employment.[8] Third, safety regulations like those discussed here may be beneficial to both parties. For example, workers may prefer better working conditions over higher wages, and employers may prefer to offer better working conditions and lower wages, but transaction costs have prevented the exchange. Still, there is the strong possibility that desired distributive outcomes will be difficult to achieve.

The final reason for prohibiting some activities because of external effects deserves more than the passing mention it gets here. It is illustrated by regulations that prohibit activity that endangers a species of animal or its habitat. In effect, these regulations grant a "right" to exist to the species or at least to those who favor preservation. The negative externality is the elimination of the animal. If left to the market and the judicial system, the problem becomes one of measuring the damages associated with the destruction of the species. In fact, some would argue that the "damages" are immeasurable.[9] Clearly, the preferences of those currently wanting to preserve the species and those who will live in the future and might wish that the species had been preserved will be drastically understated in the market due to transaction costs. But much of this may miss the point. Here the step of preemptively protecting the right seems to flow

8. Jeffrey L. Harrison, "The New Terminable-at-Will Employment Contract: An Interest and Cost Incidence Analysis," 69 *Iowa L. Rev.* 327, 340–42 (1984).

9. See *Tennessee Valley Authority v. Hill* (S.Ct.1978).

not so much from the sense that, if left to the market, it will not be protected at economically efficient levels. Instead, the right to be protected transcends traditional economic measures.

E. SOCIAL JUSTICE REGULATIONS

Many regulations seem impossible to square with conventional notions of efficiency. Instead, the sense is that these regulations exist as a result of a sense of injustice and an effort to correct that injustice. This does not mean that economic analysis is irrelevant, for a number of reasons. First, much of the search for justice really means economic justice or the sense that individuals are economically better off. This usually means there is a redistributive objective. Second, there is a cost to most efforts to adjust market outcomes to achieve just outcomes. Third, a decision must be made about who will pay the cost of increased social justice. Finally, the objectives of justice and efficiency are not necessarily inconsistent. For example, think about even the most expensive plan of redistribution you can imagine. As long as those who benefit directly from the plan and others who favor it could compensate those who are made worse off, the plan is Kaldor–Hicks efficient.

A great many social justice regulations fit into one of two categories. The first category includes those instances in which equally productive people are discriminated against. This is likely to be the case when gender or racial discrimination is involved. Here, if employers simply keep their eye on the bottom line of profitability, the discrimination should eventually disappear. For example, if employers discriminate against women who are just as productive as men by not hiring them, there will be an excess of women in the labor market. The excess will drive the wages of women down and the wages of men up. Employers hiring women would eventually experience lower costs of production and be able to increase sales. Those firms continuing to discriminate would either fold or catch on in order to survive. In effect, the employer who discriminates on the basis of race or gender has an expensive habit that is inconsistent with maximizing profits.

If the market *should* cure gender and racial job discrimination, why is any regulation necessary? The principle reason is that markets work slowly and may bog down. For example, suppose labor costs are a small part of the costs of production. In those instances, employers who discriminate may not get the message for some time. Or, if an employer has market power, he may not feel great pressure to overcome his workforce preferences. In addition, a history of discrimination may affect the training (human capital) certain groups acquire as well as their aspirations. By not acquiring the same training as men due to the perception that men's jobs are closed to them, the productivity of women may remain lower, but not for reasons that have to do with gender per se. The point is that regulations can require employers to act as though markets are working effectively, and the eventual outcome may be greater equality.

Perhaps more interesting are regulations that require employers to ignore their instincts in the market. A good example is the Americans with Disabilities Act. The Act is quite complex but basically prohibits discrimination based on disability as long as a person can, either with or without a reasonable accommodation, perform the essential functions of the job. The concept of "reasonable" under the Act does not mean "cost-justified." In other words, an employer cannot avoid the responsibility by showing that the accommodation is more expensive than the productivity gains. In economic terms, employers are required to hire and subsidize workers who, from one perspective, actually make the firm less profitable than it would otherwise be. Of course, the presence of those with disabilities may increase the morale of the workforce or have some other beneficial effect that turns out to be profitable. This is not, however, the goal. A cap on the subsidization is provided by the stipulation that employers need not undergo "undue hardship."

There are obviously great benefits associated with hiring the disabled. Aside from the impact it may have on self-esteem, the likelihood is that dependence on the government will be reduced if more disabled individuals are employed. There are, in fact, two possibilities. One is that the regulation is Kaldor–Hicks efficient. Benefits accruing to the disabled and their relatives, co-workers, and society in general as a result of a sense of living in a more just world may exceed the costs to employers. On the other hand, it may not be Kaldor–Hicks efficient but perhaps justified on more philosophical grounds. Even if this is the case, the costs are probably relevant if for no other reason than to determine whether the same benefits might be achieved at a lower cost or whether greater justice could be achieved at the same cost.

Economics also enters the picture when determining how to finance efforts to achieve social justice. Under the ADA, the costs of accommodation will be shared by the firm's customers and shareholders. Whether the cost should be shared more generally by all taxpayers who favor the subsidy is another possibility, and it may actually lower the costs–as far as utility goes–if these costs are more broadly distributed.

CHAPTER TEN

INTELLECTUAL PROPERTY

Interest in intellectual property law has exploded in recent years, and it is an area that is readily amenable to economic analysis. Interestingly, the area has not been the subject of as much scrutiny from an economic perspective as others discussed in this book. This may be because copyright and patent law, in particular, are very complex and may be viewed as the domain of creative and eccentric people. Since the law and economics of intellectual property can be linked to antitrust law and economics, we are likely to see more analysis of this field. This chapter is limited to patent, copyright, and trademark law. Much of the analysis can be carried over to the law of trade secrets as well as state common law intellectual property doctrines.

Before starting, a cautionary note is in order. After reading about the costs of monopolies in Chapter Eight, you may wonder why the government would set up systems to protect intellectual property and seem to grant the owners monopoly power. If that was your line of thinking, you have fallen into a common misperception. Patent, copyright, and trademark law do not in and of themselves result in market power. They do, as you know, afford owners a right of exclusive use, but that does not mean that owners will reap monopoly power unless the underlying property has consumer appeal. To understand this, think of the last illustration that you saw on a restaurant napkin. In all likelihood it was copyrighted, but there are probably thousands of illustrations that would serve the same purpose. The point is that patent, copyright, and trademark define property rights and limit access to private property. In many cases they are necessary but not sufficient to create monopoly power.

A. THE ECONOMIC RATIONALE

There are a variety of theories or rationales for the development of a system of intellectual property. The economic approach, however, principally centers around the idea of providing incentives. This is captured by the Supreme Court in *Mazer v. Stein*, a landmark copyright decision: "The economic philosophy behind ... patents and copyrights is the conviction that encouragement of individual effort by personal gain is the best way to advance public welfare through the talents of authors and inventors...." (347 U.S, at 333 (1954)).

In many respects, this is no different from the economic logic for defining any kind of property rights. For example, suppose you "own" a plot of excellent land that is great for grazing cattle, but you cannot erect a fence. Not only that, you cannot enjoin others from entering or even expect to collect damages if their cattle come onto your land to sample the fare there. You are not likely to find that your land is worth very much, and you would be foolish to invest in finding and cultivating the best quality grazing area. Just shift the idea to a really good device, a well-done photograph, or the name of a product you are attempting to promote. Now suppose anyone who would like to can take your device, figure out how it works, and manufacture his or her own. Or, having taken your photograph, suppose anyone who wants to can reproduce it and call it his or her own. Finally, suppose you develop a chain of restaurants that bear the name "Joe's Chop House," and you strive for uniformity and quality, but anyone who cares to can call his or her restaurant "Joe's Chop House." In all these cases–patent, copyright, and trademark–you are a victim of free-riding. In other words, you may be unable to fully internalize the gains from your efforts. If you are unable to profit from your efforts, you are less likely invest in those efforts in the first place. This is why you often hear the argument that pharmaceutical manufacturers need patent protection in other to justify high research and development expenses.

This is the problem, but in order to justify a public system of intellectual property you must also consider whether a private system could be practical or less expensive. For example, every person who comes into your art gallery could be required to sign a contract in which he or she promises not to make copies of what was displayed there. The transaction costs here would be high, and it does not take long to realize that the costs of operating a system that protects intellectual property are probably lower if it is publicly maintained.

This basic incentive rationale applies to patent, copyright, and trademark, but there are important differences. Both patent and copyright are designed to reward those who create something new. They are similar in this respect but different in another. For a device or process to be patentable, it must be novel, meaning the first. In copyright, the protection is for something that is original. This does not mean that it must be the first, but it must not be copied. For example, a person who writes a poem that is the same as one already copyrighted would not be guilty of an infringement if he or she had not actually copied the first version.

Trademark is a somewhat different matter and works on a broader scale. The goal is to reduce transaction costs–specifically the costs buyers face in identifying products. For example, if you had a great meal at Joe's Chop Shop, which happens to serve the best soy chops around, you would probably like to repeat the experience. If everyone could use Joe's Chop Shop as the name of his or her restaurant, the problem for you would be obvious. Of course, the original Joe's could begin calling itself "The Original Joe's Chop Shop" but you can see that this would ultimately not do much good.

Despite these differences, the same issues affect all intellectual property. The questions are: how broad is the protection and how long should it be?

Going back to the example of the cattle ranch, the issue can be visualized as one of determining the boundaries around one's property. In the context of intellectual property, one can see the process as putting a fence around an idea. There can be narrow protection, in which only exact copies might be viewed as infringing, or broad protection, in which the inventor or author is protected from those who do not make exact copies. In addition, protection can be defined in terms of duration. In patent and copyright the duration is in years while a trademark is lost when it is abandoned. Longer protection is obviously comparable to owning more property.

Although the notion of property ownership generally can be seen as an economic device for reducing uncertainty, allowing exchange, and creating incentives, the rationale for most property ownership doctrines also lie in history and tradition. From an economic standpoint, however, a system of intellectual property exists and is designed to increase social welfare. In essence, people are permitted to create and claim certain property rights as long as the net effect is socially beneficial.

Social welfare, in the instance of intellectual property, involves a tradeoff. The tradeoff is between the benefits derived from creative efforts and the costs resulting from exclusivity and the operation of a system of intellectual property protection.[1]

1. See generally, William M. Landes & Richard A. Posner "An Economic Analysis of Copyright Law," XVIII J. Leg. Stud. 325 (1989).

Some of the costs of exclusivity are related to possible market power. For example, a powerful new drug may be very expensive due to the inventor's monopoly. Other exclusivity costs are related to challenges to other creative people whose costs of creativity go up because they cannot make use of ideas claimed first by others.

In theory, and only in theory, the breadth of protection can be balanced against the costs to maximize the social benefits from the production of intellectual property. In fact, a number of the doctrines that define the breadth of protection can be reconciled with an effort to strike an efficient balance.

B. LIMITING PROTECTION

A challenge that arises in patent, copyright, and trademark is defining just what is protected. Although governed by different doctrines, the basic idea is not to extend protection so far that it grants more exclusivity than is necessary. In copyright this is captured by the notion that one can copyright an original expression of an idea but not the idea itself. For example, suppose you had the idea to paint a picture of a dog running through a field of wheat. Your concept would not be protected, but your execution of the idea on canvas would be, subject to exceptions too numerous to discuss here. Similarly, one may not copyright facts no matter how much work was involved in discovering them.

The economic rationale for this distinction—between ideas and facts as opposed to expression—is fairly obvious. First, to allow you to have exclusive rights to the painting of dogs running through fields is likely to be much broader protection than necessary to bring forth your painting. In effect, the protection would be inefficiently broad. Second, assessing whether there has been infringement of an idea as opposed to an expression is likely to be a complicated and expensive task. For example, suppose someone paints a dog running through a corn field with a fence around it and a car and Lou Reed, both sitting on cinder blocks, in the middle. Would that be an infringement? The point is that it is a simpler—but by no means simple—matter to examine your actual expression and determine whether it has been copied than it is to define your idea and then assess whether it has been copied. If ideas were protected, the costs of exclusivity and administration would almost certainly outweigh the benefits. In the existing system, costs of administration are further reduced by the requirement that the expression must be "fixed" in order to be copyrightable.

A similar theme is found in patent law with the requirement that patents are available only in the case of "any new and useful process, machine, manufacture or composition of matter." As in copyright, an idea or concept is not patentable. In addition, unlike copyright, patent law includes a utility requirement. One may take an idea and from there create something that is novel and useful, but the protection extends only to that which is created and does not relate back to the idea itself. From an economic standpoint this limits the amount of exclusivity granted and lowers costs of administration.

In trademark, a similar objective is approached by allowing the owner of the mark to identify a specific source but not to extend to a broader or more generic claim. The critical concern is that the mark distinguish one seller from another. For example, "Bill's Best Hamburgers," distinguishes one provider. On the other hand, granting trademark protection to "Hamburgers" has an effect similar to the impact of allowing an idea to be copyrighted or patented: it would allow the user an unnecessary measure of monopoly power and raise the costs to competitors who also sell hamburgers. This is not to say that trademarks may not be descriptive, but they must also have what is called a secondary meaning that distinguishes a specific supplier.

C. **STRIKING THE BALANCE**

The doctrines discussed above are, from an economic perceptive, the measures through which holders of intellectual property are prevented from preempting entire areas. Aside from these broad limitations, there are numerous other rules, requirements, and exceptions that play a role in the balancing process. This is not to suggest that all of these measures can be explained by reference to efficiency. In fact, one reading of the Copyright Act of 1976 reveals that far more than efficiency, the underlying motivations are about distributive outcomes. Still, it makes sense to examine how economic analysis can be applied to some of the more important doctrines.

1. THE DOCTRINE OF EQUIVALENTS

As you would expect, it is relatively easy to establish a patent infringement when the infringer has exactly duplicated the patented device or process. More difficult is the softer analysis that must take place when there is not literal duplication but a great deal of similarity. This is where the doctrine of equivalents comes into play. The issue arises in the context of an infringement action when the alleged infringement is not exactly the same as the patented process. In effect, the question is just how close one may come to the original before it is viewed as an infringement. Ultimately, the decision determines how far a patent holder's property right extends.

The larger economic importance of this decision should not be understated.[2] You can understand this if you take the perspective of the party who comes into a field of research after the original patent is granted and thinks about the way research investment might be most efficiently directed. Broad protection of the original patent will discourage investment that runs the risk of being too close to the original. This may seem like a good

2. See Hilton Davis Chemical Co. v. Warner–Jenkinson Co., Inc. (Fed.1995).

idea. It will force competitors to concentrate efforts on inventions that are true breakthroughs. In addition, the patent holder will have an incentive to make improvements to the original work without the risk of losing the gains to a second-comer who makes slight changes. On the other hand, perhaps there are small and important improvements that could be made and which have not been undertaken by the patentee. If so, broad protection may allow the original work to stagnate.

Narrow protection, on the other hand, encourages investment in research that may be very similar to that which led to the patented work. This may mean that research investment is channeled away from "breakthroughs" that will seem relatively risky. Some small improvements may only be product differentiation improvements with little social value. On the other hand, if the incumbent is enjoying monopoly position, narrow protection is advantageous to consumers because it lowers entry barriers and may mean lower prices.

2.   FAIR USE

Within copyright law, probably no doctrine has been scrutinized more closely than fair use. Unlike the doctrine of equivalents, a fair use analysis takes place after it is determined that the copying would otherwise be an infringement. It is a defense. Like the doctrine of equivalents, the process is one of defining the limits of one's property rights.

A fair use analysis involves weighing four factors. First is the "purpose and character of the use." A relevant distinction here is whether the use is educational or commercial. An additional inquiry is whether the use is transformative. In general terms, if someone is permitted to copy the work of someone else it is more likely to be a fair use if something new is created. The second factor is the nature of the original work. Creative works, as opposed to those based primarily on fact, are likely to be afforded greater protection, and a fair use defense will be more difficult to mount. A third factor is the amount of the original work that is used relative to the whole. Copying should be no greater than necessary to serve the new work's purpose. Moreover, as the amount of copying increases, the character of the new work should be of greater importance. The fourth factor is the impact on the value of the original work. The greater the impact, all other thing being equal, the less likely that the use is "fair."

The radical nature of fair use can be understood by comparing it to patent law, which has no similar doctrine. In effect, fair use says that you may, in some circumstances, copy the work of another and make adjustments to it in order to produce a new work. In patent law this would be like permitting an inventor to copy the work of another inventor and then employ a defense that the new product is socially useful and did no great harm to the original inventor. Or, in the conventional grazing example, it would be similar to but not quite the same as being required to allow others the use of your land as long as they have a socially beneficial use. The extreme nature of the exemption can also be understood by noting how much further it goes than a liability rule. That is, in the land example, a person could make an involuntary transfer (trespass) and pay the fair market value. In fair use the user does not pay fair market value. In effect, the copyright is limited in the first place.

There are a number of ways to square fair use with efficiency. In some instances, a user might be willing to pay and the copyright holder willing to accept a fee for the use, but transaction costs are so high that the exchange is impractical. Fair use here is Kaldor–Hicks efficient. The transaction cost possibility extends beyond just the obvious one-to-one relationship. For example, suppose consumers value the work of a book, film, or play reviewer and that an effective review requires copying some portion of the original. The value of the information and, thus, an informative review may exceed the value the copyright holder places on continued exclusivity. Here, free-riding and transaction costs may prevent the reviewer from generating enough revenue from his or her own work to pay the copyright holder's asking price. Here again, fair use may lead to a Kaldor–Hicks efficient outcome.

One implication of the transaction costs justification for a fair use defense would be that the defense would not be available when transaction costs are low. This is not, however, how cases have been decided. Repeatedly, defendants have successfully employed fair use as a defense even when transaction costs are low. Conversely, the fact that transactions costs are high does not work in the favor of the infringer. For example, a bar band in, say, Archer, Florida covering a Lucinda Williams song will not be able to assert as part of its fair use defense that the cost of contacting and negotiating with Williams far exceeded any benefits derived from performing the work.

Another possibility is that transaction costs are low but that copyright holders possess a level of monopoly power. The demand for a high licensing fee would exacerbate the transaction cost problem described above by further decreasing the likelihood that the second user will be able to pay the copyright holder's asking price. Also, the asking price may be inflated if the copyright holder anticipates the copying is part of direct criticism or parody. In fact, the elevated price may be of a predatory nature since it is driven by a desire to limit consumer information that might undermine the copyright holder's market power. In all these instances, fair use may allow the original work to be used in ways that are socially beneficial but which would not take place if a transaction were required.

In fact, many instances in which fair use is employed can be explained by a sense that the copying party will put the copyrighted work to a better use. When the "better use" is not reflected in economic terms, the fair use exception permits that use to take place nonetheless. This might be the case when the purposes are primarily educational.

What is most difficult to fit into an efficiency framework are instances in which transaction costs are low, the copier's use is for commercial purposes, and there is little or no critical element in the second work. In some of these instances the fair use defense is unavailable, but not always. A case to examine from this perspective is *Campbell v. Acuff–Rose Music, Inc.*, a 1994 Supreme Court decision, in which the rap group Two Live Crew recorded a parody of "Pretty Woman" after attempting to purchase the right to do so. That case can be explained by the monopoly/predatory price rationale discussed above, but it seems unlikely that the owner of Pretty Women was worried about the impact its use by a rap group would have on Pretty Women fans. Still, even when the three conditions—low transaction costs, commercial use, no critical element—exist, it still may make economic sense to permit fair use. First, the copyright holder cannot claim that the original creation was motivated by a use he or she had intended to exploit. Thus, fair use has no adverse incentive effect. In addition, from a Paretian perspective, the copyright owner suffers no harm while society and the copying party are made better off.

In instances like the one discussed above, it is tempting to argue that the fair use defense amounts to a redistribution from the owner of the original work to the infringer. This is probably incorrect. First, if the derivative work is one that would not have been anticipated by the owner, it is difficult to see wealth as having been taken from one party and distributed to the second one as opposed to new wealth simply being created by the second party. Second, the notion of a redistribution presupposes that the owner of the original work possessed something in the first place. As a technical matter, the copyright owner never possessed the right to block what is fair use. Thus, there is no redistribution. Granted, there is some circularity in this reasoning, but it is important to keep in mind that intellectual property is a legislative creation, and one cannot lose what the legislature did not grant in the first place.

D. DURATION

Part of the definition of one's intellectual property rights lies in the length of time for which those rights exist. From the standpoint of investment, the longer the term, the greater the likely return and the higher the amount of investment. Thus, as a matter of economic analysis, the balance struck is between the increased incentive effects and the additional costs of exclusivity and administration resulting from additional years. There is not a single term that maximizes efficiency across all areas of inventiveness and creativity. In addition, there is a tendency to overstate the impact of distant earnings on current investment. This is because earnings that accrue fifteen or twenty years hence must be discounted quite heavily to present value in order to be compared with current research dollars.

On the other hand, duration is still important to those considering creative effort investments and to those who hold existing patents and copyrights. In fact, for those holding existing patents and copyrights, a term extension, unless anticipated at the time the rights were purchased, can be viewed as a windfall. This does not make the additional income less attractive to those holding current rights, but it does weaken the incentive rationale for extending the term of existing intellectual property. This is a matter that will be discussed more fully below, but first it is important note that trademark terms work differently from copyright and patent terms and that the trademark approach may make more economic sense.

While patent and copyright terms are of fixed duration, the right to a trade-mark can last indefinitely depending on use by the owner. The indefinite duration seems harmless given the infinite number of potential trademarks. The right to the trade mark ends when the mark is abandoned either intentionally or by actions, or the lack thereof, that cause the mark to lose its distinctiveness. In effect, the loss of the right to the mark ties in with the rationale for trademark in the first place. When the mark loses its effectiveness as a way to lower search costs for consumers, the mark is abandoned.

As already noted, fixed terms are rather arbitrary. There seems to be constant political pressure to extend terms by those who stand to benefit. Recently the issue of term extension was addressed by the Supreme Court in *Eldred v. Ashcroft* (2003). The Court examined the Copyright Term Extension Act of 1998 which had the effect of extending most copyright terms from the life of the author plus 50 years to the life of the author plus 70 years. The specific question was whether the extension could be retroactive. Part of the Court's analysis dealt with the economic incentive issues. The problem with a retroactive extension is that it cannot easily be said to be responsible for works already in existence. Thus, to the extent that the Constitutional provision authorizing patent and copyright law seems to call for a functional or utilitarian approach to term lengths, retroactive extension would appear to be off-limits.

Rather than deny the functional goals of term duration, the Court sought to reconcile approval of retroactive extension with providing incentives even in the case of works already in existence. The reasoning offered by the Court was that term extensions had always been retroactive. Thus, when the implicit bargain was struck between those investing in creative efforts and the public, it was understood that the inventors or authors would receive the benefit of the existing term and any extensions that might take place during that term. In effect, retroactive extension was part of a bargain that had already been struck, and Congress, by making the extension retroactive, was merely holding up its end of the bargain. In other words, the calculating author or inventor of 1940 or the parties acquiring the rights to protected works would figure into their future income stream any income likely to be earned during the current term plus some figure for additional years if and when Congress decided to extend the term.

E. REMEDIES

Like most rights, copyrighted and patented works as well as trademarks could be protected by liability rules, property rules, or rules of inalienability.[3] None of the rationales for inalienability, however, apply very easily to property that comes about as a form of investment, so that possibility is largely irrelevant.

As you recall, in a general sense, liability rules may work better from an economic standpoint when transactions costs are high relative to the gains from the exchange and property rules are preferred when transaction costs are low relative to the gains from the exchange. Although it is a broad generalization, intellectual property often is, when compared to typical high transaction cost contexts, a domain of relatively low transactions costs. Most owners of intellectual property rights are anxious to make their identities known and to inform potential infringers that the rights are already claimed.

Under a liability rule, an infringer would essentially be able to force a sale of a license. In theory, the infringer who was able to make a more profitable use of the work could use the work and pay damages to the owner at an amount less than that

3. A thorough analysis is found at Roger D. Blair & Thomas F. Cotter, "An Economic Analysis of Damages Rules in Intellectual Property Law," 39 Wm. & Mary L. Rev. 1585 (1998).

earned by the infringement. The analysis is similar to the efficient breach of contract. The same questions about the efficiency of a contract breach can be raised with respect to the efficient infringement. In effect, are the damages set high enough that the person whose property right has been violated is left in a position that is no worse? The problem is that damages equal to fair market value may not serve this function. In effect, there is no guarantee than an infringement will be Pareto Superior or Kaldor–Hicks efficient. Another element of liability rule protection ties to the issue of incentives. Incentives are likely to be higher if the owner is about to fully internalize the gains generated by the work. It is interesting to note that some copyrighted works are subject to compulsory licensing which is not unlike a liability rule and may involve the same inefficiencies. The possibility of an involuntary exchange and an award of damages can only reduce the incentives created by intellectual property law. A property rule, on the other hand, requires a voluntary exchange, and the outcome should be Pareto and Kaldor–Hicks efficient.

All three regimes of intellectual property examined here permit a plaintiff to obtain injunctive relief and, thus, have elements of a property rule. Beyond that, there is an important difference that bears on the analysis. An infringing party in the case of both copyright and trademark can be liable for damages and any gains resulting from the infringement. In effect, there is a possibility of disgorgement of the gains. For example, an infringing party that uses a copyrighted song in a Broadway show would be liable for the portion of the profits generated by the show that were attributed to the song that was used without permission. This allocation is not an easy process, but it is still a far cry from patent law, at least as the law is written. In patent law, the owner is entitled to damages that are no less than an established or reasonable royalty. At least expressly, disgorgement is not possible.

The different between copyright and trademark, on the one hand, and patent, on the other, is fairly extreme. Patent law remedies reflect a liability rule approach in that the infringer is liable for the fair market value. The possibility of "efficient infringement" is, therefore, a real one, except that some courts are quite generous with awards with the possibility that they approach disgorgement levels. In addition, the authority of the courts to award treble damages, to the extent the power is used, offsets the liability rule-like nature of patent remedies.

As a result of the disgorgement possibilities in the context of copyright and trademark, the remedies come closer to a property rule regime in their effect because they tend to channel secondary users into voluntary transactions. This is because if detection were one-hundred percent, the potential infringer would be faced with disgorging all the gains made possible by the infringement or entering into a transaction that would likely permit him or her to keep at least a portion of the gains. Obviously, detection is not 100% which indicates that some kind of punitive damages would be appropriate to raise the expected costs of infringement. Copyright law does provide enhanced damages when a plaintiff is awarded statutory as opposed to actual damages, but there is no express provision for punitive damages.

The overriding question is which is the more appropriate regime for intellectual property? In the context of providing maximum incentives for creativity, the key element is the ability of the creative or inventive person to capture all the rewards for his or her efforts. A system that allows for efficient infringement by allowing damages equal to the owner's losses falls short of this goal, and, perhaps more importantly, does not assure that use by the infringing party is the more efficient one. The efficiency of property or disgorgement rules are, however, affected by transaction costs and bilateral monopoly problems which may mean that efficient uses are not realized.

In the context of copyright, most of the remedies analysis must be viewed in the context of fair use which can be analogized to compulsory licensing at no price. There is no particular guarantee that the fair users are more efficient users. In fact, copyright can be viewed as consisting of a variety of prices ranging from zero, in fair use, to disgorgement. In between are prices established by compulsory licenses. Any comprehensive view of efficiency would have to account for all these possibilities.

CHAPTER ELEVEN
PUBLIC CHOICE

Most of this book and most of the applications of economic analysis to law involve implied or expressed *market* transactions. The implicit transactions concern issues like the "price" of driving negligently or the "price" of a contract breach. Expressed prices arise in the fields of antitrust, regulated industries, and some contract law. In these instances, preferences and choices are involved and resources allocated with the purpose, at least in theory, of maximizing individual utility.

Over the years, economists have studied another mode of choice-making and resource allocation—that which occurs through political action. In recent years, those who apply economics to law have also turned their attention to this area of inquiry. The study of "public choice" involves the application of economic analysis to political rather than market choices.

Three important factors distinguish decision-making in the political arena from typical market transactions. First, rather than spending dollars which are allocated unevenly, people "spend" or express their preferences with votes, which are often distributed evenly. Second, the voting takes place in the context of other voters whose preferences will effect the eventual outcome. Consequently, there is less certainty as to what one will get when his or her vote is "spent." Third, preferences are often expressed through intermediaries. These intermediaries may be elected officials, interest groups, or lobbyists. The presence of these intermediaries may dilute or amplify the preference expressed.

The study of public choice covers a number of topics.[1] Some are very broad like: why do individuals choose to have governments at all and is it rational to vote? Others are narrow and more technical, such as the advantages and disadvantages of various forms of voting. Still others involve efforts to predict how voters will vote on a given issue. In this Chapter, only a few of these topics can be discussed, and the discussion will only scratch the surface.

A. WHY HAVE A GOVERNMENT?

The threshold question in the study of public choice is why individuals choose to have a government in the first place. "Government," in this context, means an environment in which one will not have free rein to exercise all of one's choices. In other words, it implies that there is some element of control by the government. To keep the discussion from veering too far from reality, it should be

1. See generally Iain McLean, *Public Choice: An Introduction* (1987).

acknowledged that this is a choice few people get to make. They do have the choice, however, to escape from one form of government in favor of another and continually to press for more or less coercion within any given government.

In traditional economic terms, one will consent to an actual or potential loss of liberty when it appears to be utility-maximizing to do so. The basic reason for giving up some portion of one's liberty is that it is a necessary part of an implicit or social contract with others who will be similarly limited. It is, in essence, what one must give up in order to induce the cooperation of others. Not only does the agreement to limit one's own freedom constitute the consideration in the "social contract" necessary for the formation of the government, it may actually increase one's own power to influence others. For example, the knowledge that others have that one will keep a promise or observe certain rules of conduct may mean that others will depend on the promisor and conform their behavior in ways the promisor has requested.

While giving up a portion of one's own liberty may be necessary in order to "buy" some of the liberty of others, the question still remains: how could this make an individual better off? The basic reason can be traced to the notion of externalities—both positive and negative.

These concepts are discussed in Chapters Three and Nine, but by way of review, positive externalities occur when it is impossible for the producer of some benefit to keep others from enjoying those benefits. The problem is that the producer's inability to "internalize" all the benefits may discourage production of something that all find valuable but are unwilling to pay for in hopes someone else will produce it. These goods are often called public goods.

An example of a public good might be a watchdog purchased by one neighbor, but whose barking actually frightens potential burglars away from the entire neighborhood. In instances in which the number of people involved is small, the production of public goods may come about through a series of private agreements. Each person could agree to contribute toward a fund to be used for the purchase or production of an item from which all would benefit. When the number of people involved becomes large, the transaction costs of a series of private contracts increases. In addition, there may be "hold-outs" who hope to benefit from the group effort without actually making a contribution. These factors are likely to make the private agreement route impractical.

As the terms suggest, negative externalities are the opposite of positive externalities. With positive externalities, the producer incurs all the costs of production but is unable to capture all the benefits. In the case of negative externalities, all the benefits of production are captured by the producer but the costs of production are incurred, in part, by others. The typical example is that of the factory that pollutes the air or water but does not incur any costs for the use of the air or water. The best illustration of how everyone is made worse off is the "tragedy of the commons." In this scenario, each firm produces as though it were the only user of fresh water. Of course, if they each operate accordingly, at some point the water supply will be used up and unavailable to anyone. Here again, there is some possibility that externalites could be controlled through private agreements, but this would be difficult without first taking the critical step of determining who has a right to use the water. In addition, when numerous parties are involved, more complex agreements are required, and the problem of transaction costs also arises.

The existence of public goods and the "tragedy of the commons" both suggest that the overall wellbeing of individuals may be improved through cooperation. The problem is that cooperation on a large scale is expensive to "produce" and is threatened by free-riders and hold-outs.[2] Consequently, even rational maximizers of self-interest may consent to the loss of liberty associated with being governed.

This discussion suggests that people may consent to being governed essentially because they are better off under a body of laws. Another way of putting this, which highlights the economic character of this choice, is that there are circumstances under which a system of government is more efficient than a "state of nature" or the absence of government. The amount of personal liberty individuals

2. Chapter Two includes a more detailed discussion of these concepts.

are willing to cede will be, in theory, determined by weighing the value of that liberty against the value to be gained by "pooling" each person's liberty in a "government."

The complexity does not end here. As noted in Chapter Two, "efficiency" has a variety of definitions or interpretations. If one is interested in Pareto efficiency, then the argument would be that there can be no government unless all of those subject to the government consent. On the other hand, the system would be efficient from a Kaldor–Hicks standpoint as long as those who benefit from the government could compensate those who are worse off, whether or not actual compensation takes place.

This means that a government that really coerces individuals would be unlikely to satisfy the Pareto test. On the other hand, the government might simply be established by a majority of people who felt they would be better off and agree to subordinate the wishes of the minority. This not only would not be Pareto efficient, but there is no guarantee that it would be Kaldor–Hicks efficient since it is impossible to know whether the benefits enjoyed by the majority would be sufficient to offset the losses incurred by the minority.

Using the notion of *ex ante* compensation, one might argue that those who stick around to be governed knowing they may later ultimately be part of a minority are actually consenting to the government and must, therefore, be better off. Whether this is consent in any meaningful way is questionable. The obvious point is that, even though the existence of government can be squared with the efficiency-oriented decisions of rational maximizers of self-interest, there is no guarantee that such efficiency will be achieved.

B. APPROACHES TO GOVERNMENT

The fact that rational self-interested people may choose to have some form of government does not mean they will agree on the proper role of government. This is true even if they are interested in the goal of maximizing individual utility. The central point of debate is just how much risk they are willing to expose themselves to in the quest for utility. Put differently and in an extreme fashion, do they prefer a society in which the advantaged may be extremely well off and the disadvantaged may be in terrible condition, or do they prefer a system in which even the worst off are taken care of? These two possibilities are, to some extent, illustrated by the two approaches discussed here: utilitarianism and John Rawls' *Theory of Justice*. They are not exhaustive of the possibilities by any means and the discussion is, by necessity, an overview.[3]

1.   UTILITARIANISM

The model that fits a view that people are willing to ''assume the risk'' that maximizing society's util-

3. See David Barnes and Lynn Stout, *Cases and Materials on Law and Economics* 418–435 (1993).

ity will maximize their own utility is "utilitarianism." In its law and economics form, utilitarianism is closely related to Kaldor–Hicks efficiency, with "wealth maximization" substituting for "utility maximization."[4]

"Utilitarianism" as a model for social goals is beset with a number of problems.[5] Some of these are "boundary" problems. In other words, how large is the society for which utility is to be maximized? Are there specific geographical limits? If so, is there any rational or moral basis for imposing these limits? Also, do animals count, or is it only the utility of humans that is to be maximized?

Another problem is whether the goal is to maximize total or average utility. One can imagine a society with a huge population and a tremendous total utility even though everyone is miserable. On the other hand, maximizing average utility may require controlling the size of the population.

Perhaps the most difficult problems center around the possibility that one may find that her utility must be sacrificed in the interest of maximizing overall utility. The most extreme example of this is the so-called utility monster. This involves the individual who derives tremendous pleasure

4. There are differences between maximizing utility and maximizing wealth. For a discussion of the possible differences the reader may want to refer to Chapter Two.

5. J.J.C. Smart and Bernard Williams, *Utilitarianism: For and Against* 77–150 (1973); Richard Posner, *The Economics of Justice* 51–60 (1980).

from activities that others find unpleasant. If the pleasure derived is sufficiently high, it can "justify" whatever disutility the others may suffer. Of course, the utility monster may be a single person or even a small minority.

A case can be made that a wealth-maximization approach "solves" some of these problems. For example, the need to have money as a means of expressing oneself may lower the "utility monster" risk. And, since animals are unable to express themselves in the market, they will not count. Although wealth maximization provides answers to some of the problems, it can hardly be viewed as solving them in any way that has an independent moral basis.

The most common risk in a context in which there is majority control is that one will find that he or she is part of a minority whose freedoms must be limited in order to satisfy or increase the utility of the majority. For example, in *Bowers v. Hardwick* (S.Ct.1986), a case eventually overturned, the U.S. Supreme Court, in upholding Georgia's anti-sodomy law, expressly relied on the "presumed belief of a majority of the electorate in Georgia that homosexual sodomy is immoral and unacceptable." Similar reasoning can be found in *Korematsu v. United States* (S.Ct.1944) which dealt with the constitutionality of the internment of Japanese–Americans during World War II. The Supreme Court expressly weighed the hardship and disruption experienced by the internees against the perceived threat of espionage and sabotage.

What these cases illustrate is that in a utilitarian world there will be losers as well as winners. The same is true if the goal is wealth-maximization; depriving some of their property or wealth will be viewed as acceptable as long as the benefits to those to whom it is transferred value it more than the original owners. Of course, in a wealth-maximization world there is a further drawback in that maximizing wealth may or may not lead to maximizing overall wellbeing.

Obviously, a person's attitude towards the utilitarian model or wealth-maximization will depend on the position he or she is likely to occupy in that society. Will they tend to be net beneficiaries of rules or redistributions that are necessary in the name of utility or wealth-maximization, or will they tend, on balance, to be contributors? No one can be absolutely certain, and one's view will be shaped, in part, by an assessment of his or her own attributes and how averse she is to the risk that she will ultimately be a "net contributor" as opposed to a "net recipient." To those who are risk-averse, the possibility of being on the losing end of the "bargain" may make utilitarianism an unattractive option.

2.   RAWLS' THEORY OF JUSTICE

An alternative to utilitarian reasoning, which expressly recognizes the aversion individuals may have to the risk of being members of a disadvantaged minority in a utilitarian system, is developed in what John Rawls calls "a theory of justice." Rawls addresses the question of what type of society individuals would choose if they did not know their personal attributes or the positions they would end up occupying in the society. They would be sheltered from any knowledge that would help them determine the likelihood that they would be "net contributors" or "net recipients" under the chosen system. The Rawlsian view is that the truly just state is the one selected when people do not know whether they are likely to be in the best or worse off group in that society.

Behind this "veil of ignorance," Rawls concludes that two principles would be chosen. The first would be that each individual would have a right to the most extensive basic liberty compatible with a similar liberty for others. The second would be that social and economic inequalities would be arranged so that they are reasonably expected to be to everyone's advantage.[6] This second principle—called the "difference principle"—would allow for inequalities in income and wealth, but those who become better off could only do so if those at the bottom of the distribution are also made better off. One can see the similarity between Rawls' difference principle and Paretian standards of efficiency. This is to be distinguished from utilitarianism and its Kaldor–Hicks counterpart, which permit individuals to be made worse off as long as overall welfare or wealth is increased.

6. John Rawls, *A Theory of Justice* 60–61 (1971).

Central to the Rawlsian model is the belief, which is somewhat supported in actual experience, that people are risk-averse. They are so risk-averse that they adopt a decision-making rule called "maximin." Under a maximin rule, the individuals assume they will ultimately be among the worst off in society and then choose the governing principles that would maximize the welfare of the worst off. Whether people would be so risk-averse behind the veil of ignorance that they would select the maximin decision rule is impossible to know.

In sum, there are sound economic reasons for individuals to express a preference for the existence of some form of a state. The exact form of a state that would be preferred is more difficult to predict. Moreover, imbedded in the decision about the guiding principles of a state is the moral and theoretical question of how much individuals should be permitted to know about their likely position in that state.

C. WHY VOTE AT ALL?

One of the issues that has perplexed social scientists for many years is why people bother to vote in the first place. Conventional economic analysis suggests that it is irrational to vote.[7] Under this analysis, the rational maximizer of self-interest compares the costs and benefits of voting. In the United States, voting requires that the individual undergo

7. Anthony Downs, *An Economic Theory of Democracy* 260–276 (1957); Gordon Tullock, *Toward a Mathematics of Politics* 110–112 (1967).

some inconvenience. The benefit from that vote is the probability that the vote will make a difference in the outcome times the change in one's wellbeing should the overall vote go the desired way. In any large election, the expected benefit is unlikely to out-weigh the cost of gasoline, parking, and the time consumed in the voting process.

In order to explain the decision to vote, one must expand the notion of the sorts of things from which people derive utility. One possibility is that people vote out of a sense of duty. In essence, they vote to avoid the feeling that they have shirked some responsibility. Another possibility is that they are not voting to enhance their self-interest narrowly speaking, but have a desire to look out for the welfare of others—children or the elderly. In this case, although the probability of one's vote affecting the outcome does not change, the benefit that accrues if the outcome is affected increases substantially.[8] In either case, the simplistic cost-benefit analysis does not apply.

More specifically, this suggests that the decision to express political preferences may be influenced by factors that are outside those that are traditionally viewed as consistent with self-interest. Not only may the decision *to* vote be affected by these factors, the decision about *how* to vote may also be affected. It has been suggested that the way people vote is likely to be influenced by generalized "values" while more traditional market transactions are

8. Harold Margolis, *Selfishness, Altruism and Morality* 88–95 (1982).

influenced by individual "tastes."[9] The decisions discussed in a study of law and economics probably fall somewhere between these two extremes.

D. PROBLEMS OF ASCERTAINING PREFERENCES THROUGH VOTING

1. UNANIMITY AND MAJORITY VOTING

As noted in Chapter Three, even in the traditional marketplace it is difficult to ascertain preferences. First, choices may not accurately reflect preferences. Second, since wealth and income limit one's ability to express preferences or their intensity, there is no guarantee that the eventual allocation of goods and services will maximize utility.

In the political context, rather than using money to express preferences, votes are the "currency." This too leads to problems in determining preferences, and different types of voting rules have different advantages and disadvantages in this regard.

The most basic rule and one that would seemingly appeal to the risk-averse would be the rule of unanimity. In other words, no actions can take place without the approval of all. Obviously, such a rule finds its economic counterpart in the form of Pareto efficiency, and its chief advantage is that it affords maximum respect to individual liberty. Even a strong majority is unable to subordinate a minori-

9. Kenneth Arrow, *Social Choice and Individual Values* 81–83 (1963).

ty or use the minority to achieve the majority's ends.

A number of things are, however, sacrificed under such a voting scheme. The obvious one is that complete respect for personal liberty may be inconsistent with utility maximization. It is not hard to imagine a situation in which 19 members of a group of 20 eligible voters feel very strongly that a certain policy should be adopted. The remaining voter disagrees but is almost indifferent. Still, he has, in essence, veto power. Of course, it is possible that the 19 voters in favor of the measure are just barely in favor of it and that the one voter in opposition is very opposed. In this case, the requirement of unanimity may not decrease an opportunity to raise total utility.

The veto possibility also raises a slightly different problem. Suppose voter number 20 really is indifferent about the issue or is actually slightly in favor of the majority view. Here there is a chance for that individual, by holding out, to force the others into certain concessions, and perhaps monetary compensation, in order to induce him to join the fold. Of course, every voter is a potential "voter number 20," and the probability of achieving unanimity—even in a situation in which all will be better off—may be reduced.

The obvious response to the problems inherent in a unanimity requirement is some form of majority vote. It could be a requirement for a simple majority or for a two-thirds or three-fourths majority. One of the advantages of these voting rules is that they lower the "costs" of reaching an outcome by greatly reducing the power of hold-outs. This follows from the critical feature of such voting schemes, which is that policies can be adopted without the consent of all those voting. In economic terms, it is more like utilitarianism or Kaldor–Hicks efficiency than Pareto efficiency.

This is not meant to imply that the elimination of the hold-out problem is altogether good. It is tempting to think of the problem as only arising when one voter acts opportunistically in a commercial context to extort payment from the other members of the electorate. This is, however, only one possibility. Another is that the hold-out honestly believes in her position and holds out in an attempt to convince the others that they are misguided. This might be the case when the voters are members of a jury. If the jury can render a verdict with less than a unanimous vote, the so-called hold-out with good ideas—ideas that might enlighten the majority— may be ignored.[10]

Similarly, one should be careful not to assume that some form of majority voting ensures utility or wealth maximization. There are no guarantees on this score at all. Just as one's ability to pay may be only tenuously connected to the utility he or she derives from that purchase, the capacity to cast one's vote for one alternative rather than another may be the result of only the slightest preference for that alternative. Similarly, the minority of vot-

10. *Apodaca v. Oregon* (S.Ct.1972) (J. Douglas in dissent).

ers, on the losing end of the vote, may have very strong desires for the alternative for which they voted. Voting rules that require more than a simple majority also fall short of assuring utility maximization, although they do lessen the risk.

Similarly, such voting rules do not assure Kaldor–Hicks or wealth-maximizing results. Again, the fact that one position may be voted for by more people than the alternative tells us nothing about whether the net gainers from the vote could compensate those who lost. In fact, if the voting leads to a direct redistribution of income, there is no Kaldor–Hicks improvement, as the level of wealth in the community remains the same. And, to the extent the transfer involves incurring some costs, the redistribution may leave the community worse off. Of course, the redistribution could increase welfare or utility if the recipients value the additional dollars more than those from whom the dollars were taken.

This again raises the primary concern with majority voting, which is that the majority will exploit the minority. One can imagine a situation in which the majority votes to finance some project from which they will benefit by levying a tax on the consumption of a product that is consumed by a minority of the population. In fact, virtually every tax and spending decision has some redistributive effect. While it may be that the majority of voters are the net beneficiaries of many redistributions, it is also true that many publicly approved projects seem to be designed to assist relatively small groups.

In addition, when it comes to the issue of redistribution, it is more useful to think not in terms of majority and minority, but whether the redistribution tends to benefit the relatively rich or poor. For example, the use of general tax revenues to subsidize medical or legal education may mean redistribution in favor of the relatively well-to-do. On the other hand, the use of the same funds to finance a food stamp program redistributes income in favor of the poor.

The direction of any redistribution is important because, as a general matter, most people assume that the marginal utility of money declines. This means that a wealthy person will lose less utility when a dollar is taken than the poor person will gain if she receives that dollar. Thus, by answering the question of how funds have been redistributed, one may also answer the question of whether the majority has voted in a way that increases overall utility.

2. ARROW'S THEOREM AND POSSIBLE SOLUTIONS

One of the most discussed problems encountered in attempting to ascertain preferences through voting is called Arrow's Impossibility Theorem.[11] The Theorem can best be illustrated through the use of a simple example. Suppose a class of 36 law students is asked to vote on what type of exam they will take. There are three possibilities: a three hour,

11. Kenneth arrow, supra note 9.

open-book essay exam (OB), a three hour closed-book, multiple choice exam (CB), and a 48 hour open-book, take-home exam (TH). Suppose that 12 of the students prefer OB to CB and CB to TH. Twelve other students prefer CB to TH and TH to OB. Finally, the last group of twelve prefer TH to OB and OB to CB. Their preferences can be ranked as follows:

Group I:	OB > CB > TH
Group II:	CB > TH > OB
Group III:	TH > OB > CB

If the professor then asks them to vote, it is clear that 24 of the students prefer OB to CB. On the other hand, 24 students also prefer CB to TH. Finally, 24 of the students prefer TH to OB. The problem is that there is instability in the voting results; it is impossible to determine which alternative the group actually prefers because the answer changes depending upon how the alternatives are voted on. This problem is known as "cycling."

If cycling occurs, it opens the possibility that the order in which alternatives are voted on may determine the outcome. Power to set the agenda can then determine the outcome of the voting. For example, suppose in the test hypothetical, the professor wants to give a closed-book, multiple choice exam but also wants to be popular and give the students the sense they have participated in the decision about the type of exam they will take. The teacher may first pose the question of whether the students prefer an open-book three hour exam or an open-book take-home exam. The answer is that a majority favor the take-home exam. Then the take home exam is paired against the last possibility—the closed-book exam. Here the closed-book exam alternative wins.

The problem with the test hypothetical is not just that there is instability. Another problem, even if there were no instability, is that an ordinal ranking means that the accuracy of the vote is in question. As long as the voters are unable to do more than rank their preferences (engage in "ordinal" voting), the intensity of their preferences will not be gauged and a majority vote for one of the alternatives may not be consistent with what actually is consistent with overall welfare. Again, it is important to note that the accuracy problem may exist even if the rankings resulted in a stable outcome.

Returning to the test hypothetical, suppose each of the students voting is equipped with 10 "points" or votes that he or she can allocate to the three choices. Each group of twelve would then have a total of 120 votes. In casting their points or votes, the ranking would remain the same, but the students could reflect the intensity of their feelings by allocating the points in a manner consistent with their feelings. The outcome might be as follows (the numbers in parentheses represent the total votes for each of the choices):

Group I:	OB(84) > CB(24) > TH(12)
Group II:	CB(74) > TH(40) > OB(6)
Group III:	TH(60) > OB(36) > CB(24)

Under the point system, the open-book classroom exam gets 126 points, the closed-book choice gets 122 votes and the take-home exam receives 112 votes. This outcome is both stable and permits voters to supply information about the intensity of their preferences.

"Cycling" has been offered as an explanation for seemingly inconsistent judicial decisions or instability in judicial positions.[12] In effect, the holding in a case may not represent the application of a majority rule but the ranking of two choices by nine Justices with different philosophies. For example, suppose the Court is faced with the issue of nude dancing. Three of the Justices are First Amendment absolutists and look upon all dancing as a form of expression (A), three feel as strongly about the First Amendment but do not believe that dancing is a protected form of expression (N), and three feel that dancing could be a form of protected expression but think the artistic efforts must be weighed against that part of the dancing that could be regarded as obscene (B). If these views are ranked by each group of three Justices, the possibility of cycling exists with respect to the "rule" that is adopted. This would be the situation if the rankings were as follows:

Group I:	A > B > N
Group II:	N > A > B
Group III:	B > N > A

12. Frank Easterbrook, "Ways of Criticizing the Court," 95 *Harv. L. Rev.* 802 (1982).

The holding in the case will swing on the balance struck by those Justices who favor a balancing approach. It is important to note the holding is not the result of a "rule" requiring balancing. Whatever the outcome of one case, the next one may appear to be decided in an inconsistent manner. Of course, it is only inconsistent if one assumes that the first decision was the product of a rule the Court had adopted with respect to nude dancing.

The preferences of the Justices could be arranged and probably do often fall in a pattern that gives rise to a "majority rule." In the above example, a pattern like this would create such an outcome:

$$
\begin{array}{ll}
\text{Group I:} & A > B > N \\
\text{Group II:} & A > N > B \\
\text{Group III:} & N > B > A
\end{array}
$$

Here the outcome is stable, and the "majority" rule is A. Suppose, however, that the Justices in Group II are just barely in favor of A over N, mainly because they are not positive that dancing is a protected form of expression, and that the Group III Justices feel passionately that dancing is not protected by the First Amendment. Now, although there is a stable position, the question arises as to whether the majority rule is an accurate reflection of the "rule" once the intensity of feelings is considered.

a. Logrolling

As already discussed, judicial opinions have been described as exhibiting instability, possibly accounted for by the voting method used. On the other hand, legislative decisions, which are not supposedly guided by precedent, seem to exhibit greater stability. One explanation for why legislative decisions may be more stable is the potential for logrolling. Logrolling involves the practice of what is, in effect, trading votes. For example, a legislator from Florida may feel very strongly about a bill dealing with off-shore drilling and not really care about the outcome on a bill concerning subsidies for soybean farmers. A legislator from Iowa may have opposite interests and be relatively indifferent to off-shore drilling but feel strongly about the soybean subsidies. The Florida legislator may agree to vote in the manner desired by the Iowa legislator on soybean subsidies if the Iowa legislator will vote her way on the off-shore drilling issue. In effect, the legislators have traded votes giving the Florida legislator two votes on off-shore drilling and the Iowa legislator two votes on soybean supports.

Logrolling allows the legislators to exercise what is, in effect, more than one vote. By trading votes away in order to garner votes to cast on the issues they care about most, they will not be required to vote "yes" or "no" on a particular issue but will be able, indirectly, to indicate the intensity of their preferences. In this respect, logrolling can produce the same result as the point voting system described above. Outcomes will tend to be stable. In addition, there may be greater accuracy in that the votes of those caring the most will, in effect, count more than votes of those who do not have strong feelings.

b. Single–Peaked Preferences

Although Arrow's Impossibility Theorem is important to consider, it is also true that it does not apply in a wide variety of instances. One of the assumptions necessary for the Theorem to hold is that voters have a free range of choices.[13] This means that individuals may rank the alternatives in any order. This is not the case, however, with respect to many issues about which people are concerned. Instead, their choices will be arranged along a predictable spectrum. When this is the case, the individuals have "single peaked preferences." For example, suppose there are three positions on gun control: Ban all guns (B), ban some guns (SB) and ban no guns (NB). Three voters might express their preferences like this:

Voter I:	B > SB > NB
Voter II:	NB > SB > B
Voter III:	SB > B > NB

These combinations seem realistic since Voter I, who is greatly in favor of gun control, is likely to prefer at least some gun control to none. Similarly, Voter II, who favors no gun control, would favor some control as opposed to banning guns altogether. In this case, the stable and winning outcome is SB. Once again, it is important to note that stability

13. See David Barnes and Lynn Stout, supra note 3, at 465–466.

does not mean that the result is the same as it would be if the strength of preferences could be determined.

E. THE ECONOMIC THEORY OF LEGISLATION

To this point, this Chapter has approached public choice as though each voter has the right to vote on each issue and the majority position becomes the law. As already indicated, the preferences indicated by voting may not be stable or accurate. Things become more complex when one considers the fact that the voters are typically voting for individuals who will then vote on legislation. Thus, much of the literature in public choice is devoted to the "theory of legislation." This area of discussion addresses the question of what motivates legislators. Are they wholly and exclusively interested in reelection? Do they vote in a manner that is consistent with an ideology that may at times be inconsistent with increasing the welfare of their constituents? How powerful are interest groups in influencing legislative outcomes? Can outcomes be, in effect, bought by means of campaign contributions and other inducements?

1. WHAT DO LEGISLATORS WANT?

As one might expect, the economic theory of legislation begins with the notion that legislators are rational maximizers of self-interest. The question then becomes: what are the sorts of variables that one might find in a legislator's utility function? One possibility is that the legislator is driven by the desire to be reelected. After all, whatever benefits are derived from office-holding are lost if the individual is not reelected. This is somewhat supported by empirical evidence that, in Senate reelection campaigns, candidates tend to move toward the positions held by the most recently elected Senator in their state.[14] On the other hand, this "flexibility" is quite limited. But this too could be consistent with the desire to be reelected, as voters may shy away from a candidate who is perceived as being too wishy-washy.

This leads to the question: what is the best way to ensure reelection? One possibility is that the legislator must make sure that, on balance, the legislation he supports would be supported by his constituents. And, assuming they are all rational maximizers of self-interest, this means he must vote in a way that benefits the majority. It is not clear whether this means that the legislator will only consider the narrowly defined economic well-being of the constituents or whether there will be some effort to gauge their more general values. The recent emphasis on abortion rights and sexual harassment by candidates suggests that more general values do motivate voters and, under this theory, political candidates. The basic problem with the theory that the legislator must be careful to vote in a way that his constituents prefer is that it assumes

14. See A. Glazer and M. Robbins, "How Elections Matter: A Study of U.S. Senators" 46 *Public Choice* 163 (1985).

a great deal about voter interest and information. For example, as already discussed, even the decision to vote seems irrational if one applies conventional economic reasoning. In other than very small elections, the costs of voting are likely to outweigh the benefits. In addition, for this theory to work, one would have to assume a fairly well-informed electorate that tended to keep track of how possibly obscure pieces of legislation affect them. Here again, the cost of information-gathering may be out-weighed by any possible benefit.

On the other hand, it may be that reelection really hinges on winning the support (or avoiding the disapproval) of specific interest groups that are capable of making political contributions and making sure those inclined to support the candidate actually do vote. When approached in this way, the legislator who wishes to be reelected may be seen as selling his votes to the interest group with the greatest clout. In fact, the theory of legislation is sometimes discussed in terms of the supply and demand for legislation, with interest groups being the primary demanders and legislators being the suppliers. A more detailed discussion of interest group theory is found below.

The economic theory of legislation has been criticized for offering too simplistic an explanation for legislative voting. In particular, Daniel Farber and Philip Frickey question whether legislators are directly responsive to their constituents or interest groups or whether they are also responsive to their own ideology. According to Farber and Frickey, the voting of legislators, as an empirical matter, is not fully explained by just the first two possibilities. Furthermore, other economic theories explain why one would expect some slippage between the interests of voters or interest groups and the votes of legislators. Thus, the authors propose a broader model in which votes are explained by constituent interest, special interest groups, and ideology.[15]

2. INTEREST GROUPS

A concept that comes up frequently in the literature of public choice is "rent seeking." In the context of public choice, "rent" is the term for income that is received that is in excess of what would be received under competitive conditions. Much of the activity of interest groups can be seen as rent seeking. That is, the members of the group want to be sheltered from competitive conditions in the market.

For example, in the casebook favorite *Williamson v. Lee Optical of Oklahoma* (S.Ct.1955), the Supreme Court reviewed an Oklahoma statute which prohibited opticians from providing lenses or eye glass frames without a prescription. This meant that most glasses would be sold by optometrists, who unlike opticians, were licensed to examine eyes and write prescriptions. In addition, any lenses that were to be copied or duplicated for a customer would have to be provided by an optometrist. The

15. Daniel Farber & Philip Frickey, "The Jurisprudence of Public Choice," 65 *Tex. L. Rev.* 873.

legislation, which the Supreme Court held was not a denial of due process, was heavily supported by the Oklahoma Optometric Association. The intended economic effects were to limit competition in the market for eye glasses and, thereby, raise the prices that optometrists could charge. Any increase in price would be regarded as a form of "rent." A similar result would follow from the successful efforts by physicians or lawyers opposing the opening of a new medical or law school.

The existence of interest groups can be explained by rent seeking, but certainly interest groups may also be formed to support consumer interests and moral or religious values. The study of interest groups from an economic perspective is similar to the study of many other issues in public choice. Issues arise concerning when it is rational to support an interest group and the impact of free-rider problems.

A critical issue is whether the benefits of interest group formation and activity are outweighed by the costs. These costs, which can be quite high, are only justified if the group is able to influence the passage of some legislation or some of the details within the legislation. Moreover, this effort may take place in a competitive environment in which one interest group is pitted against another interest group. As in the case of the individual voter's decision to vote or not, the probability of having the desired effect must be taken into account.

A major draw of interest group participation would appear to be economies of scale. For a certain level of influence, it probably costs a number of individuals working together less than if they were involved in an uncoordinated effort. A drawback is that even in cases in which the financial gains of a successful effort may be huge, these benefits are not one-hundred percent certain and they must be divided among all the beneficiaries. When all is considered, even a successful effort may end up as a net loss.

Another problem stems from possible free-riding. The efforts of an interest group are like a public good in that the benefits produced typically cannot be restricted to those who have contributed. Thus, there is a temptation to sit on the sidelines and hope that the other interested parties will contribute. Obviously, if a number of interested parties take the same view, the "group" may never be formed or, if it is, the level if its "interest" may be understated.

3. THE MARKET FOR LEGISLATION

Interest group activity and the likelihood that, all other things being equal, the interest group with the greatest financial clout will have greater influence leads to the issue of whether this is necessarily bad. After all, through participation in and contributions to interest groups, people are able to express the intensity of their preferences. This not only avoids cycling but seems, at first impression, to be consistent with maximizing wealth and, possibly, utility.

For example, suppose the "Save the Whales" group is able to collect $1,000,000 from contributors who want to be able to influence relevant legislation that will limit whaling. Suppose also that several producers in an industry are members of "Up With Industry," a group that opposes increased protection for whales and is able to collect $2,000,000. If this were an auction for legislation, the industry group would outbid the environmentalists and, one might say, they value the right to the whales more than the opposing bidders.

Obviously, there are several criticisms of such a view. First, as has been emphasized before, there is clear slippage between the willingness and ability to pay and utility. Thus, there are no guarantees that blocking the protective legislation increases overall utility.

Second, it is not clear that wealth will be maximized. To the extent free-riding exists by "supporters" of either group, the actual values will be understated. After all, the fact that one chooses to free-ride does not necessarily mean that she values the outcome any less than the next person; she may simply be attempting to maximize utility or wealth by enjoying the fruits of the efforts of others.

In addition, "Save the Whales" could be made up of hundreds of thousands of small contributors and "Up With Industry" may be made up of 12 producers. If so, free-riding is more likely to take place among supporters of "Save the Whales" because the diffuseness of the membership means that free-riders are likely to escape detection. Consequently, the likelihood that there could be sanctions or that they could be excluded from any benefits would be very low.

Members of "Up With Industry," on the other hand, would quickly know who the free-riders were, and there is a higher probability that they could react in a way that the free-rider would like to avoid. Thus, the relative contributions of the two groups do little to indicate the values attached to the legislation being "sold." This suggests that small groups composed of relatively affluent parties will be the most effective at achieving their aims.

The proposition that relatively small groups of intensely interested parties may be disproportionately "loud" in the market for legislation has some empirical support. Support for political action committees (PAC) tends to be less in industries with numerous firms, possibly due to free–riding fears. Increased industrial concentration leads to increased PAC activity up to a point.[16] After a point of concentration, the group may find that rent seeking efforts are more productive when directed to avenues other than political activity.

The possibility that expensive lobbying by a high powered interest group will somehow maximize

16. See Kevin Grier, Michael Munger & Brian Roberts, "PAC IT OR LEAVE IT: Concentration and Corporate Political Participation," paper delivered at the 1990 meetings of the Public Choice Society.

wealth is further reduced if the interest group is a rent seeker. Not only is a successful outcome inefficient, but the competition to achieve that outcome is also a loss since the efforts of competing groups may simply cancel each other out. In fact, even if the outcome could be viewed as otherwise efficient, the costs of achieving that outcome may be exceeded by the costs of getting there.

*

INDEX

References are to Pages

CONTRACT LAW

†